Nelson Grammar

Teacher's Book 2
For Books 3, 4, 5 & 6

OXFORD
UNIVERSITY PRESS

OXFORD
UNIVERSITY PRESS

Great Clarendon Street, Oxford, OX2 6DP, United Kingdom

Oxford University Press is a department of the University of Oxford.
It furthers the University's objective of excellence in research, scholarship,
and education by publishing worldwide. Oxford is a registered trade mark
of Oxford University Press in the UK and in certain other countries

Text © Wendy Wren 2014
Illustrations © Simon Smith 2014

The moral rights of the author have been asserted

First published 2014

All rights reserved. No part of this publication may be reproduced, stored in a retrieval system, or transmitted, in any form or by any means, without the prior permission in writing of Oxford University Press, or as expressly permitted by law, by licence or under terms agreed with the appropriate reprographics rights organization. Enquiries concerning reproduction outside the scope of the above should be sent to the Rights Department, Oxford University Press, at the address above.

You must not circulate this work in any other form
and you must impose this same condition on any acquirer

British Library Cataloguing in Publication Data

Data available

ISBN: 978-1-4085-2386-5

5 7 9 10 8 6 4

Paper used in the production of this book is a natural, recyclable product made from wood grown in sustainable forests. The manufacturing process conforms to the environmental regulations of the country of origin.

Printed in Great Britain by Ashford Colour Press

Acknowledgements

Series editor: John Jackman
Cover illustrations: Santiago Grasso
Page make-up: OKS Prepress, India

Oxford OWL
Discover eBooks, inspirational resources, advice and support
www.oxfordowl.co.uk

Contents

How Nelson Grammar Works	4
Nelson Grammar and the statutory curriculum requirements	6
Book 3 Scope and sequence	12
Book 3 Units 1 to 28	14
Book 3 Check-up answers	42
Book 4 Scope and sequence	44
Book 4 Units 1 to 28	46
Book 4 Check-up answers	76
Book 5 Scope and sequence	78
Book 5 Units 1 to 28	80
Book 5 Check-up answers	108
Book 6 Scope and sequence	110
Book 6 Units 1 to 28	112
Book 6 Check-up answers	140
Revision Book answers	142
Grammar Skills Finder	150
SATs Practice Paper Answers	152
Glossary	158

How Nelson Grammar works

YEAR	PUPIL BOOK		WORKBOOKS		RESOURCES & ASSESSMENT	TEACHING SUPPORT
YEAR 1	Pupil Book 1A	Pupil Book 1B	Work Book 1A	Work Book 1B	Resource Book 1 (KS1)	Teacher's Book 1 (KS1)
YEAR 2	Pupil Book 2		Work Book 2A	Work Book 2B		
YEAR 3	Pupil Book 3				Resource Book 2 (KS2)	Teacher's Book 2 (KS2)
YEAR 4	Pupil Book 4					
YEAR 5	Pupil Book 5				Resource Book 3 (KS2)	
YEAR 6	Pupil Book 6		Revision Book			

Teaching approaches

Working as a whole class

Some teachers will prefer to ask the whole class to work on the same unit, with children progressing through the activities according to their ability. The Pupil Book forms the core of the teaching. When Nelson Grammar is used in this way, it is possible to allocate a regular timetabled slot to the teaching of grammar.

Books 1A and 1B

This level is designed to be delivered orally (though there are opportunities to write at the teacher's discretion). Focus work is based on the colourful poster that begins each unit. Practice and Extension activities are provided in the Workbooks.

Books 2–6

From Book 2 onwards, the Pupil Book has Focus, Practice and Extension activities. Many of the Focus activities can be done orally as a class before pupils write. Most pupils should then go on to the Practice activities, and some can progress to the Extension activities. The workbook gives extra practice, and for struggling pupils there are Support PCMs, and for those who can be stretched, Extension PCMs are provided.

Group work

If the abilities of the class are more varied, it may be sensible to group the children, with each group working on a particular unit. This is more likely to be effective if the amount of time allocated to 'formal' grammar teaching varies according to different pupils' needs. The consistent structure of the Pupil Book units is designed to make it possible to work in this way.

Individual work

Some teachers may prefer their pupils use the Pupil Books individually; this is recommended only for Books 3–6.

Assessment

Formative assessment: Check-ups

There are frequent Check-ups throughout the Nelson Grammar course. These short assessments cover the skills which have been taught in the preceding units.

For Books 1 and 2, Check-ups are found in the Workbooks and Resource Book 1. For Books 3-6, Check-ups are found in the Resource Books.

Summative assessment: Practice Papers

For Book 2 and Book 6, practice test papers are provided. These are designed to provide children with practice in sitting tests similar to the statutory National Curriculum Tests sat by children in England at the end of Year 2 and Year 6. These practice papers draw on content from across the programme of study for each Key Stage.

Practice Papers are found in Resource Book 1 and Resource Book 3. The answers are found in Teacher's Book 1 and Teacher's Book 2.

Book 6 Revision Book

The Revision Book groups grammatical concepts together, providing revision questions for all aspects of grammar learned during the course. This comprehensive book will be a useful revision tool for children in the lead up to end-of-year tests and can be used as a reference during the next stage of their education.

Nelson Grammar and the new National Curriculum for England (2014)

Nelson Grammar provides excellent coverage of the requirements for the new National Curriculum in England. The careful spiral progression within the course allows revisiting and consolidation of key grammatical areas.

Year 3 Programme of Study

Word Structure

Word structure	Book 3
formation of nouns	Unit 22
articles	Unit 1
word families	Unit 24

Sentence Structure

Sentence structure	Book 3
conjunctions	Unit 25
adverbs	Unit 28
prepositions	Unit 18

Text Structure

Text structure	Book 3
paragraphs	Unit 26
headings & sub headings	Unit 19
perfect tense	Unit 27

Punctuation

Punctuation	Book 3
inverted commas	Unit 16/Unit 20

Year 4 Programme of Study

Word Structure

Word structure	Book 4
plurals & possessives	Unit 7/Unit 8/Unit 17/Unit 24/Unit 26
Standard English verb inflections	Unit 9/Unit 12/Unit 15/Unit 18

Sentence Structure

Sentence structure	Book 4
pronouns & nouns	Unit 8/Unit 21
noun phrases	Unit 17
determiners	Unit 17
frontal adverbials	Unit 23/Unit 27

Text Structure

Text structure	Book 4
paragraphs	Unit 19/Unit 28
noun & pronoun	Unit 8

Punctuation

Punctuation	Book 4
inverted commas	Unit 4/Unit 14/Unit 25
apostrophe of possession	Unit 17/Unit 24
comma – frontal adverbials	Unit 23/Unit 27

Year 5 Programme of Study

Word Structure

Word structure	Book 5
forming verbs	Unit 3/Unit 10/Unit 21
verb prefixes	Unit 21
relative pronouns	Unit 12/Unit 25

Sentence Structure

Sentence structure	Book 5
relative clauses	Unit 17/Unit 25
modal verbs	Unit 24
adverbs	Unit 5/Unit 20/Unit 23/Unit 28

Text Structure

Text structure	Book 5
paragraphs	Unit 20
nouns & pronouns	Unit 16

Punctuation

Punctuation	Book 5
brackets	Unit 27
dashes	Unit 27
commas	Unit 26/Unit 27

Year 6 Programme of Study

Word Structure

Word structure	Book 6
informal vocabulary	Unit 19/Unit 24/Unit 28
formal vocabulary	Unit 19/Unit 14/Unit 28

Sentence Structure

Sentence structure	Book 6
active & passive voice	Unit 18/Unit 23/Unit 27
noun phrases	Unit 12
determiners	Unit 12
ellipsis	Unit 11
informal structure	Unit 19/Unit 24/Unit 28
formal structure	Unit 19/Unit 24/Unit 28
subjunctive	Unit 27

Text Structure

Text structure	Book 6
semantic cohesion	Unit 22
adverbials	Unit 22
headings	Unit 13
sub-headings	Unit 13
columns	Unit 13
bullets	Unit 13
tables	Unit 13

Punctuation

Punctuation	Book 6
semi colon	Unit 21
colon	Unit 21
hyphens	Unit 15/Unit 25

Nelson Grammar and the statutory requirements for Wales, Scotland and Northern Ireland

Nelson Grammar provides an ideal way to underpin your wider literacy work by giving children a firm grasp of the principles of grammar.

Wales

Nelson Grammar is fully in line with the aims and objectives of the National Curriculum for Wales and the Welsh National Literacy and Numeracy Framework (2013) (LNF). The LNF sets out yearly expectations that children should achieve in Grammar and Punctuation, and Nelson Grammar will help children attain these. Nelson Grammar builds skills in:

- Using language appropriate to writing, including standard forms of English
- Using a variety of sentence structures, introducing and building on knowledge of phrases and clauses
- Using adjectives, adverbs and adverbials to improve writing by adding interest and precision
- Using a variety of connectives link ideas and show relationships of time and cause
- Using punctuation to demarcate sentences and for clarity, including the correct use of direct speech punctuation and apostrophes.

Scotland

The Curriculum for Excellence sets out expectations for all children in literacy and language. Nelson Grammar provides a structured progression through the vital language skills that underpin children's achievement throughout the First and Second levels. As children master these language skills, they will be able to apply them across the curriculum. These skills will stand them in good stead as they read, discuss and create texts of their own, whether traditional or multimedia.

Nelson Grammar supports the Experiences and Outcomes for literacy, in particular:

- **Tools for writing** – using knowledge of technical aspects to help my writing communicate effectively within and beyond my place of learning
- **Organising and using information** – considering texts to help create short and extended texts for different purposes
- **Creating texts** – applying the elements which writers use to create different types of short and extended texts with increasingly complex ideas, structures and vocabulary

Northern Ireland

Nelson Grammar provides the vital language skills that will support children's writing in Literacy lessons and in all other areas of the curriculum. It supports many of the objectives of the Northern Ireland Curriculum for Language and Literacy. Nelson Grammar provides the underpinning framework that will help children to:

- understand and use a range of vocabulary by investigating and experimenting with language;
- begin to check their work in relation to specific criteria;
- organise, structure and present ideas and information using traditional and digital means;
- understand some of the differences between spoken and written language;
- use a variety of skills to spell words in their writing;
- develop increasing competence in the use of grammar and punctuation.

Assessment

Formative assessment opportunities are found frequently within Nelson Grammar. Regular marking of children's completed exercises and of their written work from across the curriculum will give you an initial idea of how well they completed the task and provide a basis for further teaching. Regular Check-ups occur after a group of units; these test whether children have retained the information learned previously. Summative tests at the end of Book 2 and Book 6 provide further opportunities for assessment.

The Cambridge International Primary Curriculum

The tables below show the coverage of the Grammar and Punctuation strand of the Cambridge International Primary Curriculum, Stages 3 to 6.

The other strands of the Cambridge International Primary Curriculum: Phonics, spelling and vocabulary; Reading; Writing; Speaking and listening, are covered by the Nelson English Skills series.

The text in bold denotes a unit where a curriculum requirement is specifically addressed. The text not in bold shows where a curriculum requirement is not specifically addressed, but the unit listed may still be helpful in teaching this requirement.

Where the units are not displayed in numerical order, the unit which specifically addresses the curriculum requirement is listed first.

STAGE 3

Curriculum requirement			Nelson Grammar Book 3
GRAMMAR AND PUNCTUATION			
Reading			
	1	Use knowledge of punctuation and grammar to read age-appropriate texts with fluency, understanding and expression.	n/a
	2	Recognise the use of the apostrophe to mark omission in shortened words, e.g. can't, don't.	n/a
	3	Collect examples of nouns, verbs and adjectives, and use the terms appropriately.	Unit 3, 8, 9, 13, 14, 16, 17, 21
	4	Identify pronouns and understand their function in a sentence.	**Unit 11**
	5	Understand that verbs are necessary for meaning in a sentence.	**Unit 4**
	6	Understand pluralisation and use the terms 'singular' and 'plural'.	**Unit 2, 5, 15**
Writing			
	1	Maintain accurate use of capital letters and full stops in showing sentences.	**Unit 4, 19**
	2	Learn the basic conventions of speech punctuation and begin to use speech marks.	**Unit 10, 20**
	3	Use question marks, exclamation marks, and commas in lists.	Unit 4
	4	Continue to improve consistency in the use of tenses.	**Unit 8, 14, 27**
	5	Ensure grammatical agreement of pronouns and verbs in using standard English.	Unit 11
	6	Use a wider variety of sentence types including simple, compound and some complex sentences.	Unit **28**, 21, 23, 25
	7	Begin to vary sentence openings, e.g. with simple adverbs.	Unit 6, 12, 23

STAGE 4

	Curriculum requirement	Nelson Grammar Book 4
	GRAMMAR AND PUNCTUATION	
	Reading	
1	Use knowledge of punctuation and grammar to read with fluency, understanding and expression.	n/a
2	Identify all the punctuation marks and respond to them when reading.	Unit 4, 14, 25
3	Learn the use of the apostrophe to show possession, e.g. *girl's, girls'*.	**Unit 13, 24, 26**
4	Practise using commas to mark out meaning within sentences.	Unit 25, 27
5	Identify adverbs and their impact on meaning.	**Unit 6, 10, 16, 23, 27**
6	Investigate past, present and future tenses of verbs.	**Unit 1, 5, 9, 12, 15, 18**
7	Investigate the grammar of different sentences: statements, questions and orders.	n/a
8	Understand the use of connectives to structure an argument, e.g. *if, although*.	Unit 2, 23
	Writing	
1	Use a range of end-of-sentence punctuation with accuracy.	Unit 4, 11, 12, 13, 14, 19, 20, 22, 23, 25, 28
2	Use speech marks and begin to use other associated punctuation.	**Unit 4, 14, 25**
3	Experiment with varying tenses within texts, e.g. in dialogue.	Unit 1, 9, 12, 14, 15, 18, 25
4	Use a wider variety of connectives in an increasing range of sentences.	Unit 2, 27
5	Re-read own writing to check punctuation and grammatical sense.	n/a

STAGE 5

	Curriculum requirement	Nelson Grammar Book 5
	GRAMMAR AND PUNCTUATION	
	Reading	
1	Learn how dialogue is set out and punctuated.	**Unit 4, 7**
2	Identify prepositions and use the term.	n/a
3	Understand conventions of standard English, e.g. agreement of verbs.	All units
4	Understand the difference between direct and reported speech.	**Unit 4, 7**
5	Investigate clauses within sentences and how they are connected.	**Unit 17, 25,** 5, 12, 16
	Writing	
1	Begin to use the comma to separate clauses within sentences and clarify meaning in complex sentences.	**Unit 5, 19, 26, 27**
2	Use apostrophes for both possession and shortened forms.	**Unit 6, 14**
3	Begin to set out dialogue appropriately, using a range of punctuation.	**Unit 4, 7**
4	Use an increasing range of subordinating connectives.	Unit 5, 12, 16, 25, 28
5	Explore ways of combining simple sentences and re-ordering clauses to make compound and complex sentences.	**Unit 5, 12, 16, 17, 25,** 28
6	Use pronouns, making clear to what or to whom they refer.	**Unit 2, 12, 16, 17**
7	Practise proofreading and editing own writing for clarity and correctness.	**Unit 11, 28**

STAGE 6

Curriculum requirement			Nelson Grammar Book 6
GRAMMAR AND PUNCTUATION			
Reading			
	1	Identify uses of the colon, semi-colon, parenthetic commas, dashes and brackets.	**Unit 21**
	2	Revise different word classes.	All units
	3	Investigate the use of conditionals, e.g. to express possibility.	Unit **20**, 5, 17
	4	Begin to show awareness of the impact of writers' choices of sentence length and structure.	Unit 1, 2, 11, 12
	5	Revise language conventions and grammatical features of different types of text.	**Unit 19, 24, 27, 28**
	6	Explore use of active and passive verbs within a sentence.	**Unit 18, 23, 27**
	7	Understand the conventions of Standard English usage in different forms of writing.	**Unit 19, 24, 27, 28**
	8	Distinguish the main clause and other clauses in a complex sentence.	**Unit 6, 8, 10, 20, 26**
Writing			
	1	Punctuate speech and use apostrophes accurately.	**Unit 16**
	2	Use a wider range of connectives to clarify relationships between ideas, e.g. *however, therefore, although*.	**Unit 10, 20**
	3	Use connectives to structure an argument or discussion.	**Unit 22**, 4, 6, 10, 20
	4	Develop grammatical control of complex sentences, manipulating them for effect.	**Unit 6, 8, 10**
	5	Develop increasing accuracy in using punctuation effectively to mark out the meaning in complex sentences.	Unit 15, 21, 25

Book 3 Scope and Sequence

Unit	Pupil Book	Pupil Book Focus	Pupil Book Practice	Pupil Book Extension	Resource Book Support	Resource Book Extension
1	articles: indefinite a/an	choosing a/an for given nouns	sorting simple words under a & an headings	completing sentences with a or an/a or an before words beginning with eu, h and u	adding a or an to simple nouns/supplying own words for a/an table/writing sentences	correcting a/an mistakes in sentences/supplying a/an before adjectives
2	singular & plural: noun/verb agreement	completing sentences with correct part of verb/sentence writing with was & were	correcting noun – verb agreement in sentences	agreement with collective nouns/food & money writing sentences	completing sentences with is, are, was or were/correcting noun – verb agreement in sentences	correcting noun – verb agreement in continuous prose/writing sentences with collective nouns
3	adjectives: comparative with er; superlative with est	changing adjectives to superlative adjectives in sentences	writing comparative & superlative adjectives/writing sentences with superlative adjectives	completing sentences with irregular comparative & superlative adjectives	completing sentences with comparatives & superlatives from picture clue/filling in comparative & superlative tables	writing sentences using comparatives & superlatives
4	sentences: verb, punctuation, making sense	punctuating sentences	completing sentences with suitable verbs	completing sentences with past tense verbs/writing sentences	punctuating sentences/identifying verbs in sentences/writing sentences	writing sentences from given beginnings
5	singular and plural: nouns ending in y	forming plurals of given nouns	forming plural nouns/forming singular nouns/writing sentences	solving clues with y plurals	forming plural nouns/forming singular nouns/writing sentences with plural nouns	completing plural noun crossword/forming plural nouns & writing sentences
6	adverbs: comparative & superlative	identifying adverbs in sentences	completing adverb table	completing sentences with irregular comparatives & superlatives	completing adverb table/classifying adverbs	writing sentences with given pairs of adverbs
7	prepositions: prepositions of place	identifying prepositions in sentences	choosing the best preposition to use in sentences	listing prepositions and their opposites	matching prepositions to their opposites and using in written sentences	writing sentences with prepositions based on picture clues
8	verbs: irregular past simple tense	matching present simple & past simple verbs	supplying past simple tense verbs to complete sentences	matching verb family names to their irregular past simple tense/choosing correct verb to make past tense sentences	identifying present simple & past simple sentences/completing verb table with irregular past simple tense verbs	using dictionary to find irregular past simple tenses/writing sentences
9	adjectives: comparatives with more/superlatives with most	choosing correct adjectives to complete sentences	completing adjective table	writing comparatives & superlatives/writing sentences	writing and classifying comparatives/writing and classifying superlatives	using given comparatives & superlatives in sentences
10	sentences: direct speech – speech marks	identifying spoken words in sentences/punctuating direct speech sentences	punctuating a conversation	using synonyms for said/writing sentences	identifying spoken words in sentences/adding missing speech marks in sentences	writing speech bubbles as conversation
11	pronouns: subject & object pronouns	replacing nouns with pronouns in sentences	changing nouns & proper nouns to pronouns in sentences	completing sentences with reflexive pronouns	identifying pronouns in sentences/replacing nouns with pronouns	using given pairs of pronouns in own sentences
12	adverbs: comparative & superlative with more & most	forming comparatives & superlatives of given adverbs	forming comparative & superlative adverbs in sentences	replacing phrases with single adverbs/using adverbs in sentences	identifying adverbs in sentences/using adverbs in sentences	completing adverb table/using adverbs in own sentences
13	adjectives: number & number order adjectives	matching cardinal & ordinal adjectives	identifying number & number order adjectives & nouns they describe	completing passage with number order adjectives from picture stimulus	identifying number & number order adjectives & nouns they describe/matching number & number order adjectives	using number & number order adjectives in own sentences
14	verbs: future tense with shall & will	identifying future tense verbs in sentences	changing verbs from present tenses to future tense/changing verbs from past tenses to future tense	completing verb table/using shall and will for strong statements	identifying future tense verbs in sentences/classifying verb tenses/writing future tense sentences	changing sentences from past to future tense

* denotes content that is not specified in the National Curriculum for England (2014) but which will support children's wider knowledge and understanding of grammar.

Unit	Pupil Book	Pupil Book Focus	Pupil Book Practice	Pupil Book Extension	Resource Book Support	Resource Book Extension
15	**singular and plural:** nouns ending in *f* & *fe*	forming plurals of given nouns	forming plural nouns/forming singular nouns/using in sentences	nouns taking *s* & *ves*/completing sentences	identifying plural nouns in sentences/completing sentences with plural nouns/writing own sentences	solving clues with plural nouns/choosing correct form of plural/writing own sentences
16	**nouns:** abstract	identifying common & abstract nouns in list	identifying common & abstract nouns in sentences	forming abstract nouns from common nouns, adjectives & verbs	classifying nouns/using abstract nouns in sentences	forming abstract nouns from adjectives & verbs/using abstract nouns in sentences
17	**adjectives:** formed from verbs & nouns	identifying adjectives in sentences & verb or noun root	forming adjectives from verbs & nouns/completing sentences	using nouns as adjectives in sentences	identifying adjectives in sentences/forming adjectives to complete sentences/sentence writing	forming adjectives from nouns & verbs/writing noun phrases/sentence writing
18	**prepositions:** place/opposites	identifying prepositions/matching opposites	choosing correct preposition to complete sentences/writing own sentences	completing passage with appropriate prepositions	identifying prepositions/using prepositions in own sentences	using prepositions in own sentences/writing description with prepositions
19	**capital letters:** headings & subheadings	adding capital letters to proper nouns	film and book titles/main & subheadings	adding missing capital letters to information passage	correcting sentences missing capital letters/writing headings & subheadings correctly	listing favourite books and authors/creating headings & subheadings for given topics
20	**sentences:** direct speech	punctuating direct speech sentences	punctuating direct speech sentences where direct speech comes first	punctuating direct speech sentences where direct speech comes second	punctuating various forms of direct speech sentences	punctuating and setting out a passage of direct speech
21	**adjectives:** phrases	identifying adjective phrases in sentences	using adjective phrases in sentences/forming adjective phrases for given nouns	differentiating between adjective phrases & simple sentences /writing & punctuating sentences	identifying adjective phrases in sentences/writing adjective phrases for given nouns/writing own sentences	writing own sentences with adjective phrases for given nouns
22	**prefixes:** opposites and specific meanings	adding prefixes to make opposites/adding prefixes to make sentences opposite	matching words & definitions	finding words beginning with specific prefixes/sentence writing/definitions	making opposites with prefixes/matching prefixes with definitions	finding words beginning with specific prefixes from definitions
23	**adverbs:** phrases	identifying adverb phrases in sentences	using adverb phrases in sentences/forming adverb phrases for given verbs	differentiating between adverb phrases & simple sentences / writing and punctuating sentences	Identifying adverb phrases in sentences/writing adverb phrases for given verbs/writing own sentences	writing own sentences with adverb phrases for given verbs
24	**suffixes:** *er/ing/ed*	completing verb table	completing sentences with correct suffix	changing past tense sentences into present progressive/changing present tense sentences into past tense	forming comparative adjectives/ forming present progressive tense verbs & past simple tense verbs from verb family name	writing present progressive tense sentences & past simple tense sentences from given verb family names
25	**conjunctions:** when/before/while/after	identifying conjunctions in sentences	completing sentences with suitable conjunctions	joining sentences & using pronouns	identifying short sentences & conjunctions/writing sentences with given conjunctions	joining sentences and using pronouns
26	**paragraphs:** time in stories	answering questions about structure in extended writing	ordering paragraph openings by time	writing a three paragraph story with support	identifying the first word of paragraphs in a story/continuing the story	rewriting a story to include paragraphs
27	**verbs:** perfect tense with *have/has*	identifying the perfect tense in sentences	changing sentences from the present simple to the perfect tense	completing sentences with perfect tense verbs	identifying prefect tense verbs in sentences/completing a verb table	completing sentences with the perfect tense/writing sentences with the past simple and perfect tense
28	**sentences:** clauses	identifying main clauses in sentences	identifying main & subordinate clauses in sentences	adding main & subordinate clauses to complete sentences	identifying main & subordinate clauses in sentences/adding main & subordinate clauses to complete sentences	writing own sentences with main & subordinate clause

BOOK 3 UNIT 1 Articles

Indefinite a/an

Both 'a' and 'an' are indefinite articles used with singular countable nouns. They are used with nouns that are unspecified.

This is the only unit in the course that deals with articles as they are fairly easy for children to grasp. The Extra section of the Teacher's Notes introduces the definite article 'the'.

Pupil Book

Focus
- Read the information box on page 6.
- Explain/discuss the terms *vowel* and *consonant*.
- Do the activities orally.

Answers
1. **an** elephant
2. **a** bush
3. **an** apple
4. **a** snake
5. **a** caravan
6. **an** omelette
7. **an** insect
8. **a** cabbage
9. **an** ant

Practice
- The activity should be done individually.
- When completed, get the children to read out their answers.

Answers

with a	with an
cap	elf
sun	eel
rug	egg
rat	ear
table	inch
card	owl
box	ant
log	oar
fox	arm
mat	eye

Extension
- Activity A should be done individually.
- Read and discuss the information box on page 6.

Answers
(A)
1. There is **an** ice cube in my drink.
2. We had **an** argument this morning.
3. **A** spider has eight legs.

(B)
1. a uniform
2. a house
3. an hour
4. an umbrella
5. a unicorn
6. a euro

Resource Book

Support PCM
- Children should work on Activity A individually.
- Activity B: children can work in pairs.
- Discuss answers in class when activity is complete.

Answers
(A)
1. **an** oar
2. **an** army
3. **a** book
4. **an** ear
5. **a** window
6. **an** arm

(B) Individual answers

(C) Individual answers

Extension PCM
- Activity A should be done individually.
- Read and discuss the information box on page 5.
- Ask children for other adjectives that use *a* or *an*.

Answers
(A)
1. A army of ants built an nest. ✗
2. I am buying a house. ✓
3. We have to wear an uniform for school. ✗
4. A eel swam in the stream. ✗
5. In a hour we can go home. ✗
6. May I have an apple? ✓

(B)
1. **An** army of ants built **a** nest.
3. We have to wear **a** uniform for school.
3. **An** eel swam in the stream.
5. In **an** hour we can go home.

(C)
1. **a** white dress
2. **an** empty box
3. **a** big monster
4. **an** ugly toad
5. **an** orange scarf
6. **a** tiny ant
7. **an** unhappy boy
8. **an** awful song
9. **a** great day

Extra
- Introduce the term *the* as the *definite article* used with specific countable and uncountable nouns in both singular and plural forms.
- Demonstrate specific and non-specific nouns in context.

BOOK 3 UNIT 2 Singular and plural

Noun–verb agreement

Certain tenses require a change in verb formation depending on person. The tenses children know so far are:
- present simple – I walk/he walks
- present progressive (also known as 'continuous') – I am walking/she is walking/they are walking
- past progressive (also known as 'continuous') – I was walking/We were walking

The present progressive and past progressive are sometimes also known as the present progressive and past progressive.

This unit examines the use of singular nouns with singular verbs, and plural nouns with plural verbs. The Extension work concentrates on the use of singular verbs with 'each' and 'every', collective nouns, money and food items.

Pupil Book

Focus
- Begin by revising the terms: *singular/plural/verb*
- Read and discuss the information box on page 8.
- Do more oral examples with the children.
- Children should work individually on the activities.

Answers
(A) 1 The cottages **are** empty.
    2 We **are** going to buy them.
    3 I **am** going to live in one of them.
    4 The walls **are** dirty.
    5 The chimney **is** broken.

(B) 1 flowers **were**   2 book **was**
    3 shoes **were**   4 garages **were**
    5 children **were**   6 tree **was**

Practice
- Children should work individually on the activity.

Answers
1 The cake **crumbles** when you cut it.
2 The icing **looks** very soft.
3 I **like** to eat this cake.
4 We **buy** this cake at the bakery.

Extension
- Read and discuss the information box on page 9.
- Ask children for other examples of collective nouns.
- Children work individually.

Answers
(A) 1 the sandals – **plural** verb
    2 the spoonful – **singular** verb
    3 each boy – **singular** verb
    4 peaches and cream – **singular** verb
    5 this bunch – **singular** verb
    6 80p – **singular** verb

(B) Individual answers

Resource Book

Support PCM
- The incorrect use of *is/are, was/were* is common in children's speech and writing. The activities allow you to assess whether children have grasped the difference.

Answers
(A) 1 The crowd **is** huge.
    2 The flowers **are** wilting.
    3 Each cup **is** broken.
    4 That cow **is** brown.
    5 The orchestra **is** playing.

(B) 1 The herd **was** grazing.
    2 The soldiers **were** marching.
    3 Every book **was** damaged.
    4 The musician **was** practising.
    2 The library **was** closed.

(C) 1 The queue of people **is** very long.
    2 A swarm of bees **was** flying across our garden.
    3 The puppies **were** born last night.

Extension PCM
- Work orally on Activity A before children write. Read through the passage asking children to raise a hand if they spot a mistake.
- Activity B: children work individually

Answers
(A) We **go** to the library on a Saturday morning.
    I **like** to read adventure stories but my sister **likes** funny books.
    We **take** three books home every week.
    The man in the library **is** very helpful.
    If he can't **find** the book I **want**, he **orders** it for next time.

(B) Individual answers

Extra
Make verb cards, e.g.

| I walk. He _?_. They _?_. |

| I am singing. She __?__. We __?__. |

Individuals pick a card and complete the verbs.

15

BOOK 3 UNIT 3 Adjectives

Comparative and superlative

Adjectives are initially explained as 'describing' words. They pinpoint a quality or a feature of a noun or pronoun. Throughout the course, children will encounter single adjectives, comparative and superlative adjectives, adjective phrases possessive adjectives and adjective (relative) clauses.

Children have encountered comparative adjectives formed with the suffix *er* and superlative adjectives formed with the suffix *est*.

This unit revises the concept of comparatives and superlatives using short, common adjectives (usually one syllable) with the suffixes *er* and *est*. The Pupil Book Extension activity deals with a small group of irregular comparatives and superlatives which children should learn.

The construction of forming comparatives with 'more' and superlatives with 'most' (usually adjectives of three or more syllables) will be introduced later.

Pupil Book

Focus
- Revise/explain the term *adjective* and ask for examples.
- Discuss what children understand by *comparing* things.
- Read and discuss the information box on page 10.
- Point out that when we are comparing three or more things, we put the word *the* in front of the adjective, e.g. *the oldest car*.

Answers
1. The building is the **highest** in town.
2. That is the **brightest** star in the sky.
3. Kim is the **youngest** girl in the class.
4. Tuesday was the **coldest** day last week.
5. This is the **strongest** rope we sell.

Practice
- For both Activities, read through the vocabulary box to ensure children understand the words.
- For Activity A, children can complete the activity by writing individually, or this can be done orally as a class with you acting as scribe on the board.
  Ask children to use the comparatives and superlatives in sentences.
- Children should work individually on Activity B.

Answers

comparative	superlative
cloudier	cloudiest
braver	bravest
fatter	fattest
spookier	spookiest
wiser	wisest
redder	reddest

B Individual answers

Extension
- Read and discuss the information box on page 11.
- Children should tackle the activity individually.
- Discuss answers as a class.
- Ask children to suggest sentences using other adjectives from the table.

Answers
1. This is the **best** birthday party I have ever had.
2. You can get **more** water in this jug than that one.
3. Today's weather made it the **worst** day of the holiday.
4. I have **more** sums to do than you.

Resource Book

Support PCM
- If necessary, do Activity A orally before children write.
- If children are struggling, have three children stand at the front of the class with the name cards Aisha (tall), Tom (smaller) and Sara (smallest).
- Activity B can be done individually.

Answers
A
1. Aisha is **tall**.
2. Sara is **small**.
3. Tom is **smaller** than Aisha and **taller** than Sara.
4. Sara is **smaller** than Tom and Aisha.
5. Aisha is the **tallest** of the three children.
6. Sara is the **smallest** of the three children.

B
adjective	comparative	superlative
green	greener	greenest
tasty	tastier	tastiest
wide	wider	widest
lovely	lovelier	loveliest
blue	bluer	bluest
tiny	tinier	tiniest

Extension PCM
- Discuss the example to ensure children are clear what is required.
- Children should then work individually.

Answers
1. a This is a **heavier** parcel.
   b This is **the heaviest** parcel.
2. a I went a **longer** way around.
   b I went **the longest** way around.
3. a That was a **better** film.
   b That was **the best** film.
4. a He needs **more** help.
   b He needs **the most** help.
5. a The weather has been **worse** today.
   b The weather has been **the worst** today.
6. a I had a **better** day today.
   b I had **the best** day today.
7. a This is **more** than I can eat.
   b This is **the most** I can eat.

Extra
Write simple sentences on the board, e.g.
I am happy.
You are brave.
He is good. etc.
Have children say the comparative and superlative forms of the sentences.

# BOOK 3 UNIT 4 Sentences

Punctuation

The concept of a sentence as a unit of language that 'makes sense' can be a difficult concept for some children to grasp. The course builds children's confidence in this area through giving them the opportunity to look at punctuation of statements, questions and exclamations to familiarise themselves with what a 'sentence' looks and sounds like.

Throughout the course, children will encounter: sentence punctuation; the concept of 'making sense'; direct and indirect speech; clauses which combine to make multi-clause sentences; parts of sentences – subject/object, subject/predicate; focusing on the sentence as a unit of language that can be improved; and Standard English constructions.

This unit revises punctuation for statements, questions, and exclamations. Children will be familiar with the term *verb*. A sentence must have a verb – with the warning that the verb has, of course, to be a finite verb and this concept can cause problems for young children. At this stage it is better to tackle individual mistakes, e.g. I singing (I am singing) than to explain finite and non-finite verbs. This will be introduced in the latter stages of the book.

Pupil Book

Focus
- Revise/explain the term sentence and ask for examples which include statements, questions and exclamations.
- Introduce/revise the terms:
  verb, capital letter, full stop, question mark, exclamation mark.
- Read the information box on page 12.
- Ask children for some more oral examples of complete sentences.
- The activity can be done on the board or children can write.

Answers
1 **T**he wind <u>blows</u> around the house.
2 **M**y family <u>lives</u> in the country.
3 **I** <u>am sitting</u> on my chair.
4 **W**here <u>are</u> you <u>going</u> on holiday?
5 **T**he stone <u>cracked</u> the window.

Practice
- Activity A: Read and discuss the verbs in the box.
- Ask: *Which verbs are one word? Which verbs are made up of two words?*
- Children complete the activity individually.
- Discuss answers.

Answers
1 I **am looking** at the picture.
2 It **is** very beautiful.
3 The picture **looks** very old.
4 It **was painted** a long time ago.
5 The artist **used** lots of colours.

Extension
- For Activity A: Revise the simple and past progressive tenses.
- Children should work individually.
- Individuals read out sentences for Activity B. Class decide if they are complete sentences.

Answers
(A) Suggested answers
1 Louis **walked** into the house.
2 He **heard** thunder.
3 The rain **fell** quickly.
4 The lightning **was flashing** across the sky.
5 Louis **hid** under the bedclothes.

(B) Individual answers

Resource Book

Support PCM
- Children should work individually.
- Activity B: Remind children that a verb can be one or two words.

Answers
(A) 1 **T**he boy tripped on the step**.**
    2 **T**he gate was creaking in the wind**.**
    3 **W**ere they playing in the snow**?**

(B) 1 The child <u>plays</u> with his toys.
    2 The child <u>is playing</u> with his toys.
    3 The child <u>played</u> with his toys.
    4 The child <u>was playing</u> with his toys.

(C) Individual answers

Extension PCM
- Children should work individually.
- When completed, individuals read out their sentences. The class decide if they are complete sentences.

Answers
Individual answers

Extra
Play 'Building sentences'.
- Write 'The' on the board.
- One child comes out and writes the next word of the sentence.
- Other children add further words.
- How long a sentence can be made?

BOOK 3 UNIT 5 Singular and plural

Words ending in y

Most nouns have a singular form (one) and a plural form (more than one). The vast majority of nouns form their plural by adding *s*.

Throughout the course, children will encounter plurals with *s* and *es*, pluralisation for words ending in *y/f/fe/o/oo*, and irregular plurals.

This unit revises the work on singular and plural with nouns that form their plurals by adding *s* or *es*, and extends the work to nouns ending in *y*.

As the course progresses, the Extra section of the Teacher's Notes will suggest examining the plural form of nouns with foreign origins.

Pupil Book

Focus
- Revise/explain *more than one (noun)* and ask for examples with *s* and *es*.
- Introduce/revise the terms:
  – *singular* = one
  – *plural* = more than one
- Read the information box on page 14.
- Revise/discuss the terms *vowel* and *consonant*.
- The activity should be tackled individually.

Answers

1	flasks	2	classes	3	disasters
4	spots	5	trays	6	churches
7	hobbies	8	flies	9	flashes
10	lorries	11	bodies	12	days

Practice
- Activity A: Ask children *Does a vowel or consonant come before the* y? *What is the rule?*
- Activities B and D: Remind children that sentences can be statements, questions or exclamations. Revise punctuation at the end of sentences before children write.

Answers

(A) 1 ladies 2 puppies 3 lilies 4 cities

(B) Individual answers

(C) 1 cherry 2 army 3 bay 4 diary

(D) Individual answers

Extension
- Children can work in small groups against the clock!

Answers
1. Small horses are called ponies.
2. Big roads for fast-moving traffic are called motorways.
3. There are 196 countries in the world.
4. Valleys are areas of low land between hills.
5. Keys are used to lock doors.
6. When the weather is hot, people often eat ice lollies.

Resource Book

Support PCM
- Children should work individually on all the activities.

Answers

(A) 1 boys 2 trays
    3 cities 4 boxes
    5 donkeys 6 torches
    7 poppies 8 dresses

(B) 1 class 2 party
    3 crash 4 hobby
    5 spy 6 way
    7 lunch 8 toy

(C) Individual answers

Extension PCM
- Activity A: If children are not familiar with the crossword format, explain how it works before children write. They can work in pairs.
- Activity B should be tackled individually.

Answers

(A) Fill in the crossword.
    1 down: bunches
    2 down: atlases
    3 down: frogs
    1 across: bays
    2 across: toys
    3 across: armies
    4 across: flashes

(B) 1 canaries
    2 birthdays
    3 families
    4 turkeys
    Sentences = individual answers

Extra
Give children some singular foreign nouns to look up in a dictionary to find their plurals.

e.g. *stimulus (stimuli)* *fungus (fungi)* Latin
      gateau (gateaux) *bureau (bureaux/bureaus)* French

Discuss word meanings.

BOOK 3 UNIT 6 Adverbs

Comparative and superlative

Adverbs are usually explained as words which 'add' to a verb, giving the detail of how, where or when an action is done.

Throughout the course, children will encounter: single adverbs (manner/time/place); comparative and superlative adverbs; adverbial phrases; adverb pairs and adverbial clauses.

This unit revises the concept of comparatives and superlatives using short, common adverbs (usually one syllable) with the suffixes er/est. The Extension activities revise a short list of irregular comparatives and superlatives for children to learn.

Pupil Book

Focus

- Revise/explain the term *adverb* and ask for examples.
- Discuss what children understand by *comparing* things.
- Read the information box on page 16.
- Discuss the comparative 'later'. The adjective is 'late'. Ask: *Do we add* er *or* to it? Can children formulate the rule?
- Point out that when comparing three or more actions, the word 'the' is used in front of the adverb, e.g. *He worked the hardest.*
- Do the Activity orally.

Answers

Ⓐ 1   The girl sang the **loudest** of all.
    2   A tortoise moves **slower** than a hare.
    3   I go to bed **earlier** during the week.
    4   The red racing car travelled the **fastest**.
    5   I'm working very **hard**.

Practice

- Children can complete the activity by writing individually, or this can be done orally as a class with you acting as scribe on the board.

Answers

adverb	comparative	superlative
hard	harder	hardest
fast	faster	fastest
late	later	latest
high	higher	highest
slow	slower	slowest
loud	louder	loudest
near	nearer	nearest

Extension

- Before children look at the table of irregular adverbs, write the first column on the board. Can the children remember the comparatives and superlatives?
- Children tackle the activity individually.

Answers

Ⓐ 1   He ran **further** than his friend.
    2   You are looking **worse** today than you did yesterday.
    3   I play football **better** than my brother.
    4   Sam sings the **best** in his class.
    5   She had collected the **most** game cards.

Resource Book

Support PCM

- Children tackle the activities individually.

Answers

Ⓐ

adverb	comparative	superlative
little	less	least
fast	faster	fastest
late	later	latest
well	better	best
near	nearer	nearest
hard	harder	hardest
much	more	most
badly	worse	worst

Ⓑ

adverb	comparative	superlative
slow	later	furthest
high	faster	earliest
well	better	least
hard	louder	nearest

Extension PCM

- Read and discuss the first answer with the children so they understand what is required.

Answers

Individual answers

Extra

- Make irregular adverb cards, e.g.

| worse | much | furthest |

- Children choose a card and use the adverb on the card in a sentence.

19

BOOK 3 UNIT 7 Prepositions

Prepositions of place

Prepositions show how words in sentences are related to one another either in place [space] or time. Some prepositions, e.g. 'on', can be used for both place and time.

Prepositions can be single words (e.g. towards / beneath / during); pairs of words (e.g. because of / near to); or three words (e.g. in front of/ in addition to).

This unit begins the work on prepositions with prepositions of place, which are the easiest form for children to grasp.

Pupil Book

Focus
- Introduce the term *preposition*.
- Read the information box on page 18.
- Point out that *preposition* has the word *position* in it.
- Do the Activity orally, getting the children to do actions as they say the *preposition*.

Answers
1. up
2. over
3. on
4. in

Practice
- For the Activity, read through the vocabulary box to ensure children understand the words.
- Children can complete the activity by writing individually, or this can be done orally as a class with you acting as scribe on the board.

Answers
1. The boy jumped **over** the step.
2. I climbed **up** the stairs.
3. The apples are **in** the bowl.
4. The dog is **on** the chair.
5. The desk is **under** the window.

Extension
- Introduce / revise the term *opposite*.
- Encourage the children to do actions for each of the *prepositions* in the box to help them identify the *opposites*.

Answers
(A) & (B)

under	over
down	up
in	out
outside	inside
on	off

Resource Book

Support PCM
- Children are required to match *opposite prepositions*, and write sentences.

Answers
(A) in / out
up / down
inside / outside
under / over
on / off
behind / in front

(B) Individual answers

Extension PCM
- Discuss the picture before children write.

Answers
Individual answers

Extra
- Make *preposition* cards e.g.

| on | over | down |

- Individuals come to the front and act out the *preposition* with an object e.g. a book.
- Class guess by forming sentences e.g. *The book is on the table*.

BOOK 3 UNIT 8 Verbs

Irregular past simple tense

Verbs are often explained as 'doing words' or 'being words'. They are possibly the most complex part of speech for young children to grasp because of their many forms and tenses.

Throughout the course, children will encounter the present simple, present progressive (also known as continuous), past simple, past progressive, present perfect (labelled simply *perfect* throughout the course), past perfect, future, infinitive (labelled verb *family name* in the early parts of the course), auxiliary verbs, modals, active and passive verbs and subjunctive verbs (a construction very rarely used except in extremely formal writing).

Participles are referred to as '*ing* words' and 'regular past simple tense words'; finite verbs are referred to as 'main' or 'proper verbs', and it is for the teacher to decide the appropriate time to introduce the terms *participle* and *finite verb*.

This unit revises the past simple tense with *ed/d* and introduces irregular past simple tense verbs.

Pupil Book

Focus
- Revise/explain the term *verb* and ask for examples.
- Introduce/revise the term *past simple tense* and ask for examples.
- Read the information box on page 20.
- Say other *verb family names* and ask children for the past simple tense, e.g. *to look/looked*, etc.
- Children can do the Activities in writing, or orally with you acting as scribe on the board. All the irregular examples in this activity change one vowel or consonant from the infinitive to make the *past simple tense*.

Answers
grow/grew   draw/drew
make/made   play/played
hike/hiked   give/gave
come/came   shine/shone
throw/threw   pile/piled
jump/jumped   bake/baked
hold/held   swim/swam
run/ran

Practice
- Explain to the children that the past simple tense verbs required to complete the sentences could be regular or irregular.

Answers
1. We **arrived** at school early this morning.
2. The teacher **gave** us some jobs to do.
3. I **mixed** the paints.
4. My friend **threw** away the empty tins.
5. We **sorted** the paints.

Extension
- Read the information box on page 21.
- Explain that the verbs in Activity A do not follow the 'change one vowel of consonant' rule to make their past simple tense.
- Children should work individually.

Answers
(A) to leave/left   to catch/caught
    to think/thought   to meet/met
    to speak/spoke   to find/found
    to have/had   to sleep/slept

(B) 1 I **was** cross with Judy.
    2 The day **was** cold and damp.
    3 The children **ran** across the field.
    4 Mum **made** lovely cakes.

Resource Book

Support PCM
- Children should work individually.
- Activity A: When completed, ask children to change the present simple tense sentences into past simple tense sentences, and the past simple tense sentences into present simple tense sentences.

Answers
(A) 1 present simple
    2 past simple
    3 present simple
    4 past simple
    5 past simple

(B)

verb family name	past simple tense
to grow	grew
to draw	drew
to swim	swam
to write	wrote
to give	gave
to come	came
to sing	sang
to go	went
to find	found

(C) Individual answers

Extension PCM
- Children may already know the irregular past simple tense of these verbs but encourage them to use a dictionary if they are unsure.

Answers
1. fought
2. meant
3. bought
4. drank
5. flew

(B) Individual answers

Extra
Make infinitive cards of verbs that have irregular past simple tenses, e.g.

| to go | to buy | to write |

Individuals pick a card and give the irregular past simple tense.

BOOK 3 UNIT 9 Adjectives

> **Comparative and superlative with *more* and *most***
>
> Adjectives are usually explained as 'describing' words. They pinpoint a quality or a feature of a noun or pronoun. Throughout the course, children will encounter single adjectives, comparative and superlative adjectives, adjective phrases, possessive adjectives and adjective (relative) clauses.
>
> Children have encountered comparative adjectives formed with the suffix *er* and superlative adjectives formed with the suffix *est*.
>
> This unit revises the concept of comparatives and superlatives with *er/est*, and introduces the 'more' and 'most' form of comparatives and superlatives.

Pupil Book

Focus
- Revise/explain the term *adjective* and ask for examples.
- Discuss what children understand by *comparing* things.
- Read and discuss the information box on page 22.
- Remind children that when comparing three or more things, the word *the* is used in front of the adjective, e.g. *the oldest car*.
- Ask children for other 'long' adjectives they think we would use 'more' and 'most' with.

Answers
A
1. This is the **nicest** birthday party I have ever had.
2. This box is **heavier** than that one.
3. I am the **tallest** in my family.
4. That is the **fiercest** tiger in the zoo.
5. My hands are **cleaner** than yours.

Practice
- Children can copy the table in full or simply list the missing adjectives.
- When the table is complete, get the class to read each group of adjectives, e.g. *silly/sillier/silliest* to help them 'hear' the correct forms.

Answers

adjective	comparative	superlative
silly	**sillier**	silliest
interesting	more interesting	**most interesting**
good	**better**	best
beautiful	**more beautiful**	most beautiful
little	less	least
happy	happier	happiest
wonderful	**more wonderful**	**most wonderful**
merry	merrier	**merriest**
some	more	most
bad	worse	worst
comfortable	more comfortable	**most comfortable**
new	newer	newest
old	older	oldest
wise	wiser	wisest

Extension
- Children should tackle Activities A and B individually if possible.

Answers
A
1. more important
2. bigger
3. best
4. most surprising
5. most frightening
6. sleepiest
7. smaller
8. more attractive

B Individual answers

Resource Book

Support PCM
- Activity A: Suggest that children tick each adjective in the box when they have written the comparative under the correct heading.
- Discuss answers as a class.
- Activity B: Suggest that children tick each adjective in the box when they have written the superlative under the correct heading.
- Discuss answers as a class.

Answers

A

+ er	+ more
lighter	more wonderful
angrier	more peaceful
hotter	more horrible
wetter	more intelligent
gloomier	more famous

B

+ est	+ most
biggest	most beautiful
loneliest	most comfortable
noisiest	most terrible
shabbiest	most frightening
richest	most dangerous

Extension PCM
- The activity should be done individually.
- If necessary, model the first example, e.g. *I had the most wonderful time today*.
- Ask children for other sentences with 'most wonderful'.

Answers
Individual answers

Extra
- From children's suggestions, make a list on the board of 'long' adjectives that use 'more/most' in their comparative and superlative forms.

BOOK 3 UNIT 10 Sentences

Direct speech

The concept of a sentence as a unit of language that 'makes sense' can be a difficult concept for some children to grasp. The course builds children's confidence in this area through giving them the opportunity to look at punctuation of statements, questions and exclamations to familiarise themselves with what a 'sentence' looks and sounds like.

Throughout the course, children will encounter: sentence punctuation; the concept of 'making sense'; direct and indirect speech; clauses which combine to make multi-clause sentences; parts of sentences – subject/object, subject/predicate; focusing on the sentence as a unit of language that can be improved; and Standard English constructions.

This unit begins work on direct speech. Children often find correctly punctuating direct speech sentences problematic. Several units in the course focus on direct speech so that the various rules can be built up gradually. In this unit, the focus is on speech marks (inverted commas), and beginning a new line when a different person speaks. In fact, it is a new paragraph rather than just a new line but it is left to the teacher's judgement whether the terms 'paragraph' and 'indenting' should be introduced at this stage.

Pupil Book

Focus
- Begin by asking children how they know characters are speaking to each other in stories.
- Ask them to look in their storybook/class reader and find a part where characters are speaking to each other. How does it look different from the rest of the page?
- Read the information box on page 24.
- Ask the class to read just the spoken words in the final two examples.
- Do Activities A and B orally. Activity B can then be copied and punctuated individually.

Answers
(A) Children should say only the underlined words.
  1 "<u>I must cut the grass today,</u>" said Mum.
  2 "<u>I'll be lucky to finish this homework!</u>" said Toby.
  3 Mr Visram said, "<u>My leg is very painful.</u>"
  4 "<u>Stick out your tongue,</u>" said the doctor.

(B) 1 "This window is broken!" said the angry man.
  2 "I have lost my lunchbox," said the girl.
  3 Marion said, "I want a drink."
  4 The clown said, "I like making people laugh."

Practice
- Read the information box with the children.
- Ask pairs of children to 'have' the conversation. What words will they not read out?
- Children can work individually or in pairs on the activity.

Answers
"Did you see the rabbit go down that hole?" asked the farmer.
"No," said Mary.
"Look over there by the big tree," said the farmer.
"Oh, yes! The rabbit has just popped out again," said Mary.
"It might not be the same one. There are lots of rabbits in that hole," said the farmer.

Extension
- Activity A: These activities introduce children to synonyms for 'said'.
- Read and discuss when these synonyms might be used.
- Can children add any more synonyms?
- Activity B: Mark the sentences correct if the speech marks are in place.

Answers
Individual answers

Resource Book

Support PCM
- Activity A: remind children how they can identify spoken words.
- Activity B: Get individuals to read out the spoken words in each sentence.
- Children should then work individually.

Answers
(A) 1 "<u>Where are you going</u>?" asked Tom.
  2 "<u>I'm going to see my cousins,</u>" said Sara.
  3 "<u>Where do they live</u>?" asked Tom.
  4 "<u>They live in Scotland,</u>" said Sara.
  5 "<u>How long will you be gone</u>?" asked Tom.
  6 "<u>We are going for a week,</u>" said Sara.

(B) 1 "Have you got your school bag?" asked Mum.
  2 "Yes, I've got everything," said Anna.
  3 "Have you got your PE kit?" asked Mum.
  4 "Yes and I've got my homework," said Anna.
  5 "Have you got your lunch?" asked Mum.
  6 "No, I forgot to put it in my bag," said Anna.

(C) Individual answers

Extension PCM
- Children can work independently or in pairs.

Answers
(Children supply names for the characters.)
"Have you got your PE kit?" asked X.
"What for?" asked Y.
"We're practising for Sports Day today," said X.
"I forgot!" said Y.
"What races are you in?" said X.
"I'm doing the one hundred metres and the long jump," said Y.
"Are you doing the high jump?" asked X.
"I think so," said Y.

Extra
Children can continue the conversation from the Extension PCM.

BOOK 3 UNIT 11 Pronouns

Subject and object pronouns

Pronouns are words that take the place of nouns and noun phrases.

Throughout the course, children will encounter: personal pronouns (as subject and object); possessive pronouns; reflexive pronouns; and relative pronouns. Demonstrative pronouns are introduced in the work on noun phrases.

Interrogative pronouns are not specifically labelled as such but children encounter them in work on relative pronouns. It is up to individual teachers if indefinite pronouns, e.g. each/many/few/some, are specifically labelled as such and taught as another group of pronouns.

This unit revises the work on subject pronouns and extends it to include object pronouns. As the children have not yet encountered subject/object in a sentence, the unit works by the positioning of the pronoun in simple sentences. The Extension introduces reflexive nouns.

Pupil Book

Focus
- Revise/explain the term *noun*.
- Introduce/revise the term *pronoun* and ask for examples.
- Read the information box on page 26.
- Ask children to choose a pronoun from the pronoun box and put it in a sentence.
- Do the Activity orally.

Answers
1. The vase fell on the floor and **it** broke.
2. The dogs were tired so **they** went to sleep.
3. I told the children we would meet **them** at ten o'clock.
4. The headmaster said I should come to see **him**.
5. Dan ate quickly so **he** could go out early.

Practice
- Read and discuss the first answer so children understand what is required.

Answers
1. **They** saw **it**.
2. **He** waited for **him**.
3. **We** waved to **him/her**.
4. **They** met **them**.
5. **She** plays with **us**.

Extension
- Read and discuss the information box on page 27.
- Ask children to say sentences using reflexive nouns.

Answers
1. Tara wants to paint the cottage **herself**.
2. The dog stretched **itself** in front of the fire.
3. The postman hurt **himself** when he fell off his bike.
4. I wanted to go to the shops by **myself**.
5. You almost cut **yourself** with that knife.

Resource Book

Support PCM
- Activity A: children should work individually.
- Activity B: read and discuss the first answer so children understand what is required.

Answers

(A)
1. <u>He</u> is very upset with <u>himself</u> for missing the goal.
2. <u>You</u> should do <u>it yourself</u> if <u>you</u> want <u>it</u> done quickly.
3. Go and tell <u>them</u> that <u>we</u> are ready.
4. If <u>we</u> can find the paint, <u>we</u> will do <u>it ourselves</u>.
5. <u>They</u> bought <u>themselves</u> umbrellas.

(B)
1. **She** took **it** for a walk.
2. **She** waved at **them**.
3. **We** followed **her** on our bicycles.
4. **She/He** took **it** from **him** because **he** had broken the window.

Extension PCM
- Ask for suggestions for the first pair so children understand what is required.

Answers
Individual answers

Extra
- Point to individual, pairs/groups of children in the class.
- Say e.g. *Ben has dropped the pen*.
- Class respond: *He has dropped it.*

BOOK 3 UNIT 12 Adverbs

Comparatives and superlatives with more and most

Adverbs are usually explained as words which 'add' to a verb giving the detail of how, where or when an action is done.

Throughout the course, children will encounter single adverbs (manner/time/place), comparative and superlative adverbs, adverbial phrases, adverb pairs and adverbial clauses.

This unit revises the concept of comparatives and superlatives using short, common adverbs (usually one syllable) with the suffixes *er/est*, and introduces the forms with 'more' and 'most'.

Pupil Book

Focus

- Revise/explain the term *adverb* and ask for examples.
- Discuss what children understand by *comparing things*.
- Read the information box on page 28.
- Do the activity orally, encouraging the children to try adding *er/est* to all the adverbs so they can experience the difficulty of trying to say, for example easilyer/happilyer/patientlyer, etc.!

Answers

1. more easily/most easily
2. more happily/most happily
3. more patiently/most patiently
4. more seriously/most seriously
5. later/latest
6. more widely/most widely
7. more heavily/most heavily
8. sooner/soonest
9. more neatly/most neatly

Practice

Children should work individually on the activities.

Answers

(A) 1 If it snows, walking will be **harder**.
    2 The donkeys trotted **more quickly** when it began to rain.
    3 He swam **more strongly** after he had had a rest.

(B) 1 Ben tried **hardest** and won the race.
    2 The last choir to perform was **most tuneful**.
    3 You scored **highest** in the test.

Extension

- Activity A: Discuss the first answer so children are clear what is required.

Answers

(A) 1 The nurse helped **calmly**.
    2 Sam dribbled the ball **carefully**.
    3 Lisa answered the question **truthfully**.
    4 The cyclist rode **speedily** to win the race.

(B) Individual answers

Resource Book

Support PCM

- Children should work individually.

Answers

(A) 1 I can do that <u>easily</u>.
    2 He looked <u>carefully</u> at the instructions.
    3 The vegetables grew <u>quickly</u> after the rain.

(B) 1 Could you speak <u>more clearly</u>, please?
    2 The striker played <u>more skillfully</u> in the second half of the match.
    3 I can write <u>more neatly</u> with a sharper pencil.

(C) 1 She jumped the <u>highest</u> of the three competitors.
    2 The birds sing <u>most loudly</u> at sunrise.
    3 The first singer was the <u>most tuneful</u>

(D) Individual answers

Extension PCM

Children should work individually

Answers

(A)

adverb	comparative	superlative
gracefully	**more** gracefully	**most** gracefully
recently	**more** recently	**most** recently
completely	**more** completely	**most** completely
confidently	**more** confidently	**most** confidently
efficiently	**more** efficiently	**most** efficiently

(B) Individual answers

Extra

Working in teams, can children supply an adverb for each letter of the alphabet?

BOOK 3 UNIT 13 Adjectives

Ordinal numbers

Adjectives are usually explained as 'describing' words. They pinpoint a quality or a feature of a noun or pronoun. The information box states that adjectives describe 'people, places and things'. At this stage, the idea of describing qualities (abstract nouns) is too advanced and will be introduced later.

Throughout the course, children will encounter single adjectives, comparative and superlative adjectives, adjective phrases, possessive adjectives and adjective (relative) clauses.

In Books 1 and 2, children have encountered cardinal numbers as adjectives. This unit introduces ordinal numbers as adjectives.

Pupil Book

Focus

- Begin by revising *cardinal numbers*.
- Read the information box on page 30.
- Ensure children understand the difference by saying:
  If you are number one in a race, you come first.
  If you are number two in a race, you come second.
- Continue to ten with children supplying the ordinal number.
- Do the activity orally.
- If appropriate at this stage, point out the hyphen in 'ninety-nine/ninety-ninth' and discuss that all numbers from twenty-one/twenty-first to ninety-nine/ninety-ninth have a hyphen.

Answers

six	sixth
three	third
twenty	twentieth
ninety-nine	ninety-ninth
fourteen	fourteenth
eight	eighth

Practice

- Activity A and B: Discuss the first question in each activity to ensure children understand what they have to do.

Answers

A
1 There are <u>four</u> (glasses) on the table.
2 We saw <u>two</u> (seagulls) on the sand.
3 I got <u>ten</u> (answers) right.
4 My coat has <u>six</u> (pockets).
5 We need <u>two</u> (eggs) and <u>one</u> (lemon) to make the pancakes.

B
1 The <u>sixteenth</u> (day) of June is a Monday.
2 The <u>fourth</u> (book) on the shelf is blue.
3 That old lady is in her <u>eightieth</u> (year).
4 That's the <u>tenth</u> (time) I've told you!
5 The <u>fifth</u> (boat) in the race sank!

Extension

- Children can tackle the activity individually or in pairs.
- Alternatively, in groups of six, children can write name cards and line themselves up in the correct order.

Answers

Six children were in a running race. Ned was the **first** to cross the winning line but Holly was a close **second**. Kai came in **third** and Rose was **fourth**. Nahla and Ian were placed **fifth** and **sixth** at the end of the race.

Resource Book

Support PCM

- Children should tackle the activities individually.

Answers

A
1 King Henry's <u>sixth</u> (wife) outlived him.
2 There are <u>sixty</u> (seconds) in a minute.
3 Please go through the <u>second</u> (door) on the right.
4 Can you find <u>five</u> (buttons) that are the same?
5 Australia was discovered over <u>four hundred</u> (years) ago.

B
1	five	fifth
2	sixteen	sixteenth
3	twenty two	twenty second
4	thirty five	thirty fifth
5	seven hundred	seven hundredth
6	one thousand	one thousandth

Extension PCM

- Encourage the children to write interesting sentences.
- Remind them of punctuation and that sentences can be questions and exclamations as well as statements.

Answers

Individual answers

Extra

- Write various cardinal numbers on the board and ask children to provide the corresponding ordinal number.

BOOK 3 UNIT 14 Verbs

Future tense with *shall* and *will*

Verbs are often explained as 'doing words' or 'being words'. They are possibly the most complex part of speech for young children to grasp because of their many forms and tenses.

Throughout the course, children will encounter the present simple, present progressive (also known as continuous), past simple, past progressive (also known as continuous), present perfect (labelled simply *perfect* throughout the course), past perfect, future, infinitive (labelled *verb family name* in the early parts of the course), auxiliary verbs, modals, active and passive verbs and subjunctive verbs (a construction very rarely used except in extremely formal writing).

Participles are referred to as '*ing* words' and 'regular past simple tense words'; finite verbs are referred to as 'main' or 'proper verbs', and it is for the teacher to decide the appropriate time to introduce the terms *participle* and *finite verb*.

This unit introduces the future tense formed with *will/shall* + *infinitive*. The Extra section of the Teacher's Notes examines the construction *going to* + *infinitive*.

Pupil Book

Focus
- Revise/explain the term *verb*.
- Write a simple infinitive on the board, e.g. to *jump* and ask for the following tenses with *I*:
  – present simple
  – present progressive
  – past simple
  – past progressive
  – perfect
- Introduce the term *future tense*. What do children think the *future tense* is used for?
- Read the information box on page 32.
- Practise the *shall/will* construction orally with other verbs.
- Do the activity orally.

Answers
1. I **shall go** at seven o'clock.
2. If it rains, we **shall take** an umbrella.
3. He **will wrap** the presents in a minute.
4. The children **will know** when to sing.
5. We **shall catch** the bus to town.
6. They **will go** to the birthday party on Saturday.
7. I **shall finish** this later.
8. The dog **will bark** if someone knocks.

Practice
- Activities A and B: These can be done orally first, before children write

Answers
(A) 1. Sanjay **will answer** the question.
2. Mandy **will pay** for the apples.
3. We **shall walk** to school.

(B) 1. I **shall stroll** along the beach.
2. The teacher **will talk** to the class.
3. The cars **will race** around the track.

Extension
(A)
- Children can draw the table or list the verbs under the correct headings.
- Read and discuss the information box.
- Practise the reversal of the *shall/will* construction orally.

(B) Children should work individually.

Answers

(A)
verb family name	present simple tense	past simple tense	future tense
to believe	I believe	I believed	I shall believe
to argue	They argue	They argued	They will argue
to work	She works	She worked	She will work
to dance	We dance	We danced	We shall dance

(B)
1. You **shall** go to bed at nine o'clock!
2. I **will** ride my bike down the lane!
3. He **shall** not watch the television.

Resource Book

Support PCM
- Children should work individually.

Answers
(A)
1. We <u>shall go</u> out in five minutes.
2. After tea, <u>I shall read</u> my book.
3. The wheels <u>will squeak</u> if you don't oil them.
4. My mum <u>will meet</u> you at three o'clock.
5. The baby <u>will cry</u> if she is hungry.

(B)
present simple	past simple	future
looks	watched	will sing
shouts	bought	shall sleep
points	carried	will blow

(C) Individual answers

Extension PCM

Read and discuss the first answer so children understand what is required.

Answers
(A)
1. Tomorrow, I **shall telephone** my friend.
2. Tomorrow, we **shall visit** the museum.
3. Tomorrow, he **will mend** his bicycle.
4. Tomorrow, they **will plant** some seeds.
5. Tomorrow, I **shall go** to the library.

Extra

Introduce the construction *going to* + *infinitive* as another way of indicating the future.
Write examples on the board, e.g. I am *going to visit my cousin on Saturday*.
This is becoming a more popular way of expressing plans and predictions than the *shall/will* construction.
Ask children: *What are you going to do at the weekend/next week/on your birthday/in the holidays?* etc.

BOOK 3

Singular and plural

Nouns ending in *f* and *fe*

Most nouns have a singular form (one) and a plural form (more than one). The vast majority of nouns form their plural by adding *s*.

Throughout the course, children will encounter plurals with *s* and *es*, pluralisation for words ending in *y*/*f*/*fe*/*o*/*oo*, and irregular plurals.

This unit revises the work on singular and plural with nouns that form their plurals by adding *s*, *es* and the rules governing nouns that end in *y*. It then extends the work to nouns ending *f*/*fe*.

As the course progresses, the Extra section of the Teacher's Notes will suggest examining the plural form of nouns with foreign origins.

Pupil Book

Focus
- Revise/explain *more than one (noun)* and ask for examples with *s*, *es*, *consonant* + *y* and *vowel* + *y*.
- Introduce/revise the terms:
  – *singular* = one
  – *plural* = more than one
- Read the information box on page 34.
- Revise/discuss the terms *vowel* and *consonant*.
- The activity should be tackled individually.

Answers
1. leaves
2. roofs
3. sheaves
4. lives
5. thieves
6. cliffs
7. halves
8. wives

Practice
- Activity A: Ask children *Do any of the words not follow the rule?*
- Activities B and D: Remind children that sentences can be statements, questions or exclamations. Revise punctuation at the end of sentences before children write.

Answers
(A) 1. calves
    2. loaves
    3. shelves
    4. chiefs

(B) Individual answers

(C) 1. wolf
    2. staff
    3. safe
    4. elf

(D) Individual answers

Extension
- Read the information box with the children.
- Children tackle the activity individually.

Answers
1. **Leaves** grow on trees.
2. We use **handkerchiefs/handkerchieves** for blowing our noses.
3. **Knives** are used for cutting.
4. People who steal things are called **thieves**.
5. Horses have four **hoofs/hooves**.
6. **Sheriffs** kept law and order in the Wild West.

Resource Book

Support PCM
- Children should tackle the activities individually.
- For Activity C, remind children that a plural noun needs a plural verb in a sentence.

Answers
(A) 1. Be careful with the sharp <u>knives</u>.
    2. This bird builds its nest on top of <u>cliffs</u>.
    3. The <u>leaves</u> fall off that tree in autumn.
    4. Can you see the <u>sheaves</u> of corn in the field?
    5. This cow has had two <u>calves</u>.

(B) 1. The police caught the **thieves**.
    2. There were six **handkerchiefs/handkerchieves** in the drawer.
    3. The **roofs** were covered in snow.
    4. The **elves** lived in the forest.
    5. A horse has four **hoofs/hooves**.

(C) Individual answers

Extension PCM
- The activities should be tackled individually.
- For Activity C, remind children that a plural noun needs a plural verb in a sentence.

Answers
(A) 1. calves
    2. halves
    3. shelves
    4. safes
    5. dwarfs/dwarves

(B) 1. knives
    2. hoofs/hooves
    3. loaves
    4. roofs
    5. lives

(C) Individual answers

Extra
- Following the format in Extension PCM A, children make up clues for *f*/*fe* plural words for others to guess.

BOOK 3 UNIT 16 Nouns

Abstract

Nouns are usually explained as 'naming' words. Nouns are the most common part of speech that children of this age will encounter. Children's first words are usually nouns as they make sense of the world by naming things.

Throughout the course, children will encounter common, proper, collective, compound, abstract and possessive nouns, together with noun phrases.

This unit introduces the concept of abstract nouns. The wide variety of definitions include states, events, feelings, qualities, experiences, emotions, concepts, etc. which have no physical entity. This unit concentrates on qualities, feelings and time as an introduction to the concept.

Pupil Book

Focus

- Revise/explain the term *noun* and ask for examples of:
  - common nouns
  - proper nouns
  - collective nouns
  - compound nouns
- Introduce and explain the term *abstract noun*.
- Read the information box on page 36.
- The activity should be done orally.

Answers

Common nouns: animal/picture/station/house/teacher/book/building

Abstract nouns: slavery/kindness/envy/poverty/wisdom/freedom/dusk/pleasure/skill

Practice

- Go through the sentences orally before children write.

Answers

1 (Fear) made the boy cry.
2 The teacher admired his (talent).
3 That concert gave me great (pleasure).
4 The old woman lived in (poverty).

Extension

- Read the information box on page 37 with the children.
- Put the children into teams to tackle the activities.
- Discuss answers in class.

Answers

(A) 1 infancy   2 friendship   3 theft
(B) 1 skill   2 fame   3 action
(C) 1 deception 2 freedom   3 flattery

Resource Book

Support PCM

- Children should work individually on the activities.
- Activity A will give a good indication of whether further work is needed on any particular type of noun.

Answers

(A)

common noun	proper noun	collective noun	abstract noun
table	Karen	bunch	generosity
garden	David	herd	sympathy
cart	Cardiff	gaggle	pity
elephant	Paris	pack	bravery
water	Mars	fleet	laughter

(B) Individual answers

Extension PCM

- Children should work individually on the activities.

Answers

(A) 1 selfishness
    2 stupidity
    3 brightness
    4 poverty
    5 gratitude
    6 wisdom

(B) Individual answers

(C) 1 flattery
    2 pleasure
    3 action
    4 robbery
    5 hatred
    6 satisfaction

(D) Individual answers

Extra

- Write a variety of nouns, adjectives and verbs on the board.
- Children give the corresponding abstract noun.

BOOK 3 UNIT 1 Adjectives

Formed from nouns and verbs

Adjectives are usually explained as 'describing' words. They pinpoint a quality or a feature of a noun or pronoun. Throughout the course, children will encounter single adjectives, comparative and superlative adjectives, adjective phrases, possessive adjectives and adjective (relative) clauses.

Children have so far encountered adjectives formed by adding the suffixes *less* and *ful*.

This unit extends the work on forming adjectives from verbs and nouns.

Pupil Book

Focus
- Revise/explain the term *adjective* and ask for examples.
- Introduce/revise the term *suffix*.
- Ask for examples of *adjectives* that end with *ful* and *less*.
- Explain that you are going to look at how adjectives can be formed from nouns and verbs.
- Read and discuss the information box on page 38.
- Do the activity orally.
- When complete, ask if any of the adjectives could be made from a noun and a verb.
  (No. 1 to cry/a cry)

Answers
1. The **crying** baby was in her pram. (verb – to cry)
2. The **wooden** hut was never used. (noun – wood)
3. The **dried** flowers were thrown away. (verb – to dry)
4. The **warlike** warriors attacked at dawn. (noun – war)
5. That was a **foolish** thing to do! (noun – fool)

Practice
- Activity A: Children are required to form adjectives from given infinitives to complete sentences. Encourage the children to look back at the verb examples in the information box if they are struggling.

Practice
- Activity B: Children are required to form adjectives from given nouns to complete sentences. Encourage the children to look back at the noun examples in the information box if they are struggling.

Answers
(A)
1. The **woven** rug was made on a loom.
2. I practised diving into the **swimming** pool.
3. Four times around the **running** track is eight hundred metres.
4. The **terrifying** storm woke me up.
5. I have finished my **reading** book.
6. I can't play tennis with my **broken** arm.

(B)
1. How many **musical** instruments can you play?
2. The **stony** path hurt my feet.
3. The box is a **rectangular** shape.
4. Thank you for your **generous** donation.
5. What a **dreadful** mistake to make!
6. The **dirty** clothes needed a wash.

Extension
- Children should tackle the activity individually if possible.
- Encourage the children to write interesting sentences.
- Remind them of punctuation and that sentences can be questions and exclamations as well as statements.

Answers
Individual answers

Resource Book

Support PCM
- The activities should be tackled individually.
- For Activity A, tell the children to find the noun in each sentence which will help them locate the adjective that is describing it.
- For Activity C, encourage the children to write interesting sentences.
- Remind them of punctuation and that sentences can be questions and exclamations as well as statements.

Answers
(A)
1. I can't find my <u>colouring</u> book.
2. The <u>gigantic</u> tree was cut down.
3. The baby played with the <u>building</u> bricks.
4. You need to clean those <u>muddy</u> boots!
5. The hero of this story is very <u>adventurous</u>.

(B)
1. This is my **lucky** day!
2. I have had an **amazing** time!
3. That is a **beautiful** painting.
4. Have you ever seen such **stormy** weather?
5. I need a **comfortable** chair.

(C) Individual answers

Extension PCM
- The activities should be tackled individually.
- Activities A and B: Discuss the first example in each activity to ensure children understand what is required.
- Discuss answers in class.

Answers
(A)
1. grown
2. spoken
3. postal
4. broken
5. drawn

Phrases = individual answers

(B)
1. perilous
2. horrible
3. boyish
4. microscopic
5. charitable

Phrases = individual answers

(C) Individual answers

Extra
There are some more suffixes added to verbs or nouns which signal an adjective.
Write these suffixes on the board:
   able / ible / al / ic / ive
Can children suggest adjectives with these suffixes?

BOOK 3 UNIT 18 Prepositions

Time and place

Prepositions show how words in sentences are related to one another either in place (space) or time. Some prepositions, e.g. 'on', can be used for both place and time.

Prepositions can be single words – towards/beneath/during; pairs of words – because of/near to; or three words – in front of/in addition to.

This unit continues the work on prepositions.

Pupil Book

Focus
- Introduce/revise the term preposition and ask for examples.
- Read the information box on page 40.
- Point out that *preposition* has the word *position* in it.
- Activity A: this can be done orally before children write.
- Activity B: Children can work in pairs.

Answers
Ⓐ 1 The rope was tied **around** the tree.
    2 It was cooler when the sun went **behind** the clouds.
    3 It was very windy **during** the night.
    4 The path went **through** the woods.
    5 The duck flew **over** the lake.
Ⓑ
with	without
above	below
up	down
on	off
far	near
inside	outside
before	after
under	over

Practice
- Children should work individually on the activities.

Answers
Ⓐ 1 I am sorry **for** breaking the plate.
    2 Black is the opposite **of** white.
    3 We played football **for** two hours.
    4 No one knew the cause **of** the accident.
    5 Is this book different **from** that one?
Ⓑ Individual answers

Extension
- Children can work in pairs.
- Encourage them to read the whole passage first to see which prepositions fit best in which gaps.
- Discuss answers in class.

Answers
Martin came **in** at four o'clock. He put his jacket **over** the chair and took some bread **out** of the cupboard. He put butter **on** two slices and put jam **between** them. He poured milk **into** a glass and sat **down** on the chair to eat his sandwich. Martin looked **at** the clock. He would have to wait **for** ten minutes **before** his friends came to call **for** him.

Resource Book

Support PCM
- Children should work individually.

Answers
Ⓐ The fox ran <u>behind</u> the dustbin and jumped <u>on</u> the fence. It leaped <u>into</u> the tree and ran <u>along</u> the branch. It jumped <u>down</u> and disappeared <u>through</u> the hedge. The fox looked <u>around</u>, slipped <u>inside</u> a shed and hid <u>between</u> some old boxes.

Ⓑ Individual answers

Extension PCM
- The Activities should be done individually.
- Discuss possible scenes for description with children who are struggling to come up with an idea.

Answers
Ⓐ Individual answers

Ⓑ Individual answers

Extra
- Make preposition cards, e.g.

| on | over | down |

- Individuals come to the front and act out the preposition with an object, e.g. a book.
- Class guess by forming sentences, e.g. *The book is on the table.*

BOOK 3 UNIT 19 Capital letters

Book/film/play titles; headings and subheadings

Capital letters are used in a variety of ways within written work.

Children have so far encountered capital letters for the pronoun *I*, the beginning of sentences, and a variety of types of proper noun.

This unit examines capital letters for book, film and play titles, together with headings and subheadings. The latter items can be taught where every word in a heading or subheading has a capital letter OR where only important words have a capital letter. Both are correct but once one method had been adopted, consistency is important.

Pupil Book

Focus
- Begin by asking the children when they would use a *capital letter*.
- Read and discuss the initial list in the information box on page 42. Did they suggest all the examples?
- Read and discuss the rest of the information box.
- Look at the titles of the children's reading books as examples.
- Can they suggest film titles? (Plays may be more problematic at this age).
- What do they understand by the terms *headings* and *subheadings*?
- Use information books as examples.
- Children work individually on the Activity.

Answers
1. Queen Mary
2. Tuesday
3. November
4. Mr Harris
5. Mount Everest
6. America

Practice
- Activity A should be done individually.
- Activity B: Read and discuss the headings and subheadings. Remind children to add the missing capital letters.

Answers
(A)
1. Alice in Wonderland
2. The Secret Garden
3. Toy Story
4. Ice Age
5. Romeo and Juliet
6. Toad of Toad Hall

(B) Big Cats
   Lions
   Tigers
   Jaguars
   Pumas

Extension
- Children can work in pairs on the activity.

Answers
The Four Seasons in the UK
There are four season in the year. They are spring, summer, autumn and winter.
Spring
This is the season when everything begins to grow after winter. The weather gets warmer and baby animals are born.
Summer
This is usually the hottest time of the year when people go on holiday. We have a long break from school.
Autumn
The weather begins to get colder in autumn. Some trees lose their leaves and it gets dark very early.
Winter
Winter is my favourite time of the year if it snows. Playing in the snow is great fun.

Resource Book

Support PCM
- Children should work individually.

Answers
(A)
1. I have just read The Wind in the Willows.
2. Did you see the film Batman?
3. Our school play is Little Red Riding Hood.

(B)
1. **Cities in Australia**
   Melbourne
   Sydney
   Perth
2. **Team games**
   Playing football
   Netball matches
   Team tennis

Extension PCM
- Children can work individually on the activities but some may need support for Activity B.

Answers
(A) Individual answers
(B) Individual answers

Extra
Do a class survey.
Ask five individuals to write the title of their favourite book on the board.
Check for correct use of capital letters.
Ask the rest of the class:
1. which they have read?
2. which is their favourite?

BOOK 3 UNIT 20 Sentences

Direct speech

The concept of a sentence as a unit of language that 'makes sense' can be a difficult concept for some children to grasp. The course builds children's confidence in this area through giving them the opportunity to look at punctuation of statements, questions and exclamations to familiarise themselves with what a 'sentence' looks and sounds like.

Throughout the course, children will encounter: sentence punctuation; the concept of 'making sense'; direct and indirect speech; clauses which combine to make multi-clause sentences; parts of sentences – subject/object, subject/predicate; focusing on the sentence as a unit of language that can be improved; and Standard English constructions.

Children often find correctly punctuating direct speech sentences problematic. Several units in the course focus on direct speech so that the various rules can be built up gradually. In this unit, speech marks (inverted commas), and beginning a new line when a different person speaks are revised, and punctuation before the final speech marks is added.

Pupil Book

Focus
- Begin by asking the children why *direct speech* (characters having a conversation) looks 'different' on the page.
- Revise the terms *statement – full stop/question – question mark/exclamation – exclamation mark/speech marks (inverted commas)*.
- Read the information box on page 44.
- Do the activity orally, asking children to read only the spoken words. Children can then copy and write.

Answers
1. "The police are coming soon," said Anne.
2. "What is the time?" asked Richard.
3. "Watch out!" yelled the farmer.
4. "Don't make any noise," whispered the girl.
5. "I'm bored," complained Ben.

Practice
- Children should work individually.

Answers
1. "Grab this rope!" shouted the climber.
2. "May I have an apple?" asked Tara.
3. "I have lost my purse!" sobbed Kathy.
4. "Have you got your ticket?" asked the bus driver.
5. "That building over there is the museum," said the guide.

Extension
- Read and discuss the information box.
- Stress that when the non-spoken words come before the spoken words:
  – they are always followed by a comma;
  – the spoken words always begin with a capital letter.
  (NB The latter is obviously not true when the non-spoken words interrupt a spoken sentence, but this will be tackled later on in the course.)
- Model the first answer, then children should work individually.

Answers
1. "Where is the treasure hidden?" asked the pirate.
2. Billy said, "I have got the map."
3. "Let me see it!" demanded the pirate.
4. Billy asked, "What will you give me?"
5. With a laugh, the pirate replied, "Nothing!"
6. "That's not fair!" gasped Billy.

Resource Book

Support PCM
- Children should work individually.

Answers
(A) 1. "It will be freezing tonight," said the weatherman.
    2. "Look out!" shouted the policeman.
    3. "Have you seen a volcano erupt?" asked the scientist.
(B) 1. "We have to be very quiet," whispered the bird-watcher.
    2. "What bird is it?" asked the child.
    3. "It's a woodpecker," he explained.
(C) 1. Kali asked, "What time are they arriving?"
    2. Mum said, "In about an hour."
    3. The twins shouted, "Hurray!"
(D) 1. Sam explained, "We have to keep to the path."
    2. Ben asked, "Why can't we go into the wood?"
    3. Sam warned, "We might get lost!"

Extension PCM
- Children should work individually.
- Accept a new line for a different person speaking if children have not yet been introduced to the concept of paragraphing.

Answers
"Today we are going to learn about how to begin a story," said the teacher. "Can anyone tell me why the beginning of a story is very important?"
   "I know why. It has to make the reader want to read on and find out what happens," said Jenny.
   "Yes, that's a good reason. Can anyone think of another one?" asked the teacher.
   "It can tell us where the story is set," said Harry.
   "Anything else?"
   "It can introduce us to the characters," said Vera.

Extra
- In pairs, children can create a cartoon-type story with frames and speech bubbles.
- Pairs swap their cartoons and change them into a direct speech conversation.

BOOK 3

Adjectives

Phrases

Adjectives are usually explained as 'describing' words. They pinpoint a quality or a feature of a noun or pronoun. Throughout the course, children will encounter single adjectives, comparative and superlative adjectives, adjective phrases and adjective (relative) clauses.

This unit moves the concept of adjectives as single words (comparatives and superlatives with 'more' and 'most' can be classed as 'single word' adjectives) to a group of words that do the same job – the adjective phrase. A phrase is a group of words forming a conceptual unit, but not a sentence.

Deciding what is, and is not an adjective phrase can be complicated so the unit gives children three simple models to follow:

1 phrase beginning with 'with'
2 two adjectives joined by a conjunction
3 a series of adjectives separated by commas.

Pupil Book

Focus

- Revise/explain the term *adjective* and ask for examples.
- Read and discuss the information box on page 46.
- Ask children to substitute:
  – the phrase 'with a big, floppy hat' for other phrases that could distinguish the lady.
  – single adjectives that could describe the garden.
- Do the activity orally.

Answers

1 The weather, **cold and wet**, kept us in all day.
2 The **handsome but sulky** prince was in a bad mood.
3 The wood was **dark and frightening** in the moonlight.
4 **Five small blue** flowers had grown on the rubbish heap.
5 The dog **with the injured leg** was howling.

Practice

- Activity A: Discuss each adjective phrase to help children think of suitable sentences, e.g. Ask *What could be 'sleek and graceful'? Who might be seen 'with no shoes'?* etc.
- Activity B: Remind the children of the 'models' for adjective phrases that they can follow.
- When Activity B is completed, ask children to read out their sentences. The rest of the class identify the adjective phrase.

Answers

A Individual answers
B Individual answers

Extension

- Tell children that the capital letters and punctuation are missing, otherwise it would be too easy!
- The activities can be tackled individually or in pairs.
- When completed, discuss answers.

Answers

A Identifying adjective phrases:
  3 the poor injured
  4 shivering and frightened
  6 with a heavy bag
  Using adjective phrases = individual answers

B Identifying and punctuating sentences:
  1 "Thank you," said Jim.
  2 Sonu ran home.
  3 Give me that.

Resource Book

Support PCM

- The activities should be tackled individually.
- For Activity B, remind the children of the 'models' for adjective phrases that they can follow.

Answers

A 1 A noise, <u>strange and frightening</u>, came from the forest.
  2 The cat <u>with four white paws</u> is called Socks.
  3 <u>Seven large, black crows</u> landed on the lawn.
  4 The lady <u>with the hat</u> is old Mrs Cotton.
  5 We saw a <u>large, brightly-coloured</u> balloon in the sky.

B Individual answers
C Individual answers

Extension PCM

- Children should work individually.
- When completed, ask children to read out their sentences. The rest of the class identify the adjective phrase.

Answers

Individual answers

Extra

- Prepare adjective phrase cards that children will be able to act, e.g.

| with a fierce scowl | cold and shivering |

- Individuals take a card and mime for the rest of the class to guess.

BOOK 3 UNIT 22 Prefixes

Making opposites/special meanings

A prefix is a group of letters added to the beginning of a word to adjust or qualify its meaning.

So far in the course, children have encountered the prefix *un* to make opposite adjectives and verbs.

This unit builds on the concept of 'opposite' with the prefix *un*, and examines other prefixes which form opposites. It extends the work into prefixes with special meanings. Children should be introduced to the term *prefix* at this stage and understand that the addition of a prefix does not alter the spelling of the word it is being added to.

Pupil Book

Focus

- Introduce and discuss the term *prefix*.
- Read and discuss the first table in the information box on page 48, ensuring children understand the meaning of the words.
- Look particularly at *illegal/illegible*. Can children spot the double letter?
- Can they add *un* to a word beginning with *n*, and *im* to a word beginning with *m*, etc.?
- Read and discuss the second table in the information box on page 48, ensuring children understand the meaning of the words.
- Can children give another example for each prefix?
- Activity A: Children can work in pairs. Discuss answers in class.
- Activity B can be done individually.

Answers

(A)
1. **un**true
2. **dis**loyal
3. **im**moveable
4. **in**secure
5. **dis**honour
6. **im**pure
7. **un**well
8. **im**mobile
9. **dis**approve
10. **il**logical
11. **dis**agree
12. **in**active

(B)
1. Did you **disobey** the rules?
2. Will you **unlock** the door?
3. That is **impossible**.
4. You are very **impatient**.

Practice

- The activities should be done individually, giving children dictionary practice.
- Discuss answers in class.

Answers

1. to think that something is not true — disbelieve
2. not able to do something — incapable
3. not able to be seen — invisible
4. to put words on paper again — rewrite
5. not to be certain — unsure

Extension

- Activities A and B should be done individually, giving children dictionary practice.

Answers

(A) Suggested answers
1. interchange/intertwine/interlock
2. bicycle/biped/bikini
3. propose/propel/provide
4. prefix/prepare/presume
5. monologue/monopoly/monoplane
6. submarine/submerge/subdue
7. postpone/postscript/postgraduate
8. automatic/autobiography/autograph
9. alcove/album/always
10. reassure/recover/return
11. expand/expel/exterior
12. transplant/transform/translate

(B) Individual answers

(C) Individual answers

Resource Book

Support PCM

- Children work individually.

Answers

(A)
1. **im**possible
2. **il**legal
3. **un**wise
4. **dis**appear
5. **dis**trust
6. **un**pleasant
7. **in**visible
8. **un**certain
9. **un**selfish
10. **im**perfect

(B)
- bi = two
- ex = out of
- inter = between
- mis = wrong
- re = again
- sub = under
- super = extra good or large
- auto = oneself

Extension PCM

- The activity can be done individually or in pairs against the clock!

Answers

1. a biplane
   b biped
   c bisect
2. a precede
   b preface
   c prehistory
3. a submarine
   b suburb
   c subside
4. a redeliver
   b rewrite
   c recover
5. a exit
   b extend
   c exterior

Extra

Examine other number prefixes. What do children think they mean? Can they give examples?
tri = three (Greek)
quad/quar = four (Latin)
pent = five (Greek)
hexa = six (Greek)
hept = seven (Greek)
oct = eight (Latin)

35

BOOK 3 UNIT 23 Adverbs

Phrases

Adverbs are usually explained as words which 'add' to a verb giving the detail of how, where or when an action is done.

Throughout the course, children will encounter single adverbs (manner/time/place), comparative and superlative adverbs, adverbial phrases, adverb pairs, possessive adjectives and adverbial clauses.

This unit introduces the concept of adverbial phrases that do the same job in a sentence as single adverbs, giving more detail of how, when or where an action was done.

Pupil Book

Focus

- Revise/explain the term *adverb* and ask for examples of *how*, *when* and *where* adverbs.
- Read and discuss the information box on page 50.
- Ask children to substitute the phrase:
  – 'in a huge burst of flame' for other phrases that say 'how' the rocket took off;
  – 'on Thursday night' for when the rocket took off;
  – 'into the dark night sky' for where the rocket took off
- Do the activity orally. When children have identified the adverb phrases, ask if each is an adverb phrase of manner, time or place.

Answers

1. The giant approached the village **with loud, thudding footsteps**.
2. **Yesterday morning**, I planted some seeds.
3. The painter climbed **to the top of the ladder** to paint the window frame.
4. We ran **as quickly as we could**.
5. The eagle built its nest **on the mountain top**.

Practice

- Activity A: Discuss each adverb phrase to help children think of suitable sentences, e.g. ask *What could happen 'from time to time'? What might be done 'carefully and slowly'?*
- Activity B: Remind children that sentences can be statements, questions or exclamations.
- When Activity B is completed, ask children to read out their sentences. The rest of the class identify the adverb phrase.

Answers

(A) Individual answers

(B) Individual answers

Extension

- Tell children that the capital letters and punctuation are missing, otherwise it would be too easy!
- The activities can be tackled individually or in pairs.
- When completed, discuss answers.

Answers

(A) Identifying adverb phrases:
1. before the first lesson
3. in front of the cinema
4. gasping for breath
Using adverb phrases = individual answers

(B) Identifying and punctuating sentences:
2. We'll meet at the corner.
5. Omar rang the bell.
6. You must find that letter.

Resource Book

Support PCM

- The activities should be tackled individually.

Answers

(A)
1. The car came to a halt <u>with a loud screeching noise</u>.
2. <u>Late last night</u> there was a knock on the door.
3. I left my bicycle <u>outside the shop</u>.
4. I drew the picture <u>slowly and carefully</u>.
5. We will meet <u>in the morning</u>.

(B) Individual answers

(C) Individual answers

Extension PCM

- Children should work individually.
- When completed, ask children to read out their sentences. The rest of the class identify the adjective phrase.

Answers

Individual answers

Extra

Make scenario cards, e.g.

| walking to the shops | building a model |

Individuals take a card and say an adverb phrase of manner, time or place to describe the action. Class identify which sort of adverb phrase it is.

BOOK 3 UNIT 24 Suffixes

Ending words with ed/ing/er

A suffix is a group of letters added to the end of a word to form a derivative.

So far, the children have encountered suffixes to form nouns, comparative adjectives and verbs.

This unit revises the *ed/ing/er* suffixes. Point out to children that, unlike prefixes, suffixes do sometimes alter spelling.

Pupil Book

Focus
- Revise/explain the term *suffix* and ask for examples of suffixes:
  – making adverbs
  – making nouns
  – making verb tenses
- Read the information box on page 52.
- The activity can be done individually or as a class on the board with individuals filling in the table.

Answers

word	ed suffix	ing suffix	er suffix
warm	warmed	warming	warmer
jump	jumped	jumping	jumper
fill	filled	filling	filler
wrap	wrapped	wrapping	wrapper
clean	cleaned	cleaning	cleaner
help	helped	helping	helper
count	counted	counting	counter

Practice
- Children should work individually and check spelling carefully.
- Discuss answers in class.

Answers
1. This ice cream is **bigger** than yours.
2. The pirates were **looking** for the treasure.
3. We **searched** and **searched** but we could not find it.
4. The **runner** who was first received the medal.
5. **Cooking** is one of my hobbies.
6. The **longer** you take to get ready, the less time we will have for **swimming**.

Extension
- Activities A and B: These give children practice in changing sentences from one tense to another. They should be done individually.

Answers
(A) 1. The birds **are circling** overhead.
2. A stranger **is moving** into the village.
3. The garage door **is creaking** in the wind.
4. I **am trying** hard with my fractions.

(B) 1. We **wondered** if our decision was the right one.
2. **I posted** a letter to my friend.
3. They **elected** the team captain.
4. We **sailed** into the harbour.

Resource Book

Support PCM
- Children should work individually.

Answers
(A) 1. bigger
2. smaller
3. higher
4. frostier
5. sillier
6. fitter
7. heavier

(B) 1. I am going
2. I am sitting
3. I am worrying
4. I am smiling
5. I am laughing

(C) 1. I skipped
2. I moved
3. I hurried
4. I plodded
5. I howled

Extension PCM
Model the first answer with suggestions from the children to ensure they understand what is required.

Answers
Individual answers

Extra
Make infinitive cards, e.g.

| to run | to skip | to drive |

Individuals choose cards and say:
– present progressive verb
– noun

BOOK 3 UNIT 25 Conjunctions

Conjunctions of time – when/after/before/while

Conjunctions join words, phrases and clauses together in sentences.

Coordinating conjunctions – usually *and/but/or* – join two main clauses.

Subordinating conjunctions join subordinate clauses to main clauses.

Throughout the course, children will encounter coordinating and subordinating conjunctions to form multi-clause sentences.

This unit looks at useful conjunctions to denote time in sentences.

Pupil Book

Focus
- Revise/explain *joining word (conjunction)* and ask for examples.
- Read the first half of the information box on page 54.
- Remind the children that:
  – *and* is used when we expect the second half of the sentence, e.g.
    It was raining and I put up my umbrella.
  – *but* is used when we do not expect the second half of the sentence, e.g.
    It was raining but I did not put up my umbrella.
  – or is used when there is a choice:
    I could take my umbrella or I could leave it at home.
  – *so* and *because* often answer the question *Why?*
- Read the second half of the information box on page 54.
- Can children suggest other sentences that use these conjunctions?
- Do the activity orally.

Answers
1. I ran to the shops **before** it rained.
2. Sally had her tea **when** Mum came home.
3. I shall write the letter **while** you find an envelope.
4. The striker scored **before** full time.
5. The field was flooded **after** there was a violent storm.
6. He listens to music **while** he reads his book.

Practice
- For the Activity, read through the vocabulary box to ensure children understand the words.
- Read through the sentences and get the children to say the conjunctions they would use, then the complete sentence.
- Children can then complete the activities in writing individually.

Answers
1. Look both ways **before** you cross the busy road.
2. Sue saw her friend **while** she was walking home.
3. You can only go to bed **after** you have brushed your teeth.
4. The teacher dismissed the class **when** the bell rang.

Extension
- Model the first answer so children understand what is required.

Answers
1. The cats prowled around the dustbins **when they** wanted something to eat.
2. Sam had to find his key **before he** could unlock the door.
3. Jim could listen to music **after he** had finished his homework.
4. Lili always read a book **when she** wanted to relax.

Resource Book

Support PCM
- Activity A: Children should work individually.
- Activity B: Discuss possible sentences before children write.

Answers
(A)
1. We had a spelling test (and) I got them all right.
2. The team were good (but) they didn't win.
3. You must pack your school bag tonight (or) you must get up early to do it.
4. They found an injured bird (so) they took it to the vet.
5. I couldn't unlock the door (because) I lost my keys.
6. The bull snorted fiercely (when) it saw the boy climb over the gate.
7. We dug the garden (before) we planted the seeds.
8. They watered the seeds (after) they had planted them.
9. Some people watch the television (while) they do their homework!

(B) Individual answers

Extension PCM
Read and discuss the first answer so children understand what is required.

Answers
1. Dad and Tom got off the bus when they had reached their stop.
2. The soldiers camped by the river after they had marched all day.
3. The musicians sat in silence while they waited for the conductor.
4. Kim took the dog for a walk before she went to school.

Extra
- Put the children into four teams.
- Label the teams WHEN, BEFORE, AFTER and WHILE.
- Say pairs of sentences.
- If the WHEN team think they can be joined with WHEN, they all stand up, etc.
- If a team member stands up incorrectly, he/she is out of the game.
- The winning team, after the allotted time, is the one with the most team members still in play.

BOOK 3 UNIT 26 Paragraphs

Time in stories

A paragraph is a group of sentences within a piece of writing. It is usually signalled by:
- indenting in handwritten work and fiction (all paragraphs but the first)
- leaving a full line space (block paragraphing) in typing and non-fiction work.

The mechanics of paragraphing can be taught as a concept, but the 'reasons' for paragraphing are many and varied, and must be attached to a particular style of writing.

Throughout the course, children will encounter: paragraphing in narrative writing – time, place and for the inclusion of direct speech; paragraphing for aspects of a topic in non-fiction information writing; and paragraphing to present for and against arguments in discursive writing.

This unit deals with paragraphing in narrative writing based on the time element in stories.

Pupil Book

Focus
- Introduce and discuss the term *paragraph*.
- Use the short story in the information box on page 56 to show children what a paragraph looks like on the page.
- Introduce the term indenting and discuss not indenting for the first paragraph.
- Read and discuss the information box on page 56 and work through the Focus questions with the children.

Answers
1. six o'clock
   'It was six o'clock…'
   climbed out of bed/washed/dressed/went downstairs
2. half past six
   'It was half past six'
   drank her tea/put on her coat/went to milk the cows
3. half past seven
   'An hour later…'
   feeding the chickens/scattering the corn
4. 'Next'
5. nine o'clock
   'At nine o'clock…'
   smelled the fresh bread/took off her boots

Practice
- Children can work in pairs with your support.

Answers

From breakfast to lunch	From lunch to tea
Early in the morning	After lunch
After breakfast	In the afternoon
Before lunch	Before tea
From tea to bedtime	**After bedtime**
After tea	Late at night
In the evening	At midnight
Before bedtime	

Extension
- Children should work individually with your support.
- They can use the time signal words and phrases from the Practice activity but encourage children to think of some of their own.

Answers
Individual answers

Resource Book

Support PCM
- Activity A: Children should work individually.
- Activity B: Discuss the things children do in the morning to stimulate ideas about what Sam might have done.

Answers
(A) Haden's alarm clock went off at seven o'clock. He switched it off and went back to sleep.

Half an hour later, his mum came into the bedroom. She told Haden to get up or he would be late for school.

Haden yawned and got out of bed. He looked at the clock. It was now twenty to eight and the bus left in twenty minutes!

He dashed into the bathroom, got washed and dressed and raced downstairs.

The clock said five to eight! He grabbed a piece of toast and ran out of the house.

At eight o'clock he was at the bus stop just as the bus pulled up. He got on the bus and closed his eyes.

(B) Individual answers

Extension PCM
- Children should work individually but some discussion beforehand to help them pick out the time signal words and phrases that begin the paragraphs may be helpful.

Answers
By nine o'clock in the evening, Amy and her dad were settled down behind the big oak tree at the edge of the wood. They had come to see if they could spot the family of badgers that lived on the edge of the wood.
  Half an hour passed and still there were no badgers. Dad opened a flask and poured them each a hot cup of tea.
  At ten o'clock, Dad thought they had better be going home when they heard something. They kept very quiet and saw the badgers as they came out of the wood into the moonlight.

Extra
Children can continue the story from the Extension PCM.

Discuss what Amy and her dad might have done after they saw the badgers and the time aspect before children write.

BOOK 3 UNIT 27 Verbs

Perfect tense

Verbs are often explained as 'doing words' or 'being words'. They are possibly the most complex part of speech for young children to grasp because of their many forms and tenses.

Throughout the course, children will encounter the present simple, present progressive (also known as continuous), past simple, past progressive, present perfect (labelled simply *perfect* throughout the course), past perfect, future, infinitive (labelled *verb family name* in the early parts of the course), auxiliary verbs, modals, active and passive verbs and subjunctive verbs (a construction very rarely used except in extremely formal writing).

Participles are referred to as '*ing* words' and 'regular past simple tense words'; finite verbs are referred to as 'main' or 'proper verbs', and it is for the teacher to decide the appropriate time to introduce the terms *participle* and *finite verb*.

This unit introduces the present perfect tense. Technically, the present perfect tense is constructed with *has/have* + past participle. As this is the first introduction to the tense, it is simpler to say that it is constructed with *has/have* + the past simple tense (regular or irregular). Mistakes where the past simple tense and the past participle are NOT the same can be dealt with on an individual basis. The tense is referred to as the *perfect tense* to distinguish it from the *past perfect tense* and to avoid the use of the word *present* in a past tense verb.

Pupil Book

Focus
- Revise/explain the term verb and ask for examples of:
  – present simple
  – present progressive
  – past simple
  – past progressive
- Read and discuss the information box on page 58.
- Look at the perfect tense column in the verb box. Point out that *I/You/We/They* are followed by 'have'; *He/She/It* are followed by 'has'.
  Ask children to substitute other verbs, e.g.
  I have looked: I have walked/bought/copied etc.
- Do the activity orally.

Answers
1. He **has walked** all the way home.
2. They **have played** on the beach.
3. He **has cooked** pasta for tea.
4. The rain **has poured** down all day.
5. You **have cleaned** your room very well!

Practice
- Remind the children that they are changing:
  – from the present to a past tense;
  – from a one-word verb to a two-word verb.

Answers
1. I **have played** the piano for an hour a day.
2. You **have watched** television for too long!
3. He **has watered** the plants.
4. She **has washed** her hair.
5. It **has rained** every morning at ten o'clock.
6. We **have visited** our cousins.

Extension
- Children should tackle the activity individually, basing their answers on the picture clues.

Answers
1. I **have washed** my hands.
2. She **has scattered** the corn on the ground.
3. They **have finished** the jigsaw.
4. He **has mended** the broken vase.
5. The sun **has melted** the snowman!

Resource Book

Support PCM
- Children should work individually.

Answers
1. They <u>have finished</u> painting the room.
2. She <u>has cleaned</u> her bicycle.
3. It <u>has stopped</u> raining.
4. Dad <u>has mended</u> the gate.
5. We <u>have arrived</u> on time.

(B)

present simple tense	past simple tense	perfect tense
I talk	I talked	I have talked
They smile	They smiled	They have smiled
We wave	We waved	We have waved
You tidy	You tidied	You have tidied
He paints	He painted	He has painted
She looks	She looked	She has looked
It howls	It howled	It has howled

Extension PCM
- Activity A should be done individually.
- Activity B: Read and discuss the first answer so children understand what is required.

Answers
(A)
1. They **have planned** a surprise party for their friend.
2. He **has helped** on the farm all summer.
3. I **have watched** that film before.
4. It **has snowed** all day today.

(B) Individual answers

Extra

Make a set of personal pronoun cards, e.g.

| I | | you | | he |

Make a set of verb infinitive cards. These should only be of verbs where the past simple tense and the past participle are the same, e.g.

| to bring | | to build | | to catch |

Individuals take a pronoun card and a verb infinitive card and say the perfect tense, e.g.

| You | + | to bring | = you have brought

BOOK 3 UNIT 28 Sentences

Main and subordinate clauses

The concept of a sentence as a unit of language that 'makes sense' can be a difficult concept for some children to grasp. The course builds children's confidence in this area through giving them the opportunity to look at punctuation of statements, questions and exclamations to familiarise themselves with what a 'sentence' looks and sounds like.

Throughout the course, children will encounter: sentence punctuation; the concept of 'making sense'; direct and indirect speech; clauses which combine to make multi-clause sentences; parts of sentences – subject/object, subject/predicate; focusing on the sentence as a unit of language that can be improved; and Standard English constructions.

This unit introduces the concept of the main clause (a sentence in itself) and subordinate clauses (of less importance) to expand sentences. At this stage, the subordinate clauses are mainly adverbial, but the term is not introduced here. The term *finite verb* is introduced and the best way of explaining it is that a finite verb makes a complete tense, so 'singing' is not finite but 'am singing' is. Both main and subordinate clauses need a finite verb.

Pupil Book

Focus
- Revise/discuss the term *phrase*.
- Ask children what they understand by the term *sentence*.
- Introduce the term *clause* and explain the difference between a phrase and a clause.
- Read the information box on page 60.
- Revise/discuss the term *conjunction*.
- Do the activity orally.

Answers
1. **We were ready to go** when it started to rain.
2. **The procession came down the main street** after it came out of the park.
3. **We didn't win the match** although we played very well.
4. **I don't use a calculator** when I do my sums.
5. **I have to tidy up** if I make a mess.
6. **The volcano erupted** before lava poured down its sides.

Practice
- Activities A and B: Children can do this in their books or you can put the sentences on the board for individuals to underline.

Answers
(A) 1. The famous violinist was nervous but she played very well.
2. I am curious to know where you are going and how you will get there.
3. You will get a parking ticket if you park on a double yellow line.
4. The builder finished his work and put away his tools.

(B) 1. I am excited because it is my birthday.
2. The birds will come into the garden if you feed them.
3. I am worried about the spelling test although I think I know them all.
4. The match was good even though my team didn't win.

Extension
- Children can work individually but may need support.
- Discuss answers in class.

Answers
(A) Individual answers

(B) Individual answers

Resource Book

Support PCM
- Children should work individually.

Answers
(A) 1. I will come to the park if I finish my homework.
2. The car skidded because the road was wet.
3. I have to go to the shops when it stops raining.
4. The team was exhausted after the match.

(B) 1. We will get there more quickly if we go by train.
2. I don't want a drink because I am not thirsty.
3. I like the dress although I am not sure about the colour.
4. We need another key because I have lost mine!

(C) Individual answers

(D) Individual answers

Extension PCM
- Discuss the first answer so children understand what is required.

Answers
Individual answers

Extra
This is a difficult concept for most children so plenty of practice is needed.
Ask children for simple sentences and write on the board. Can they add a subordinate clause beginning with a given conjunction?

Book 3 Check-up answers

Check-up 1 (Units 1–6)

Articles
1. **an** orange
2. **a** mountain
3. **an** insect
4. **a** building
5. **an** owl
6. **an** hour

Verbs and nouns
1. The boy **is** on his bicycle.
2. Some people **are** fond of animals.
3. Our cat **is** lost.
4. My brother and I **are** in the team.

Adjectives
(A)
1. sicker
2. shorter
3. smoother
4. plainer
5. smaller
6. greener

(B)
1. saddest
2. smartest
3. flattest
4. bluntest
5. weakest
6. longest

(C)

adjective	comparative	superlative
bad	worse	worst
good	better	best
little	less	least
much	more	most

Sentences
(A)
1. **T**he children worked hard.
2. **T**he spider spun a web.
3. **W**e went out when the rain stopped.
4. **O**n Saturdays we go shopping.

(B)
1. The curtains <u>were hanging</u> over the windows.
2. The bird <u>is pecking</u> at the ground.
3. I <u>worked</u> hard at school.
4. I <u>catch</u> the bus to school.

Singular and plural
(A)
1. berries
2. keys
3. pennies
4. kidneys
5. toys
6. rubies

(B)
1. The **team** goes to the park to play.
2. The **boy** finds his ball in the long grass.
3. My **sisters** want their tea now.
4. **Cats** like to drink milk.

Adverbs
Individual answers

Check-up 2 (Units 7–12)

Prepositions
(A)
1. Sam is climbing **up** the stairs
2. Ben found a book **on** the shelf
3. the cat jumped **over** the fence
4. Ray took the dog **out** for a walk

(B) Individual answers

Verbs
(A)
1. We <u>went</u> to the park after school.
2. The robber <u>ran</u> down the road.
3. I <u>found</u> my coat in the cupboard.
4. They only just <u>caught</u> the bus.

(B) Individual answers

Adjectives
(A)
1. more comfortable
2. merrier
3. worse
4. neater
5. more wonderful
6. sadder
7. more amazing
8. wilder

(B)
1. best
2. most dangerous
3. proudest
4. tidiest
5. most fabulous
6. most ancient
7. coldest
8. stormiest

Sentences
1. "Let me look at your hand," said the nurse.
2. The boy muttered, "I always get the blame."
3. "What a mess!" Mum shouted.
4. "I'm very cold," moaned the little girl.

Pronouns
1. <u>I</u> am going to tidy the garage <u>myself</u>.
2. <u>He</u> watched the seagull as <u>it</u> dived for fish.
3. Mum gave <u>us</u> dinner money.
4. When <u>you</u> go out, see if <u>you</u> can find <u>it</u>.
5. <u>You</u> must get <u>yourself</u> ready in good time to meet <u>them</u>.

Adverbs
(A)
1. more wisely
2. more happily
3. higher
4. more neatly

(B)
1. most wonderfully
2. most sadly
3. fastest
4. most amazingly

Check-up 3 (Units 13–18)

Adjectives
(A)
first, second, third, fourth, **fifth**, sixth, **seventh**, eighth, **ninth**, tenth, **eleventh**, twelfth

(B)
1. He came **first**.
2. She came **fourth**.
3. He came **seventh**.
4. She came **second**.
5. He came **sixth**.

(C)
1. If you are good at music, you are **musical**.
2. If you play football with skill, you are **skilful**.
3. If you act with caution, you are **cautious**.
4. If you give things a lot of thought, you are **thoughtful**.
5. If you act like a fool, you are **foolish**.

Verbs
1. The candle **will burn** all night.
2. The bells **will jingle** in the wind.
3. I **shall listen** to the radio on Saturday morning.
4. The cabbage **will rot** in the vegetable basket.
5. The castle **will fall** down.

Singular and plural
1. calves
2. lives
3. loaves
4. gulfs
5. knives
6. cliffs
7. thieves
8. scarfs or scarves

Nouns
1. The <u>pain</u> in my arm made me cry.
2. We planned to escape at <u>midnight</u>.
3. "My <u>memory</u> is not what it used to be," said Mum.
4. It's a <u>mystery</u> where that book has gone.

Prepositions
1. The rabbit went <u>down</u> the hole.
2. To reach my house, I walk <u>through</u> the park.
3. My book fell <u>behind</u> the chair.
4. The helicopter hovered <u>above</u> the waves.

Check-up 4 (Units 19–24)

Capital letters
(A)
1. **A** **T**ale of **T**wo **C**ities
2. **T**he **T**wits
3. **T**he **R**ailway **C**hildren
4. **T**he **S**ilver **S**word

(B) My Favourite Foods
Fish
Sweet things
Juicy fruit

Sentences
1. "I will carry that for you," offered Jake.
2. "Will you come for tea?" asked Danny.
3. Mark said, "I can't find my jumper."
4. Seren shouted, "Look over there!"

Adjectives
(A)
1. Antarctica is a <u>cold and frozen</u> land.
2. The bicycle <u>with the punctured tyre</u> is mine.
3. The birds pecked at the <u>newly mown</u> lawn.
4. The <u>angry, wounded</u> tiger ran into the jungle.

(B) Individual answers

Prefixes
1. **il**legal
2. **in**accurate
3. **im**perfect
4. **dis**respect
5. **anti**climax
6. **in**capable

Adverbs
(A)
1. The class listened in <u>complete silence</u>.
2. <u>Tomorrow at midday</u>, the parade will begin.
3. <u>From the top of the tree</u>, I could see the old mill.
4. Dad was cooking a meal <u>in the kitchen</u>.
5. I could not get to sleep <u>last night</u>.

(B) Individual answers

Suffixes
1. The clean**er** swept the floor and polish**ed** the windows.
2. The teach**er** was look**ing** for some pencils.
3. I have climb**ed** a high**er** mountain than you have.

Check-up 5 (Units 24–28)

Conjunctions
(A)
1. You need to clean those football boots <u>before</u> you put them in your bag.
2. The rain came <u>after</u> we heard thunder.
3. I will cook the tea <u>while</u> you set the table.
4. He towed the car to the garage <u>when</u> it broke down.

(B)
1. I was cleaning the picture **when** the glass broke.
2. Sam checked he had everything **before** he went to work.
3. The bird laid its eggs **after** it had built the nest.
4. Dad mowed the lawn **while** Mum weeded the flowerbed.

Paragraphs
Suggested answers
1. When I woke up / Early in the morning
2. In the morning / Before lunch
3. In the afternoon / Before tea
4. In the evening / Before I went to bed

Verbs
1. I **have walked** along the road.
2. The pirate **has buried** his treasure.
3. The farmer **has milked** the cows.

Sentences
(A)
1. <u>The plant died</u> even though I watered it.
2. <u>I am going to be late</u> because I overslept!
3. <u>I must write that letter</u> before I forget.

(B) Individual answers

Book 4 Scope and Sequence

Unit	Pupil Book	Pupil Book Focus	Pupil Book Practice	Pupil Book Extension	Resource Book Support	Resource Book Extension
1	**verbs:** round-up of verb tenses*	forming verb tenses for given infinitives	identifying sentences as past, present or future	changing sentences into past and future tense	completing verb tables	classifying verbs/sentence writing
2	**sentences:** main and subordinate clauses*	matching main and subordinate clauses	identifying main and subordinate clauses	adding subordinate clauses to main clauses/adding main clauses to subordinate clauses	identifying main and subordinate clauses in sentences/completing sentences with main and subordinate clauses	writing pairs of sentences with given nouns placed in the main and then the subordinate clause
3	**nouns:** abstract*	identifying abstract nouns in sentences	forming abstract nouns from adjectives and verbs/sentence writing	solving clues with abstract nouns	classifying common, proper, collective and abstract nouns/writing sentences	forming abstract nouns from adjectives and verbs/writing sentences
4	**sentences:** direct speech	adding missing speech marks	punctuating direct speech sentences	punctuating direct speech sentences where direct speech comes second	punctuating various forms of direct speech sentences	ordering and rewriting a speech bubble conversation as direct speech
5	**suffixes:** verb ending; changing parts of speech*	adding suffix to given root words to complete sentences	forming adjectives and abstract nouns by adding suffixes	writing sentences/solving clues with words with suffixes	forming suffix word webs/sentence writing	completing sentences with words with suffixes/sentence writing
6	**adjectives and adverbs:** phrases*	identifying adjective and adverb phrases in sentences	using adjective and adverb phrases in sentences	identifying adjective phrases, adverb phrases and sentences/sentence writing and punctuation	identifying adjective and adverb phrases in sentences/writing adjective and adverb phrases	writing sentences with adjective phrases for given nouns/writing sentences with adverb phrases for given verbs
7	**singular and plural:** words ending in *o*	forming plurals	completing sentences to show noun–verb agreement	forming plurals/listing in alphabetical order	classifying nouns according to plural formation	forming plurals/sentence writing for noun–verb agreement
8	**pronouns:** possessive	identifying possessive pronouns in sentences	completing sentences with possessive pronouns	writing sentences with pairs of possessive pronouns	replacing nouns with possessive pronouns/writing sentences with possessive pronouns	substituting possessive pronouns for repeated nouns in sentences/writing sentences with pairs of possessive pronouns
9	**verbs:** present perfect tense – regular and irregular	identifying the perfect tense in sentences	changing sentences from present to perfect tense	forming unusual perfect tense verbs	completing verb tables	forming perfect tense of more unusual verbs/sentence writing
10	**adverbs:** pairs*	identifying adverb pairs in sentences	building sentences with adverb pairs	improving narrative extract with adverbs and adverb pairs	identifying adverbs and verbs/identifying adverb pairs/sentence writing with given adverb pairs	completing sentences with adverbs or adverb pairs/writing a personal account with adverbs and adverb pairs
11	**sentences:** subject and object*	identifying subjects and objects in sentences	completing sentences with objects	building sentences with adjectives for objects/composing sentences with given subjects and objects	identifying subjects, objects and verbs in sentences	composing pairs of sentences where given noun is first the subject, then the object
12	**verbs:** past perfect tense – regular verbs	identifying past tense verbs in sentences	completing sentences with past perfect verbs	constructing sentences with given pairs of actions	completing past tense verb chart/sentence writing	constructing sentences with given pairs of actions
13	**adjectives:** possessive*	identifying possessive adjectives in sentences	completing sentences with possessive adjectives	descriptive phrases for given nouns with possessive adjective + adjective/completing sentences with *its* or *it's*	completing sentences with suitable possessive adjective/writing sentences using *its* or *it's*	supplying possessive adjective + adjective for given nouns/using descriptive phrases in sentences
14	**sentences:** indirect speech	identifying direct speech and indirect speech in sentences	changing direct speech sentences to indirect speech/indirect speech sentences to direct speech	conversation writing in direct and indirect speech	changing direct speech sentences to indirect speech/indirect speech sentences to direct speech	converting passage of indirect speech narrative into direct speech
15	**verbs:** past perfect tense – regular and irregular	identifying the past perfect tense in sentences	changing sentences from present to past perfect tense	forming unusual past perfect tense verbs	completing verb tables	forming past perfect tense of more unusual verbs/sentence writing

* denotes content that is not specified in the National Curriculum for England (2014) but which will support children's wider knowledge and understanding of grammar.

44

Unit	Pupil Book	Pupil Book Focus	Pupil Book Practice	Pupil Book Extension	Resource Book Support	Resource Book Extension
16	**adverbs:** clauses	identifying adverb clauses and related verbs in sentences	choosing conjunctions to complete adverb clauses – sentences	adding adverb clauses to main clauses/ adding main clauses to adverb clauses	identifying adverb clauses in sentences/ completing sentences with adverb clauses	writing personal recount with adverb clauses
17	**nouns:** noun phrases	identifying the noun phrase in sentences/ making nouns into noun phrases	identifying noun phrases in sentences/ writing expanded noun phrases	identifying noun phrases with *ing*	indentifying noun phrases in sentences/ writing *ing* adjectives and noun phrases	Expanding noun phrases with adjectives/sentences writing
18	**verbs:** common mistakes	correcting mistakes in sentences	writing paragraph opening for a story	correctly using *borrow* and *lend*; *learn* and *teach*	completing sentences with correct forms of the verbs *to come*, *to do* and *to be*/correcting verb mistakes in sentences	using *borrow/lend*, *learn/teach*, *flowed/flown* and *ringed/rung* in own sentences
19	**paragraphs:** location in stories	answering questions about structure of extended writing	ordering paragraphing openings by location	writing a three paragraph story with support	identifying the first sentence of paragraphs in a story/ continuing the story	rewriting a story to include paragraphs
20	**sentences:** double negatives*	adding negative words to sentences to give the opposite meaning	forming contractions/ writing sentences with opposite meaning	rewriting sentences to give intended meaning	Identifying negative words in sentences/ rewriting sentences to give intended meaning	correcting double negative sentences/ sentence writing with given negative words
21	**pronouns:** ambiguity	identifying two possible meanings for sentences due to pronoun ambiguity	clear and ambiguous use of pronouns in context/rewriting sentences to clarify meaning	reordering words in sentences to clarify meaning	identifying double meanings in sentences	clarifying confusion in sentences due to pronoun ambiguity
22	**verbs:** synonyms*	synonyms for given infinitives	synonyms for *went* and *said* in sentence writing	using unusual verbs in sentence writing	classifying verbs in synonym groups	listing synonyms for given verbs/sentence writing
23	**adverbs:** clauses	identifying adverb clauses and related verbs in sentences	completing sentences with adverb clauses/ rewriting sentences so adverb clause comes first	writing sentences with given adverb clauses	identifying adverb clauses in sentences/ completing sentences with adverb clauses	writing sentences around subordinating conjunctions
24	**nouns:** singular and plural possessive	adding apostrophes to form possessive nouns	shortening phrases with possessive nouns – plural owners	adding missing apostrophes to singular and plural owners	identifying possessive nouns in sentences/ shortening phrases with possessive nouns – singular and plural owners/sentence writing with given possessive nouns	writing sentences with possessive nouns from picture stimulus/ forming plural/ sentence writing
25	**sentences:** split direct speech	identifying spoken words in sentences	punctuating split direct speech sentences	direct speech sentences writing using given synonyms for *said*	writing conversation with two direct speech sentences/one split direct speech sentence	punctuating direct speech narrative and using synonyms for *said*
26	**nouns:** plural and possessive	identifying plural nouns and possessive nouns in sentences	identifying possessive and plural nouns in sentences	punctuating sentences with missing apostrophes of possession	identifying possessive nouns in sentences and designating singular or plural/sentence writing with given plural and possessive nouns	forming plural nouns and plural possessive nouns/sentence writing
27	**adverbs:** fronted phrases and clauses	identifying adverb phrases and clauses in sentences	rewriting sentences so that adverb phrases and clauses come at the beginning	completing sentences with appropriate subordinating conjunctions	adding missing commas to sentences with fronted adverbials/completing sentences with fronted adverbial phrases and clauses	using given adverbial phrases and clauses at the beginning, end, and in the middle of own sentences
28	**paragraphs:** non-fiction – aspects of a topic	answering questions about structure of extended writing	grouping given species of animals into paragraphs	writing three paragraphs about a chosen topic	sorting information into two paragraphs/ improving writing	writing three paragraphs on the topic of *My Family*

BOOK 4 UNIT 1 Verbs

Round-up of tenses

Throughout the course, children will encounter the present simple, present progressive (also known as continuous), past simple, past progressive, present perfect (labelled simply *perfect* throughout the course), past perfect, future, infinitive (labelled *verb family name* in the early parts of the course), auxiliary verbs, modals, active and passive verbs and subjunctive verbs (a construction very rarely used except in extremely formal writing).

Participles are referred to as '*ing* words' and 'regular past simple tense words'; finite verbs are referred to as 'main' or 'proper verbs', and it is for the teacher to decide the appropriate time to introduce the terms *participle* and *finite verb*.

This unit recaps on all the verb tenses the children have learned so far:

- present simple
- past simple
- present progressive
- past progressive
- present perfect (Technically, the present perfect tense is constructed with *has/have* + past participle. It is simpler to say that it is constructed with *has/have* + the past simple tense (regular or irregular)).
- future

Pupil Book

Focus

- Revise/discuss the term *verb* and ask for examples of:
  – present simple   – present progressive
  – past simple   – past progressive
  – perfect   – future
- Read and discuss the information box on page 6.
- Do the activity orally.

Answers

	past simple	past progressive	perfect
1	I watched	I was watching	I have watched
2	I waved	I was waving	I have waved
3	I hurried	I was hurrying	I have hurried
4	I grabbed	I was grabbing	I have grabbed
5	I painted	I was painting	I have painted
6	I jumped	I was jumping	I have jumped

	present simple	present progressive	future
1	I watch	I am watching	I shall watch
2	I wave	I am waving	I shall wave
3	I hurry	I am hurrying	I shall hurry
4	I grab	I am grabbing	I shall grab
5	I paint	I am painting	I shall paint
6	I jump	I am jumping	I shall jump

Practice

- Children identify the tense of the verb in each sentence.
- When completed, get children to change the sentences into other tenses in preparation for the Extension activities.

Answers

1. I am sewing seven buttons on to my jacket. — present tense
2. The army wore bright red uniforms. — past tense
3. Your helmet will protect you. — future tense
4. She was making a cake when the doorbell rang. — past tense
5. I believe everything you say. — Present tense

Extension

- Children should work individually.

Answers

(A)
1. My neighbour **was working** in the garden.
2. This **was** a valuable vase.
3. The giant **was frightening** the villagers.
4. The dog **was stealing** the biscuits.
5. I **was going** to the shops for milk.

(B)
1. The siren **will sound** at midnight.
2. It **will happen** every day at four o'clock.
3. I **shall drink** my juice very quickly.
4. The dog **will wash** her new puppies.
5. The match **will go** ahead in spite of the bad weather.

Resource Book

Support PCM

- Children work individually for you to assess their grasp of the different verb tenses the course has covered so far.

Answers

(A)
verb family name	present simple	present progressive	future
to walk	I walk	I am walking	I shall walk
to grow	He grows	He is growing	He will grow
to bring	You bring	You are bringing	You will bring
to see	We see	We are seeing	We shall see
to live	She lives	She is living	She will live
to eat	It eats	It is eating	It will eat
to come	They come	They are coming	They will come
to make	We make	We are making	We shall make

(B)
verb family name	past simple	past progressive	perfect
to cook	I cooked	I was cooking	I have cooked
to shout	He shouted	He was shouting	He has shouted
to climb	You climbed	You were climbing	You have climbed
to plan	We planned	We were planning	We have planned
to wash	She washed	She was washing	She has washed
to happen	It happened	It was happening	It has happened
to jump	They jumped	They were jumping	They have jumped
to cry	We cried	We were crying	We have cried

Extension PCM

- The activities should be done individually.

Answers

(A)
past tenses	present tenses	future tense
was going	am reading	will fly
rowed	help	shall go
broke	are seeing	will read
Were catching	look	will buy

(B) Individual answers

Extra

Make infinitive and tense cards, e.g.

infinitive cards: | to wish | to find | to like |

tense cards: | present simple | past progressive |

Children pick an infinitive card and a tense card and make a sentence.

BOOK 4 UNIT 2 Sentences

Main and subordinate clauses

The concept of a sentence as a unit of language that 'makes sense' can be a difficult concept for some children to grasp. The course builds children's confidence in this area through giving them the opportunity to look at punctuation of statements, questions and exclamations to familiarise themselves with what a 'sentence' looks and sounds like.

Throughout the course, children will encounter: sentence punctuation; the concept of 'making sense'; direct and indirect speech; clauses which combine to make multi-clause sentences; parts of sentences – subject/object, subject/predicate; focusing on the sentence as a unit of language that can be improved; and Standard English constructions.

This unit revises the concept of the main clause (a sentence in itself) and subordinate clauses (of less importance) to expand sentences. At this stage, the subordinate clauses are mainly adverbial, but the term is not introduced here. The term *finite verb* is revised and the best way of explaining it is that a finite verb makes a complete tense, so 'singing' is not finite but 'am singing' is. Both main and subordinate clauses need a finite verb.

Pupil Book

Focus

- Revise/discuss the term *phrase*.
- Ask children what they understand by the term *sentence*.
- Revise/discuss the term *conjunction*.
- Introduce the term *clause* and explain the difference between a phrase and a clause.
- Read the information box on page 8.
- Do the activity orally.

Answers

1. The lightning flashed before we heard the thunder.
2. I need to stay in bed although I am feeling a little better.
3. The dog barked because it was frightened.
4. It was very cold so I found my thick, winter coat.
5. I will send the email if you give me the address.

Practice

- Activities A and B: Children can do this in their books or you can put the sentences on the board for individuals to underline.

Answers

(A) 1. The telephone rang so she answered it.
2. Someone spoke but she couldn't hear very well.
3. She finished the call because the connection was bad.

(B) 1. We go to the cinema when they are showing a good film.
2. We went last week although I had already seen the film.
3. We went for a pizza before we went to the cinema.

Extension

- Children can work individually but may need support.
- Discuss answers in class.

Answers

(A) Individual answers
(B) Individual answers

Resource Book

Support PCM

- Children should work individually.

Answers

(A) 1. The school was closed because of the snow.
2. I got up early so I could feed the rabbit.
3. The windows are closed so I can clean them.
4. We scored a goal when the substitute came on.

(B) 1. You must bring in the washing before it rains.
2. I will get that new book if I go into town.
3. The plant has died although I did water it.
4. You cannot use the sports club unless you are a member.

(C) Individual answers

(D) Individual answers

Extension PCM

- Discuss the first example so children understand what is required.

Answers

Individual answers

Extra

This is a difficult concept for most children so plenty of practice is needed.

Ask children for simple sentences and write on the board.

Can they add a subordinate clause beginning with a given conjunction?

BOOK 4 UNIT 3 Nouns

Abstract nouns

Nouns are usually explained as 'naming' words. Nouns are the most common part of speech that children of this age will encounter. Children's first words are usually nouns as they make sense of the world by naming things.

Throughout the course, children will encounter common, proper, collective, compound, abstract and possessive nouns, together with noun phrases.

This unit revises the concept of abstract nouns. The wide variety of definitions includes states, events, feelings, qualities, experiences, emotions, concepts, etc. which have no physical entity. This unit concentrates on qualities, feelings and time as an introduction to the concept.

Pupil Book

Focus
- Revise/discuss the term *noun* and ask for examples of:
  – common nouns
  – proper nouns
  – collective nouns
  – compound nouns
- Introduce/revise the term *abstract noun*.
- Read the information box on page 10.
- The Activity should be done orally.

Answers
1. The sailors were in great **danger** as the sea grew rougher.
2. If you use all of your **strength**, you can lift that box.
3. I think it takes great **courage** to go skydiving.
4. When **darkness** had fallen, they crept out of the camp.
5. They stared at the **beauty** of the mountain lake.
6. **Honesty** is always best.

Practice
- Read and discuss the information box on page 11.
- Children should work individually.

Answers
(A)
1. silence
2. weakness
3. fragrance
4. violence
5. forgetfulness
6. magnificence
7. brilliance
8. elegance

(B) Individual answers

(C)
1. admission
2. information
3. decision
4. multiplication
5. education
6. description
7. collection
8. imagination

(D) Individual answers

Extension
- Children should work individually.

Answers
1. If you are angry, you show **anger**.
2. If you are frightened you show **fear**.
3. If you think, you have **thoughts**.
4. Your eyes give you the sense of **sight**.
5. Going very fast is to travel at **speed**.

Resource Book

Support PCM
- Children should work individually on the activities.
- Activity A will give a good indication of whether further work is needed on any particular type of noun.

Answers
(A)

common noun	proper noun	collective noun	abstract noun
tree	London	army	friendship
lake	John	herd	weakness
mountain	River Thames	bouquet	information
kangaroo	America	orchestra	sight
valley	Jupiter	fleet	courage

(B) Individual answers

Extension PCM
- Children should work individually on the activities.

Answers
(A)
1. happiness
2. silliness
3. strength
4. tidiness
5. bravery
6. forgetfulness

(B) Individual answers

(C)
1. addition
2. discussion
3. confusion
4. election
5. confession
6. operation

(D) Individual answers

Extra
Make abstract noun suffix cards:

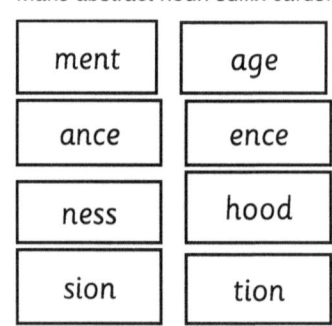

ment	age
ance	ence
ness	hood
sion	tion

Individuals pick a card and make an abstract noun with the given suffix.

BOOK 4 UNIT 4 Sentences

Direct speech

The concept of a sentence as a unit of language that 'makes sense' can be a difficult concept for some children to grasp. The course builds children's confidence in this area through giving them the opportunity to look at punctuation of statements, questions and exclamations to familiarise themselves with what a 'sentence' looks and sounds like.

Throughout the course, children will encounter: sentence punctuation; the concept of 'making sense'; direct and indirect speech; clauses which combine to make multi-clause sentences; parts of sentences – subject/object, subject/predicate; focusing on the sentence as a unit of language that can be improved; and Standard English constructions.

Children often find correctly punctuating direct speech sentences problematic. Several units in the course focus on direct speech so that the various rules can be built up gradually. In this unit, speech marks (inverted commas) begin a new line when a different person speaks and punctuation before the final speech marks are revised.

Pupil Book

Focus
- Begin by asking the children why direct speech (characters having a conversation) looks 'different' on the page.
- Revise the terms *statement – full stop/question – question mark/exclamation – exclamation mark/speech marks (inverted commas)*.
- Read and discuss the information box on page 12.
- Do the activity orally, asking children to read only the spoken words. Children can then copy and write.

Answers
1. "Is that a new mobile phone?" asked Kapil.
2. "Yes," said Sara.
3. "Show me how it works," said Kapil.
4. "Be careful with it!" said Sara.
5. "I won't drop it," said Kapil.

Practice
- Children should work individually.

Answers
1. "Look at that enormous bird!" exclaimed the farmer.
2. "What do you think it is?" asked Harry.
3. "I have never seen anything like it!" said the farmer.
4. "Look. It's flying towards us," said Harry.
5. "Run!" yelled the farmer.

Extension
- Read and discuss the information box on page 13.
- Stress that when the non-spoken words come before the spoken words:
  – they are always followed by a comma;
  – the spoken words always begin with a capital letter.
  (NB The latter is obviously not true when the non-spoken words interrupt a spoken sentence, but this will be tackled later on in the course.)
- Model the first answer then children should work individually.

Answers
1. "These are the spellings you have to learn," said the teacher.
2. Sam asked, "Do we have to learn all of these?"
3. The teacher replied, "Yes. All of them."
4. "I'll never learn all these spellings!" moaned Sam.
5. "Do a few each day," suggested the teacher.
6. Sam mumbled, "I suppose so."

Resource Book

Support PCM
- Children should work individually.

Answers
(A) 1. "I like running. What is your favourite sport?" asked the runner.
2. "I like swimming," replied the boy.
3. "Swimming is so boring!" exclaimed his friend.

(B) 1. "The rainforest is very important," explained the scientist.
2. "What should we do?" asked the interviewer.
3. "We must stop cutting it down!" he explained.

(C) 1. The policeman asked, "What are you doing?"
2. Mrs Green explained, "I am looking for my cat."
3. The policeman said, "Let me help you."

(D) 1. Ben shouted, "Look out!"
2. Fran asked, "What's the matter?"
3. Ben replied, "It's unlucky to walk under a ladder."

Extension PCM
- Children should work individually.
- Accept a new line for a different person speaking if children have not yet been introduced to the concept of paragraphing.

Answers
Suggested answer
"What time is it?" asked Anne.
"It is two o'clock," replied Sally.
"When do we get there?" asked Anne.
"At about half past two," replied Sally.
"Will we be on time?" asked Anne.
"I think we'll be late!" exclaimed Sally.

Extra
- In pairs, children can create a cartoon-type story with frames and speech bubbles.
- Pairs swap their cartoons and change them into a direct speech conversation.

BOOK 4 UNIT 5 Suffixes

Verb tense/parts of speech

A suffix is a group of letters added to the end of a word to form a derivative.

So far, the children have encountered suffixes to form nouns, comparative adjectives, adverbs and verbs.

This unit revises the *ed/ing* suffixes for changing tense, and continues the concept of suffixes changing a word from one part of speech into another.

Pupil Book

Focus
- Revise/discuss the term *suffix* and ask for examples of suffixes:
  – making adverbs
  – making nouns
  – making verb tenses
- Read and discuss the information box on page 14.
- The activity can be done individually or as a class on the board with individuals providing the correct word to complete each sentence.

Answers
1. Which **direction** do we take?
2. **Darkness** falls quickly near the Equator.
3. You need to be very **careful** if you climb on these rocks.
4. These **subtraction** sums are very difficult.
5. He is very keen on sport and **fitness**.
6. The view from the top of the mountains was **wonderful**.

Practice
- Remind children that suffixes can alter spelling.
- Children should work individually and check spelling carefully.
- Discuss answers in class.

Answers
(A) 1 beautiful 2 careful
    3 hopeful   4 enjoyable
    5 punishing 6 believable

(B) 1 weakness   2 kindness
    3 gentleness   4 encouragement
    5 satisfaction   6 situation

Extension
- Read and discuss the information box on page 15.
- Can the children suggest any other words ending with each suffix?

Answers
(A) Individual answers

(B) 1 duck**ling**
    2 fam**ous**
    3 help**ful**
    4 danger**ous**
    5 occupa**tion**
    6 dark**ness**
    7 pay**ment**

Resource Book

Support PCM
- Activity A: Children can work in teams against the clock!
- Activity B: Children should work individually.

Answers
(A) Suggested answers
    ness: happiness/kindness/sadness/fondness/gentleness/awkwardness
    less: careless/thoughtless/merciless/remorseless/hopeless/aimless
    ful: dutiful/careful/sorrowful/pitiful/shameful/dreadful
    tion: situation/magnification/location/situation/donation/imagination

(B) Individual answers

Extension PCM
- Children should work individually.

Answers
(A) 1 To win a victory is to be **victorious**.
    2 To satisfy someone is to give them **satisfaction**.
    3 If you believe what someone says it is **believable**.
    4 If a country is invaded it has suffered an **invasion**.
    5 The job that occupies your time is your **occupation**.
    6 If you imagine something, you are using your **imagination**.

(B) Individual answers

Extra
Make suffix cards:

| tion | ness | ism |
| dom | ment | ship |

Children pick a card and say an abstract noun ending in that suffix.

BOOK 4 UNIT 6 Adjectives and adverbs

Phrases

Adjectives are usually explained as 'describing' words. They pinpoint a quality or a feature of a noun or pronoun. Throughout the course, children will encounter single adjectives, comparative and superlative adjectives, adjective phrases, possessive adjectives and adjective (relative) clauses.

Adverbs are usually explained as words which 'add' to a verb giving the detail of how, where or when an action is done. Throughout the course, children will encounter single adverbs (manner/time/place), comparative and superlative adverbs, adverbial phrases, adverb pairs and adverbial clauses.

This unit revises adjective and adverb phrases. A phrase is a group of words forming a conceptual unit, but not a sentence. Adjective phrases do the same job as a single adjective, and adverb phrases do the same job as a single adverb.

Pupil Book

Focus
- Revise/discuss the terms *adjective* and *adverb*, and ask for examples.
- Read and discuss the information box on page 16.
- Ask children to substitute the phrase *with bare branches* for other phrases that could distinguish the tree.
- Ask children to substitute the phrase with *heavy thudding footsteps* for other phrases that say 'how' the boy came downstairs
- Do the activity orally. When children have identified the adverb phrases, ask if each is an adverb phrase of manner, time or place.

Answers

1. He ran the race **surprisingly well**.   **adverb** phrase
2. I'll be there **in less than an hour**.   **adverb** phrase
3. The wind was **cold and biting**.   **adjective** phrase
4. My books are **in the room upstairs**.   **adverb** phrase
5. My brother was **covered in mud**.   **adjective** phrase

Practice
- Activity A: Discuss each adjective phrase to help children think of suitable sentences, e.g. Ask *What could be built of wood*? etc.
- Activity B: Discuss each adverb phrase to help children think of suitable sentences, e.g. Ask *What could have happened in June last year*? etc.

Answers
(A) Individual answers
(B) Individual answers
(C) Individual answers
(D) Individual answers

Extension
- Tell children that the capital letters and punctuation are missing, otherwise it would be too easy!
- The activities can be tackled individually or in pairs.
- When completed, discuss answers.

Answers
(A) sentences = My name is Ben./She is upset.
(B) adjective phrases = very funny/faint and eerie
    sentences = individual answers

    adverb phrases = on the swing/with great skill
    sentences = individual answers

Resource Book

Support PCM
- The activities should be tackled individually.

Answers
(A) 1. The joke was <u>very funny</u>.
    2. The fox's coat was a <u>dull, dark red</u>.
    3. I like the apple <u>with the red skin</u>.

(B) 1. I wear this ring <u>all the time</u>.
    2. I feel very tired <u>by ten o'clock</u>.
    3. Put it <u>in the shed</u>.

(C) Individual answers
(D) Individual answers

Extension PCM
- Children should work individually.
- When complete, discuss answers.

Answers
(A) Individual answers
(B) Individual answers

Extra
Make scenario cards, e.g.

| washing up | doing homework |

Individuals take a card and say an adverb phrase of manner, time or place to describe the action. Class identify which sort of adverb phrase it is.

BOOK 4
Singular and plural

Words ending in o/oo

Most nouns have a singular form (one) and a plural form (more than one). The vast majority of nouns form their plural by adding s.

Throughout the course, children will encounter plurals with s and es, pluralisation for words ending in y/f/fe/o/oo, and irregular plurals.

This unit revises the work on singular and plural with nouns that form their plurals by adding s or es, and nouns ending in y. It extends the work to nouns ending in o/oo.

As the course progresses, the Extra section of the Teacher's Notes will suggest examining the plural form of nouns with foreign origins.

Pupil Book

Focus
- Revise/discuss *more than one (noun)* and ask for examples with s and es.
- Introduce/revise the terms:
  – singular   =   one
  – plural   =   more than one
- Read the information box on page 18.
- Revise/discuss the terms *vowel* and *consonant*.
- Do the activity on the board.

Answers
(A) 1 pianos   2 photos
    3 potatoes   4 hippos
    5 cockatoos   6 piccolos

(B) Individual answers

Practice
- These activities revise noun–verb agreement.
- Children should work individually.

Answers
(A) 1 The bamboo **is** growing tall.
    2 The hippos **are** playing in the mud.
    3 The cello **is** out of tune.

(B) 1 The tomatoes **were** ripe.
    2 The potato **was** rotten.
    3 The photos **were** very good.

Extension
- The Extension activities assess how much individuals remember about plural forms they have learned earlier in the course.
- Children should work individually.

Answers
(A) 1 factor**ies**   2 dictionar**ies**
    3 abbey**s**   4 railway**s**
    5 melod**ies**   6 balcon**ies**
    7 ceremon**ies**   8 alley**s**
    9 decoy**s**   10 ferr**ies**
    11 butterfl**ies**   12 kidney**s**

(B) abbeys   alleys   balconies   butterflies
    ceremonies   decoys   dictionaries
    factories   ferries   kidneys   melodies   railways

(C) 1 thie**ves**   2 pupp**ies**   3 loa**ves**
    4 wol**ves**   5 famil**ies**   6 cliff**s**
    7 crowd**s**   8 boy**s**   9 camera**s**

(D) boys   cameras   cliffs
    crowds   families   loaves
    puppies   thieves   wolves

Resource Book

Support PCM
- Children should work individually.

Answers

Add s	Add es
trolleys	potatoes
cellos	matches
pianos	bushes
valleys	glasses
bamboos	foxes

Take off y and add ies	Change f/fe to ves
babies	wolves
rubies	leaves
families	shelves
factories	thieves
puppies	knives

Extension PCM
- Children should work individually.

Answers
(A) 1 dingoes
    2 cargoes
    3 dominoes
    4 banjos
    5 sopranos

(B) Individual answers

(C) Individual answers

Extra
These 'o words' are foreign in origin.
Discuss meanings and plurals with the children.
    aficionado   –   aficionados
    maestro   –   maestri/maestros
    virtuoso   –   virtuosi/virtuosos

BOOK 4 UNIT 8 Pronouns

Possessive

Pronouns are words that take the place of nouns and noun phrases.

Throughout the course, children will encounter: personal pronouns (as subject and object); possessive pronouns; reflexive pronouns; and relative pronouns.

Demonstrative pronouns are introduced in the work on noun phrases.

Interrogative pronouns are not specifically labelled as such but children encounter them in work on relative pronouns. It is up to individual teachers if indefinite pronouns, e.g. each/many/few/some, are specifically labelled as such and taught as another group of pronouns.

This unit introduces work on possessive pronouns. All of the possessive pronouns are in common use except *its* which is more commonly used as a possessive adjective. It really is a very fine point – it is far more important that children are able to differentiate between *its* and *it's*.

Pupil Book

Focus
- Revise/discuss the term *noun*.
- Revise/discuss the term *pronoun* and ask for examples.
- Read the information box on page 20.
- Ask children to choose a pronoun from the pronoun box and put it into another sentence.
- Do the Activity orally.

Answers

(A) 1 That old hat is **mine**.
2 Is this **hers**?
3 My writing is neater than **his**.
4 This book is **yours**.
5 I like **ours** better.
6 That car is **theirs**.

Practice
- Read through the sentences before children write.
- This can be done individually or on the board with individuals supplying the missing pronoun.

Answers

1 "This chair is **mine** and that chair is **yours**," said Ian to his sister.
2 Carl made a model castle. Lynn helped him so it is **hers** as well.
3 The children took some baby photographs to school. The twins were not sure if they could find **theirs**.
4 The teacher asked for the homework. Karima and I hadn't brought **ours**.
5 "These footballs are **ours**!" shouted the boys.

Extension
- Read and discuss the first example so children understand what is required.

Answers

Individual answers

Resource Book

Support PCM
- Activity A: Children should work individually.
- Activity B: If children find it too difficult to compose one sentence with both possessive pronouns, they can compose two related sentences.

Answers

(A) 1 The house is **theirs**.
2 This car is **ours**.
3 This comic is **mine**.
4 These boots are **his**.
5 These skates are **hers**.
6 This bag is **yours**.

(B) Individual answers

Extension PCM
- Children should work individually.

Answers

(A) 1 mine
2 yours
3 hers
4 his
5 theirs

(B) Individual answers

Extra

Make possessive pronoun cards: (avoid its)

mine	yours	his
hers	ours	theirs

Children pick a card and compose a sentence using the possessive pronoun on that card.

53

BOOK 4 UNIT 9 Verbs

Perfect tense – regular and irregular

Verbs are often explained as 'doing words' or 'being words'. They are possibly the most complex part of speech for young children to grasp because of their many forms and tenses.

Throughout the course, children will encounter the present simple, present progressive (also known as continuous), past simple, past progressive, present perfect (labelled simply *perfect* throughout the course), past perfect, future, infinitive (labelled *verb family name* in the early parts of the course), auxiliary verbs, modals, active and passive verbs and subjunctive verbs (a construction very rarely used except in extremely formal writing).

Participles are referred to as '*ing* words' and 'regular past simple tense words'; finite verbs are referred to as 'main' or 'proper verbs', and it is for the teacher to decide the appropriate time to introduce the terms *participle* and *finite verb*.

This unit revises the present perfect tense. Technically, the present perfect tense is constructed with *has/have* + past participle. As this is the first introduction to the tense, it is simpler to say that it is constructed with *has/have* + the past simple tense (regular or irregular). Mistakes where the past simple tense and the past participle are NOT the same can be dealt with on an individual basis, and a list of words the children may need is given in the Extra section of the Teacher's Notes. The tense is referred to as the 'perfect tense' to distinguish it from the 'past perfect tense' and to avoid the use of the word 'present' in a past tense verb.

Pupil Book

Focus
- Revise/discuss the term *verb* and ask for examples of:
  – present simple
  – present progressive   – past simple
  – past progressive   – perfect
  – future
- Read and discuss the information box on page 22.
- Do the activity orally.

Answers
1. I **have listened** to the whole CD.
2. They **have bought** a goldfish.
3. We **have reached** the top of the mountain.
4. The crowd **has left** the ground.
5. That horse **has won** the race.

Practice
- Remind the children that they are changing:
  – from the present to a past tense;
  – from a one-word verb to a two-word verb.

Answers
1. I **have bought** bread every day.
2. We **have met** at the station.
3. I **have taught** the children.
4. It **has caught** the ball.
5. I **have brought** lunch to school.
6. I **have felt** a draught from the window.

Extension
- Read and discuss the first one with the children so they understand what is required.

- Children can work in pairs.
- When complete, discuss answers.

Answers
1	I have eaten	2	I have seen
3	I have drawn	4	I have been
5	I have known	6	I have grown
7	I have broken	8	I have spoken
9	I have rung	10	I have shaken

Resource Book

Support PCM
- Children should work individually.
- Point out that the verbs in Activity E have an irregular perfect tense, i.e. they do not use the past simple tense of the verb.

Answers

(A)
verb family name	past simple	perfect
to walk	I walked	I have walked
to arrive	I arrived	I have arrived
to listen	I listened	I have listened
to laugh	I laughed	I have laughed

(B) Individual answers

(C)
verb family name	past simple	perfect
to bring	I brought	I have brought
to catch	I caught	I have caught
to think	I thought	I have thought
to fight	I fought	I have fought

(D) Individual answers

(E)
verb family name	past simple	perfect
to eat	I ate	I have eaten
to grow	I grew	I have grown
to break	I broke	I have broken
to fly	I flew	I have flown

(F) Individual answers

Extension PCM
- Some of the verbs in this activity are unusual. Read through them and ensure children understand their meanings.

Answers
1	have arisen	2	have fled	3	have forbidden
4	have sought	5	have thrived	6	have undergone
7	have flung				

Sentences: Individual answers

54

BOOK 4 UNIT 9

Extra

Here is a useful list of verbs that have a different past simple tense form to their past participle.
Use these as the basis of team games.

Infinitive	past simple tense	past participle
to be	was/were	been
to begin	began	begun
to blow	blew	blown
to break	broke	broken
to choose	chose	chosen
to come	came	come
to do	did	done
to draw	drew	drawn
to drink	drank	drunk
to drive	drove	driven
to eat	ate	eaten
to fall	fell	fallen
to fly	flew	flown
to forget	forgot	forgotten
to forgive	forgave	forgiven
to freeze	froze	frozen
to give	gave	given
to go	went	gone
to grow	grew	grown
to hide	hid	hidden
to know	knew	known
to ride	rode	ridden
to ring	rang	rung
to rise	rose	risen
to run	ran	run
to shake	shook	shaken
to sing	sang	sung
to sink	sank	sunk
to speak	spoke	spoken
to steal	stole	stolen
to swim	swam	swum
to take	took	taken
to tear	tore	torn
to throw	threw	thrown
to write	wrote	written

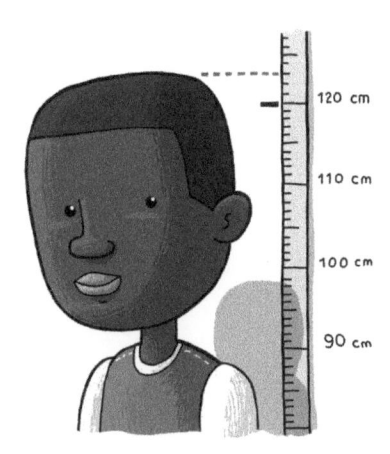

BOOK 4 UNIT 10 Adverbs

Pairs

Adverbs are usually explained as words which 'add' to a verb giving the detail of how, where or when an action is done.

Throughout the course, children will encounter single adverbs (manner/time/place), comparative and superlative adverbs, adverbial phrases, adverb pairs and adverbial clauses.

This unit introduces the concept of adverb pairs where one adverb clarifies the exact meaning of the following adverb.

Pupil Book

Focus

- Revise/discuss the term *adverb* and ask for examples of *how*, *when* and *where* adverbs.
- Read and discuss the information box on page 24.
- Do the activity orally.
- When complete, ask: *What is the difference between rather slowly and slowly; quite happily and happily?* etc.

Answers

1. The cat crept **rather slowly** towards the bird.
2. The bird was **quite happily** pulling a worm from the ground.
3. **Very quietly**, the cat crept closer.
4. **Almost silently**, the cat jumped towards the bird.
5. The bird flew away **very quickly** and landed in a tree.

Practice

- Tell the children to read the words in the box and all of the incomplete sentences before they begin to write.

Answers

1. Put away the glasses **very/extremely/more** carefully.
2. You need to paint **more/less/rather/very** colourfully.
3. When we move away, we will visit **very/less/more** often.
4. The train is running **very/rather/extremely** late.
5. The girl sang **so** beautifully that the audience clapped **very/extremely** loudly.

Extension

- Tell children to read the whole passage before they begin to write.

Answers

Suggested answers
Night fell **quickly** and the wood became dark and gloomy. The two friends rode along **rather slowly** and talked **quietly**. They **suddenly** heard rustling in the trees and stopped their horses. One of the men got off his horse **rather nervously** and listened **carefully**. There it was again.
"What shall we do?" whispered the man on the horse **very softly**.
"I don't know," the other replied. "I think we should ride on **immediately** and get out of this wood."

Resource Book

Support PCM

- Children should work individually.

Answers

A
1. The crowd (cheered) loudly at the match. — how
2. Dan (jumped) up when the bell rang. — where
3. The snake (hisses) suddenly. — when
4. You can (go) early if you have finished. — when
5. The spider (spun) busily to make its web. — how

B
1. The time went rather quickly.
2. You must draw the map very neatly.
3. I go to that shop most often.
4. He spoke so quietly that I could hardly hear him.
5. This is quite firmly stuck together!

C Individual answers

Extension PCM

- *Children should work individually.*

Answers

A Individual answers
B Individual answers
C Individual answers

Extra

Make adverbs cards, e.g.

| very | quite |
| rather | extremely |

Children pick a card and make an adverb pair.

56

BOOK 4 UNIT 11 Sentences

Subject and object

The concept of a sentence as a unit of language that 'makes sense' can be a difficult concept for some children to grasp. The course builds children's confidence in this area through giving them the opportunity to look at punctuation of statements, questions and exclamations to familiarise themselves with what a 'sentence' looks and sounds like.

Throughout the course, children will encounter: sentence punctuation; the concept of 'making sense'; direct and indirect speech; clauses which combine to make multi-clause sentences; parts of sentences – subject/object, subject/predicate; focusing on the sentence as a unit of language that can be improved; and Standard English constructions.

This unit introduces 'subject' and 'object' in sentences.

- The 'subject' is what the sentence is about and usually does the action expressed by the verb. The 'subject' can be a single noun, a noun phrase or pronoun – the latter being in the subject form.
- The object is what has been directly affected by the verb. The 'object' can be a single noun, a noun phrase or pronoun – the latter being in the object form.

Pupil Book

Focus

- Ask children what they understand by the term *sentence*.
- Revise/discuss the terms *noun* and *pronoun*.
- Introduce the terms *subject* and *object*.
- Read the information box on page 26.
- Do more oral examples asking children to identify subject and object in simple sentences.
- Do the activities orally.

Answers

1. **We** are buying tickets.
2. **I** bought a jacket.
3. **The squirrel** ate the nuts.

(B) 1. The nurse wore **a uniform**.
2. The bus crashed into **a tree**.
3. The car is in **the garage**.

Practice

- Children can work in pairs. What are the most unusual objects they can come up with?

Answers

Individual answers

Extension

- Activity A: Children should work individually.
- Activity B: Model the first answer to help children who are finding the concept difficult. Ask: *What could we do with the ball?*

Answers

(A) Individual answers
(B) Individual answers

Resource Book

Support PCM

- Children should work individually.

Answers

(A) 1. The <u>teacher</u> piled up the (books).
2. <u>Mr Smith</u> cleaned the (windows).
3. The <u>gardener</u> cut off the (branches).
4. Three <u>children</u> forgot their (packed lunches).
5. <u>Larry</u> rode the winning (horse).

(B) 1. _s_ _v_ _o_
The policeman caught the robbers.
2. _s_ _v_ _o_
Sam finished the jigsaw.
3. _s_ _v_ _o_
Our relay team won the race.
4. _s_ _v_ _o_
The hairy spider spun silky webs.

Extension PCM

- Model the first answer so children understand what is required.

Answers

Individual answers

Extra

- Make subject and object cards, e.g.

subject cards: | The man | | She |

| Our new teacher |

object cards: | the dog | | the umbrella |

| us |

Children choose a subject card and an object card and make a sentence.

BOOK 4 UNIT 12 Verbs

Past perfect

Verbs are often explained as 'doing words' or 'being words'. They are possibly the most complex part of speech for young children to grasp because of their many forms and tenses.

Throughout the course, children will encounter the present simple, present progressive (also known as continuous), past simple, past progressive, present perfect (labelled simply *perfect* throughout the course), past perfect, future, infinitive (labelled *verb family name* in the early parts of the course), auxiliary verbs, modals, active and passive verbs and subjunctive verbs (a construction very rarely used except in extremely formal writing).

Participles are referred to as '*ing* words' and 'regular past simple tense words'; finite verbs are referred to as 'main' or 'proper verbs', and it is for the teacher to decide the appropriate time to introduce the terms *participle* and *finite verb*.

This unit introduces the past perfect tense. Technically, the past perfect tense is constructed with *had* + past participle. It is simpler to say that it is constructed with *had* + the past simple tense (regular or irregular). Mistakes where the past simple tense and the past participle are NOT the same can be dealt with on an individual basis, and irregular past perfect tense verbs are examined in Unit 15.

Pupil Book

Focus
- Revise/discuss the term *verb* and ask for examples of:
  – present simple
  – present progressive
  – past simple
  – past progressive
  – perfect
  – future
- Read and discuss the information box on page 28.
- Do the activity orally.
- When complete, discuss when children would use the various past tenses.

Answers
1. We **were looking** for our cat all day.
2. The comedian **laughed** and **joked** with the audience.
3. I **have watered** the plants and **fed** the birds.
4. They **had lived** in a cottage before they **moved** to a new house.
5. I **was getting** into bed when the telephone **rang**.
6. Mr Green **had finished** the ironing so he **made** a cup of tea.

Practice
- Read and discuss the first answer so children understand what is required.

Answers
Individual answers

Extension
- Read and discuss the first answer so children understand what is required.

Answers
Individual answers

Resource Book

Support PCM
- Children work individually for you to assess their grasp of the different verb past tenses the course has covered so far.

Answers

A

verb family name	past simple tense	past progressive tense	perfect tense (have/has)	past perfect tense (had)
to talk	I **talked**	I **was talking**	I **have talked**	I **had talked**
to yell	We **yelled**	We **were yelling**	We **have yelled**	We **had yelled**
to guess	You **guessed**	You **were guessing**	You **have guessed**	You **had guessed**
to touch	They **touched**	They **were touching**	They **have touched**	They **had touched**
to arrive	It **arrived**	It **was arriving**	It **has arrived**	It **had arrived**
to laugh	He **laughed**	He **was laughing**	He **has laughed**	He **had laughed**
to finish	She **finished**	She **was finishing**	She **has finished**	She **had finished**

B Individual answers

Extension PCM
- The activity should be done individually.

Answers
Individual answers

Extra
Make infinitive and tense cards, e.g.
infinitive cards:

| to arrive | to sail | to hike |

Two tense cards:

| perfect | past perfect |

Children pick an infinitive card and a tense card and make a sentence.

58

BOOK 4 UNIT 13 Adjectives

Possessive

Adjectives are usually explained as 'describing' words. They pinpoint a quality or a feature of a noun or pronoun.

Throughout the course, children will encounter single adjectives, comparative and superlative adjectives, adjective phrases, possessive adjectives and adjective (relative) clauses.

This unit introduces possessive adjectives. They differ from possessive pronouns in that they are followed by a noun, but do not stand in place of a noun.

Pupil Book

Focus
- Revise/discuss the term *adjective*, and ask for examples.
- Read and discuss the information box on page 30.

Answers
1. The computer in **our** classroom is not working properly.
2. If you can remember that far back, **your** memory is very good.
3. The castle was well preserved but **its** tower was in ruins.
4. The champion beat **his** opponent easily.
5. **Their** quarrel lasted for days.
6. I found **my** keys in the bottom of my bag.
7. I'm sure **her** sister plays the piano.

Practice
- Children should work individually.

Answers
1. I'll let you have **my** new address when we move.
2. The committee found it difficult to make **their** decision.
3. Katy was pleased because **her** friend was coming to stay for the weekend.
4. **Our** tap was leaking so we called a plumber.

Extension
- Activity A: Read and discuss the first example so children understand what is required.
- When complete, discuss answers.
- Read the information box on page 31.
- Ask children to give sentences using *its* and *it's*.
- Activity B: Children should work individually.

Answers

(A) Individual answers

(B)
1. The dog slept in **its** kennel.
2. "**It's** a grizzly bear!" screamed Jenny.
3. **It's** windier today than it was yesterday.
4. The kitten put out **its** sharp claws.

Resource Book

Support PCM
- Children should work individually.

Answers
(A)
1. The bird couldn't fly because **its** wing was broken.
2. I heard **his** radio so I knew he was in **his** room.
3. **My/His/Her/Our/Your/Their** bag is heavier than **my/his/her/our/your/their** bag.
4. We live in that street and **our** house is on the left.
5. "**Your** work is very neat," said the teacher to Frankie.

(B) Individual answers

Extension PCM
- If necessary, model the first answer so children understand what is required.

Answers
Individual answers

Extra
Make possessive adjective and possessive pronoun cards, e.g.

| my | mine | his |
| her | hers | its |

Children pick a card and put the pronoun/adjective into a sentence.
What do the children notice about *his*?
It is not that important that children can say which is a pronoun and which an adjective at this stage. Far more important is that they can use the words correctly in sentences.

BOOK 4 UNIT 14 Sentences

Indirect speech

The concept of a sentence as a unit of language that 'makes sense' can be a difficult concept for some children to grasp. The course builds children's confidence in this area through giving them the opportunity to look at punctuation of statements, questions and exclamations to familiarise themselves with what a 'sentence' looks and sounds like.

Throughout the course, children will encounter: sentence punctuation; the concept of 'making sense'; direct and indirect speech; clauses which combine to make multi-clause sentences; parts of sentences – subject/object, subject/predicate; focusing on the sentence as a unit of language that can be improved; and Standard English constructions.

This unit introduces the concept of 'indirect speech', giving children the opportunity to change direct speech sentences into indirect speech, and indirect speech into direct speech sentences, as well as writing conversations and reported conversations. Indirect speech is also known as 'reported speech', which is helpful for children as they understand the idea of 'reporting' what someone has said.

Pupil Book

Focus
- Begin by asking the children why direct speech (characters having a conversation) looks 'different' on the page.
- Revise the terms *statement – full stop/question – question mark/exclamation – exclamation mark/speech marks (inverted commas)*.
- Introduce the term *indirect (reported) speech*.
- Read the information box on page 32.
- Do the activity orally.

Answers
Direct speech   =   1/3
Indirect speech =   2/4/5

Practice
- Activities A and B: Explain that the children are going to change direct speech into indirect speech, and indirect speech into direct speech.
- Do the first question from each activity orally first so children understand what is required.

Answers
(A) 1 A voice boomed over the loudspeaker asking all passengers to go to Platform 9.
2 Dad said that he liked porridge for breakfast.
3 One of the customers asked snappily how long he/she had to wait to be served.
4 The actor said with a groan that he had forgotten his lines.

(B) 1 "My book is very dull," said Chris.
2 "How far do we still have to go?" asked Latif.
3 "Have many people come to the show?" asked the singer.
4 "Sandy, tell me what has happened," said Martha encouragingly.

Extension
- Activity A: Children can work in pairs to produce the conversation and read it as a duologue to the class.

- Remind them to include some synonyms for *said*.
- Activity B: Children should work individually.

Answers
Individual answers

Resource Book

Support PCM
- Children should work individually on the activities.

Answers
(A) 1 "The school bus has broken down," said the teacher.
2 "We are going to visit your aunty," said Mum.
3 "I am closing soon," said the shopkeeper.
4 "We will be taking off in five minutes," said the pilot.

(B) 1 The nurse asked to look at my hand.
2 Tim moaned that he didn't want to go.
3 The teacher explained how to do division sums.
4 The runner exclaimed that he was so pleased that he had won.

Extension PCM
- Children should work individually.
- Remind them of the punctuation needed and beginning a new line (paragraph) when a different person speaks.

Answers
"I have forgotten my homework," I told the teacher. She wasn't very pleased.
"How did you manage to forget it?" she asked.
"I got up late and was in a rush," I explained.
"You should have put it in your bag last night,"
she said.
"Yes, I should have done that," I agreed. "I'm sorry."
"Being sorry isn't good enough," she said. "You will have to stay in at break time and do it again."
"Can I go home and get it?" I asked.
" No. I can't let you leave school so you will just have to learn the hard way."

Extra
For extra practice, choose a passage of direct speech from the class reader and ask children to change it into indirect speech.

BOOK 4 UNIT 15 Verbs

Past perfect regular and irregular

Verbs are often explained as 'doing words' or 'being words'. They are possibly the most complex part of speech for young children to grasp because of their many forms and tenses.

Throughout the course, children will encounter the present simple, present progressive (also known as continuous), past simple, past progressive, present perfect (labelled simply *perfect* throughout the course), past perfect, future, infinitive (labelled *verb family name* in the early parts of the course), auxiliary verbs, modals, active and passive verbs and subjunctive verbs (a construction very rarely used except in extremely formal writing).

Participles are referred to as '*ing* words' and 'regular past simple tense words'; finite verbs are referred to as 'main' or 'proper verbs', and it is for the teacher to decide the appropriate time to introduce the terms *participle* and *finite verb*.

This unit revises the past perfect tense. Technically, the past perfect tense is constructed with *had* + past participle. It is simpler to say that it is constructed with *had* + the past simple tense (regular or irregular). Mistakes where the past simple tense and the past participle are NOT the same can be dealt with on an individual basis.

Pupil Book

Focus
- Elicit/explain the term *verb* and ask for examples of:
  – present simple
  – present progressive
  – past simple
  – past progressive
  – perfect
  – past perfect
  – future
- Read and discuss the information box on page 34.
- Point out that the verbs in the verb box do not make the perfect and past perfect with the past simple tense. If appropriate, introduce/revise the term participle.
- Do the activity orally which revises the regular past perfect tense.

Answers
1. They **had searched** for the sheep all day.
2. I **had wondered** where they were.
3. Elephants **had knocked** down the tree.
4. Swallows **had nested** in the old shed.
5. Three pupils **had finished** the test.
6. I **had enjoyed** the concert very much.

Practice
- Remind the children that they are changing:
  – from the present to a past tense;
  – from a one-word verb to a two-word verb.

Answers
1. I **had walked** to school.
2. Sally **had caught** the train.
3. Ben **had gone** by bus.
4. The twins **had travelled** by car.
5. Fred **had ridden** his bike.

Extension
- This can be done in teams as a competition.

Answers
1	to go	I have **gone**	I had **gone**
2	to see	I have **seen**	I had **seen**
3	to forget	I have **forgotten**	I had **forgotten**
4	to fly	I have **flown**	I had **flown**
5	to know	I have **known**	I had **known**
6	to choose	I have **chosen**	I had **chosen**
7	to become	I have **become**	I had **become**
8	to speak	I have **spoken**	I had **spoken**
9	to ring	I have **rung**	I had **rung**
10	to shake	I have **shaken**	I had **shaken**

Resource Book

Support PCM
- Children should work individually.
- Point out that the verbs in Activity E have an irregular past perfect tense, i.e. they do not use the past simple tense of the verb.

Answers

(A)
verb family name	past simple	past perfect
to type	I **typed**	I had **typed**
to start	I **started**	I had **started**
to miss	I **missed**	I had **missed**
to race	I **raced**	I had **raced**

(B) Individual answers

(C)
verb family name	past simple	past perfect
to bring	I **brought**	I had **brought**
to fight	I **fought**	I had **fought**
to keep	I **kept**	I had **kept**
to spend	I **spent**	I had **spent**

(D) Individual answers

(E)
verb family name	past simple	past perfect
to draw	I **drew**	I had **drawn**
to forgive	I **forgave**	I had **forgiven**
to hide	I **hid**	I had **hidden**
to sink	I **sank**	I had **sunk**

(F) Individual answers

Extension PCM
- Some of the verbs in this activity are unusual. Read through them and ensure children understand their meanings.

Answers
1. had sawed/sawn
2. had proved/proven
3. had lit/lighted
4. had spilled/spilt
5. had struck/stricken
6. had woken/waked
7. had shone/shined

Sentence = individual answers

Extra

Here is a useful list of verbs that have a different past simple tense form to their past participle.
Use these as the basis of team games.

Infinitive	past simple tense	past participle
to be	was/were	been
to begin	began	begun
to blow	blew	blown
to break	broke	broken
to choose	chose	chosen
to come	came	come
to do	did	done
to draw	drew	drawn
to drink	drank	drunk
to drive	drove	driven
to eat	ate	eaten
to fall	fell	fallen
to fly	flew	flown
to forget	forgot	forgotten
to forgive	forgave	forgiven
to freeze	froze	frozen
to give	gave	given
to go	went	gone
to grow	grew	grown
to hide	hid	hidden
to know	knew	known
to ride	rode	ridden
to ring	rang	rung
to rise	rose	risen
to run	ran	run
to shake	shook	shaken
to sing	sang	sung
to sink	sank	sunk
to speak	spoke	spoken
to steal	stole	stolen
to swim	swam	swum
to take	took	taken
to tear	tore	torn
to throw	threw	thrown
to write	wrote	written

BOOK 4 UNIT 16 Adverbs

Clauses

Adverbs are usually explained as words which 'add' to a verb giving the detail of how, where or when an action is done.

Throughout the course, children will encounter single adverbs (manner/time/place), comparative and superlative adverbs, adverbial phrases, adverb pairs and adverbial clauses.

Children have encountered the concepts of main and subordinate clauses earlier in the course. A main clause is a sentence in itself whereas a subordinate clause (beginning with a conjunction) is of less importance. Both main clauses and subordinate clauses contain a finite verb, i.e. a verb that makes a tense.

This unit introduces adverbial clauses. As with adverbial phrases, an adverbial clause does the same job as a single adverb, answering the basic questions how, when or where. It also expresses *reason* with conjunctions such as 'because', 'since', 'as'; *purpose* with conjunctions such as 'so that', 'in order to'; *contrast* with conjunctions such as 'although', 'as though'; and *comparison* with conjunctions such as 'as if', 'as though'.

Pupil Book

Focus

- Revise/discuss the terms *phrase, sentence, conjunction, main clause, subordinate clause, finite verb*.
- Write sentences with a *main* and *subordinate* clause on the board.
- Children identify:
  - the main clause
  - the subordinate clause
  - the conjunction which begins the subordinate clause
  - the verb in the main clause
  - the verb in the subordinate clause.
- Read the information box on page 36.
- Explain that one type of subordinate clause is an adverb clause.
- Ask children to substitute:
  - *because the engine broke down* with another *because* clause;
  - *when they fix the engine* with another *when* clause;
  - *if they fix the engine* with another *if* clause.
- Do the activity orally.

Answers

Adverb clause = bold; verb = circled

1 The prisoner (escaped) **because the guard was asleep**.
2 I (will do) my homework **when I have had something to eat**.
3 I (can't polish) my shoes **if there is no polish**.
4 The squirrel (ran) up the tree **when the dog chased it**.
5 We (will go) for a picnic **if it doesn't rain**.

Practice

- Point out that more than one conjunction can be used and still make sense although the meaning will be different.
- When completed, discuss answers.

Answers

1 We will go to the village shop **if/because** we have time.
2 You cannot ride your bike **even if/unless** you wear your helmet.
3 The doctor works very late **because/if** there are lots of people waiting to see her.
4 I have to find my bag **although/even though/even if** I am late for school.

Extension

- Activity A: Remind children that the adverbial clause they add must begin with a conjunction but NOT *and/but/or*.
- Activity B: Remind children that the main clause they add must be a sentence in itself.
- When activities are complete, discuss answers.

Answers

(A) Individual answers
(B) Individual answers

Resource Book

Support PCM

- Activity A: Remind children they are looking for a conjunction that signals the beginning of the adverbial clause.
- Activity B: Remind children that the adverbial clause they add begins with a conjunction.

Answers

(A) 1 The singer signed autographs <u>after the concert had finished</u>.
2 The sheep had escaped <u>because the farmer left the gate open</u>.
3 I like cooking <u>although this recipe is difficult</u>.
4 The tiger roared <u>when the hunter approached it</u>.

(B) Individual answers

Extension PCM

- Have an initial discussion about the sort of exciting things children could do after school.
- Children then work individually on the activity.
- Check work in progress and help children to see opportunities for including adverbial clauses.

Answers

Individual answers

Extra

Make conjunction cards, e.g.

when	because
even though	although

Children pick a card and use the conjunction as the beginning of an adverbial clause in a sentence.

BOOK 4 UNIT 17 Nouns

Phrases

Nouns are usually explained as 'naming' words. Nouns are the most common part of speech children of this age will encounter. Children's first words are usually nouns as they make sense of the world by naming things.

Throughout the course, children will encounter common, proper, collective, compound, abstract and possessive nouns, together with noun phrases.

This unit introduces the concept of noun phrases introduced by:
- articles
- demonstrative adjectives [also called demonstrative pronouns when not followed by a noun]
- adjectives including 'ing' participles

Later in the course the concepts of noun phrases with possessive adjectives and possessive nouns is introduced, along with the idea of indicating something specific or something general.

Pupil Book

Focus
- Revise / discuss the term *noun* and ask for examples of:
  - common nouns
  - proper nouns
  - collective nouns
  - compound nouns
  - abstract nouns
  - singular possessive nouns
- Revise / discuss the term *phrase*.
- Introduce / discuss the term *noun phrase*.
- Read and discuss the information box on page 38.
- The activity should be done orally.

Answers
(A) 1 That tennis racquet is broken!
    2 Plain flour is used for making bread.
    3 A rare bird was seen yesterday.
    4 The savage dog growls at people.
    5 These old books are valuable.

(B) 1 **the** cottage
    2 **a** storm
    3 individual answer
    4 individual answer
    5 **the [adjective]** mountain
    6 **a [adjective]** book

Practice
- Read / discuss the first answer so children understand what is required.

Answers
Noun phrases:
1 A noisy grasshopper is under the lilac bush.
2 The lion is hunting the antelope.
3 The moon is shining on the water.
4 A tree is blocking the road.
5 The clouds are bringing the rain.

Expanded noun phrases = individual answers

Extension
- Read and discuss the information box on page 39.
- Children should work individually.

Answers
1 The barking dog kept everyone awake.
2 I saw those flashing lights over there.
3 Don't prod that sleeping tiger!
4 We were watching the climbing monkey.
5 They visited a working farm.

Resource Book

Support PCM
- Children should work individually.

Answers
(A) 1 We were playing on the sandy beach.
    2 Simon was making a huge sandcastle.
    3 Ari was swimming in the freezing water.
    4 Butch ran off with that striped beach towel.
    5 Dad gave us a delicious picnic.

(B) Individual answers

(C) Individual answers

Extension PCM
- Activity A: Model a possible answer to question 1 so that children understand what is required.

Answers
Individual answers

Extra
Make noun cards e.g.

| hedgehog | forest | library | cake |

Individuals take a card and expand the noun into as long a noun phrase as they can.

64

BOOK 4 UNIT 18 Verbs

Common mistakes

Verbs are often explained as 'doing words' or 'being words'. They are possibly the most complex part of speech for young children to grasp because of their many forms and tenses.

Throughout the course, children will encounter the present simple, present progressive (also known as continuous), past simple, past progressive, present perfect (labelled simply *perfect* throughout the course), past perfect, future, infinitive (labelled *verb family name* in the early parts of the course), auxiliary verbs, modals, active and passive verbs and subjunctive verbs (a construction very rarely used except in extremely formal writing).

Participles are referred to as '*ing* words' and 'regular past simple tense words'; finite verbs are referred to as 'main' or 'proper verbs', and it is for the teacher to decide the appropriate time to introduce the terms *participle* and *finite verb*.

This unit examines areas of common mistakes when constructing verb tenses and matching person to the correct form of the verb. It is linked to units on Standard and Non-standard English which come later in the course.

Pupil Book

Focus

- Revise/discuss the term *verb* and ask for examples of:
  - present simple
  - present progressive
  - past simple
  - past progressive
  - perfect
  - past perfect
  - future
- Revise/explain the terms *tense* and *person*. (Link person to pronouns.)
- Read and discuss the information box on page 40.
- *Do the activity orally.*

Answers

1. I **like** fish.
2. We have **done** our homework.
3. We **were** going to a party.
4. He **came** here yesterday.
5. They **play** in the park.
6. Yesterday, she **bought** a new book.
7. I **wrote** a letter and posted it.
8. The cat **drank** the milk.

Practice

Children can work in pairs.

Answers

1. The teacher **ringed** the mistakes in red ink.
2. Who had **rung** the fire alarm?
3. The river **flowed** to the sea.
4. The bird had **flown** from its cage.
5. She **hung** the picture in the bedroom.
6. The highwayman was **hanged** for his crimes.

Extension

- Discuss the difference between *borrow/lend, teach/learn* before children write.

Answers

(A)
1. May I **borrow** your book, please?
2. Will you **lend** me a pencil?
3. Sally will **lend** you some money for the bus.
4. If you **borrow** money, you must pay it back.

(B)
1. The little children **learn** to write their names.
2. I shall **teach** you how to do it.
3. I would like to **learn** a foreign language.
4. Can you **teach** me how to play this game?

Resource Book

Support PCM

- Children should work individually.

Answers

(A)
1. Tim **comes** to school late.
2. Sally **does** the cooking on Saturdays.
3. I have **done** the crossword!
4. We **were** playing a game of cards.
5. You **are** very early.

(B)
1. When it's sunny, I **go** out for a walk.
2. I **did** it yesterday.
3. I have **given** the book to my friend.
4. We **were** wearing our new shoes.
5. Music lessons **are** my favourite.

Extension PCM

- Remind children that sentences can be statements, questions or exclamations needing the appropriate punctuation.

Answers

Individual answers

Extra

- Based on common mistakes with verbs that the class make, write incorrect sentences on the board for children to correct.

65

BOOK 4 UNIT 19 Paragraphs

Location in stories

A paragraph is a group of sentences within a piece of writing. It is usually signalled by:

– indenting in handwritten work and fiction (all paragraphs but the first)

– leaving a full line space (block paragraphing) in typing and non-fiction work.

The mechanics of paragraphing can be taught as a concept, but the 'reasons' for paragraphing are many and varied, and must be attached to a particular style of writing.

Throughout the course, children will encounter: paragraphing in narrative writing – time, place and for the inclusion of direct speech; paragraphing for aspects of a topic in non-fiction information writing; and paragraphing to present for and against arguments in discursive writing.

This unit deals with paragraphing in narrative writing based on the location of the action in stories.

Pupil Book

Focus

- Revise/discuss the term *paragraph*.
- Ask children what they have learned about paragraphing in stories.
- Use the short story in the information box on page 42 to show children what a paragraph looks like on the page.
- Introduce the term *indenting* and discuss not indenting for the first paragraph.
- Read and discuss the information box on page 42 and work through the Focus questions with the children.

Answers

1	Treasure Seeker	=	anchored in a small bay off a deserted island.
	Captain Black and Smithy	=	on board
	They are	=	looking at a treasure map.
2	Captain Black and Smithy	=	on the beach
	They are	=	looking at the map/ pointing to the cliff.
3	Captain Black and Smithy	=	on the cliff Climbing up the cliff/ almost falling off the cliff.
4	Captain Black and Smithy	=	in the forest Walking through the forest/chopping leaves to get through.

Practice

- Children can work in pairs with your support.

Answers

Individual answers

Extension

- Discuss location phrases that children could use to begin each of the three paragraphs.
- Children should work individually with your support.

Answers

Individual answers

Resource Book

Support PCM

- Activity A: Children should work individually.
- Activity B: Discuss the things the twins might have done when:
  – sitting in their seat
  – the plane landed.

Answers

(A) Paragraph 1: <u>The</u> suitcases were packed and stood by the front door.
Paragraph 2: <u>In</u> the taxi, the twins began to feel sick.
Paragraph 3: <u>They</u> arrived at the airport in plenty of time.
Paragraph 4: <u>Having</u> checked their bags and got through security, they found themselves in the Departure Lounge.
Paragraph 5: <u>Eventually,</u> the gate opened and they queued to give in their tickets and board the plane.
Paragraph 6: <u>The</u> twins looked at the narrow tube they would be travelling in.

(B) Individual answers

Extension PCM

- Children should work individually but some discussion beforehand to help them pick out when the action of the story moves to a new place may be helpful.

Answers

The café was quite full but Mr and Mrs Green found a table. They ordered tea and looked over their shopping list to decide what to do next.

They left the café and walked down the high street towards the library.

The librarian smiled at them and took the books that Mr Green had brought back. Mrs Green said she would leave him to choose some new books and would see him in half an hour.

She left the library and headed for the shoe shop. She needed some new boots as her old ones were falling to bits.

In the shoe shop, the assistant was very helpful. Mrs Green found a pair of boots she liked and left the shop.

Back in the library, she saw her husband sitting comfortably in a chair, reading.

Extra

Children can continue the story from the Extension PCM. Discuss other places Mr and Mrs Green might have gone after they left the library.

BOOK 4 UNIT 20 Sentences

Double negatives

The concept of a sentence as a unit of language that 'makes sense' can be a difficult concept for some children to grasp. The course builds children's confidence in this area through giving them the opportunity to look at punctuation of statements, questions and exclamations to familiarise themselves with what a 'sentence' looks and sounds like.

Throughout the course, children will encounter: sentence punctuation; the concept of 'making sense'; direct and indirect speech; clauses which combine to make multi-clause sentences; parts of sentences – subject/object, subject/predicate; focusing on the sentence as a unit of language that can be improved; and Standard English constructions.

This unit examines 'negative' words in sentences, recapping on contractions. The Extension section introduces 'double negatives' in sentences. This is an aspect of 'making sense' where a grammatical error causes a sentence to be the opposite of what the writer intended.

Pupil Book

Focus
- Ask children what they understand by the term *sentence*.
- Revise/discuss the terms *contraction* and *apostrophe*.
- Introduce the term *negative* and ask children what they understand by it.
- Read the information box on page 44.
- Do the activity orally, stressing that adding one negative word to a sentence is grammatically correct.

Answers
1 I **don't/didn't/can't/won't** have an apple for lunch.
2 She has no **time** to tidy her room.
3 The children do **not** want to go to the park.
4 There is **no/never** space in the cupboard.
5 Greg **never** goes to the library on Saturday.
6 I **can't/won't/didn't** lift this heavy box.

Practice
- Activity A can be done on the board with children writing the contractions.
- Activity B: Children should work individually.

Answers
(A)
1 can't	2 won't	3 shan't
4 mustn't	5 haven't	6 shouldn't
7 wouldn't	8 doesn't	9 don't
10 isn't	11 couldn't	12 hadn't

(B) 1 The thief said he knew <u>nothing</u> about the burglary.
The thief said he knew about the burglary.
2 He did <u>not</u> have a ticket to get in.
He did have a ticket to get in.
3 The boys had <u>nowhere</u> to go.
The boys had somewhere to go.
4 "I <u>mustn't</u> feed the cat," said Dad.
"I must feed the cat," said Dad.

Extension
- Discuss what children think the writer meant in each case.

Answers
1 I wanted to win the race but I didn't have **any** luck.
2 Pam didn't want to go **anywhere**.
3 I mustn't throw **anything** away.
4 Mum will not get **a** bus today.
5 Tom didn't score **any** goals in the match.
5 I never go **anywhere**.

Resource Book

Support PCM
- Activity A: Children should work individually.
- Activity B: Discuss what children think the writer meant in each case.

Answers
(A) 1 I <u>couldn't</u> finish the crossword!
2 He will <u>not</u> go swimming today.
3 There's <u>nothing</u> you can say to make me change my mind.
4 It <u>never</u> snows in August.
5 I have <u>nowhere</u> to go.

(B) 1 He doesn't want **any** more soup.
2 The tiger will **not** find food tonight./The tiger will find **no** food tonight.
3 I'm not going to the cinema **ever** again.
4 I could not go **anywhere** today.

Extension PCM
- Children should work individually.

Answers
(A) 1 If you do not want no soup, you want **some** soup.
2 If you are not going nowhere, you are going **somewhere**.
3 If you don't know nothing, you know **something**.
4 If you do not never listen to the radio, it means you **sometimes** listen to the radio.

(B) Individual answers

Extra
Make negative word cards, e.g.

| didn't | never | nowhere |

Children pick a card and use the negative word in a sentence.

BOOK 4 UNIT 21 Pronouns

Correct choice for clear meaning

Pronouns are words that take the place of nouns and noun phrases.

Throughout the course, children will encounter: personal pronouns (as subject and object); possessive pronouns; reflexive pronouns; and relative pronouns.

Demonstrative pronouns are introduced in the work on noun phrases.

Interrogative pronouns are not specifically labelled as such but children encounter them in work on relative pronouns. It is up to individual teachers if indefinite pronouns, e.g. each/many/few/some, are specifically labelled as such and taught as another group of pronouns.

This unit examines using pronouns unambiguously, and the confusion caused when pronouns are used carelessly.

Pupil Book

Focus

- Revise/discuss the term *noun*.
- Revise/discuss the term *pronoun* and ask for examples.
- Read the information box on page 46.
- Ask the children if they could make the sentence *Ben told James that his dog was missing* clear without using direct speech, i.e.
  Ben told James that Ben's dog was missing./Ben told James that James's dog was missing.
- Do the Activity orally.

Answers

1. John does not want to play cards with his brother because he always wins.
   a John always wins.
   b His brother always wins.
2. The suitcase was on the plane but now it has gone.
   a The suitcase has gone.
   b The plane has gone.
3. Amy saw Shireen while she was shopping with her mother.
   a Amy was shopping with her mother.
   b Shireen was shopping with her mother.
4. The twins were looking for their cats. Have you seen them?
   a Have you seen the twins?
   b Have you seen the cats?
5. Billy suggested to Owen that he coach the football team.
   a Billy should coach the football team.
   b Owen should coach the football team.

Practice

- Activity A: Discuss:
  – what the children think each sentence means;
  – why are they sure?
  In these cases the context is the clue to the intended meaning of the writer.
  Activity B: When complete, discuss the various ways in which the sentences have been restructured to make the meaning clear.

Answers

(A) The context leads the reader to understand that:
1. The man had his car stolen and he told a policeman.
2. The teacher marked Sally's story and said it was excellent.
3. The doctor said that the patient was improving.

(B) 1. Kim had a hole in her jumper and told her mother. Kim said to her mother, "I have a hole in my jumper."
2. It was Tim's birthday and he went to visit Fred. It was Fred's birthday so Tim went to visit him.
3. Take the radio off the shelf and then fix the shelf. Take the radio off the shelf and then fix the radio.

Extension

- Read and discuss the information box on page 47.
- Children should work individually on the activity.

Answers

1. The teacher collected the books, put them on the desk and looked at her students.
2. When the plants were tall enough we planted them in pots.
3. When Dad drove into the wall, he damaged his car.
4. He cleaned the cage before he put the bird into it.

Resource Book

Support PCM

- Children can work in pairs.
- When completed, discuss how the sentences can be restructured to make the meaning clear.

Answers

1. a Mary's bicycle is missing.
   b Beth's bicycle is missing.
2. a Fred was waiting for the bus.
   b Joe was waiting for the bus.
3. a The ball has gone.
   b The basket has gone.

Extension PCM

Children should work individually.

Answers

1. Dan hurled his racket at the branch and broke the branch/the racket.
2. Nina had a day off and phoned Sophie./When Sophie had a day off, Nina phoned her.
3. He cleaned the table before he put the dish on it./He cleaned the dish before he put it on the table.
4. The boys picked the blackberries and ate them while watching the squirrels.
5. "I am/You are in no danger," the man assured his friend.

Extra

In small groups, can children construct ambiguous sentences for the class to restructure?

BOOK 4 UNIT 22 Verbs

Synonyms

Verbs are often explained as 'doing words' or 'being words'. They are possibly the most complex part of speech for young children to grasp because of their many forms and tenses.

Throughout the course, children will encounter the present simple, present progressive (also known as continuous), past simple, past progressive, present perfect (labelled simply *perfect* throughout the course), past perfect, future, infinitive (labelled *verb family name* in the early parts of the course), auxiliary verbs, modals, active and passive verbs and subjunctive verbs (a construction very rarely used except in extremely formal writing).

Participles are referred to as '*ing* words' and 'regular past simple tense words'; finite verbs are referred to as 'main' or 'proper verbs', and it is for the teacher to decide the appropriate time to introduce the terms *participle* and *finite verb*.

Children have tackled a few activities based on synonyms for 'said'. This unit continues this concept in greater detail looking to improve children's writing through more adventurous verb choices.

Pupil Book

Focus

- Revise/discuss the term *verb* and ask for examples of:
  – present simple
  – present progressive
  – past simple
  – past progressive
  – perfect
  – past perfect
  – future
- Revise/discuss the term *synonym*.
- Read and discuss the information box on page 48.
- Do the activity in teams as a timed game.
- When complete, make lists on the board from the children's suggestions and vote for the best synonym for each verb.

Answers

Suggested answers
1. to like = enjoy/fancy/love/adore/relish/approve
2. to walk = stroll/march/stride/hike/ramble/saunter
3. to run = rush/hurry/hasten/race/sprint/accelerate/dash/scurry
4. to follow = hunt/chase/stalk/pursue/shadow/trail
5. to answer = reply/respond/explain
6. to break = smash/shatter/split/fracture/destroy
7. to catch = grasp/snatch/grip/seize/clutch
8. to close = shut/bolt/lock/fasten/block/obstruct
9. to come = arrive/appear/reach/approach/enter
10. to get = earn/receive/obtain/fetch/bring/acquire
11. to eat = chew/munch/gobble/devour
12. to pick = choose/select/collect/gather

Practice

- Children should work individually.
- When complete, discuss children's answers and the reasons for choosing particular synonyms.

Answers

(A) Suggested answers
1. The stone **smashed** through the window.
2. They **walked/hurried/strolled** to the shops.
3. The rabbit **dived/scrambled/plunged** into the hole.
4. The horse **cantered/trotted/galloped** across the field.
5. I **travelled/sailed/voyaged** on a ship.
6. The bus **travelled** quickly.

(B) Suggested answers
1. "I am very angry with you," she **snapped/bellowed**.
2. "This is what you do," the teacher **explained**.
3. "I hate spiders!" she **screeched/screamed/shuddered**.
4. "Where are you going?" Tom **asked/inquired/demanded**.
5. "It's a secret," he **whispered**.
6. "Sports day will begin at two o'clock," the head teacher **announced**.

Extension

- Children should use a dictionary to ensure they understand the meaning of each verb.

Answers

Individual answers

Resource Book

Support PCM

- Some words may be unfamiliar to the children so go through them orally to ascertain meaning before they write.

Answers

(A)

Synonyms for said	Synonyms for walked
muttered	strolled
boasted	rambled
announced	marched
ordered	sauntered
suggested	hiked
Synonyms for caught	**Synonyms for got**
grabbed	earned
gripped	received
grasped	brought
clutched	obtained
snatched	fetched

(B) Individual answers

Extension PCM

- Children should work individually.

Answers

Suggested answers
1. to fly = soar/swoop/glide
2. to look = glance/stare/peer
3. to shout = shriek/yell/bellow
4. to hurt = injure/wound/harm
5. to jump = leap/spring/bound

Extra

- Make infinitive cards of common verbs, e.g.

| to smile | to jump | to shout |

Children pick a card and give an interesting synonym.

BOOK 4 UNIT 23 Adverbs

Clauses

Adverbs are usually explained as words which 'add' to a verb giving the detail of how, where or when an action is done.

Throughout the course, children will encounter single adverbs (manner/time/place), comparative and superlative adverbs, adverbial phrases, adverb pairs and adverbial clauses.

Children have encountered the concepts of main and subordinate clauses earlier in the course. A main clause is a sentence in itself whereas a subordinate clause (beginning with a conjunction) is of less importance. Both main clauses and subordinate clauses contain a finite verb, i.e. a verb that makes a tense.

This unit revises adverbial clauses, introducing the idea of adverbial clauses at the beginning of a sentence. As with adverbial phrases, an adverbial clause does the same job as a single adverb, answering the basic questions how, when or where. It also expresses *reason* with conjunctions such as 'because', 'since', 'as'; *purpose* with conjunctions such as 'so that', 'in order to'; *contrast* with conjunctions such as 'although', 'as though'; and *comparison* with conjunctions such as 'as if', 'as though'.

Pupil Book

Focus

- Revise/discuss the terms *phrase, sentence, conjunction, main clause, subordinate clause, finite verb*.
- Write sentences with a main and subordinate clause on the board.
- Children identify:
  – the main clause
  – the subordinate clause
  – the conjunction which begins the subordinate clause
  – the verb in the main clause
  – the verb in the subordinate clause.
- Read the information box on page 50.
- Explain that one type of subordinate clause is an adverb clause.
- Ask children to substitute:
  – *because it was very dirty* with another *because* clause;
  – *before the children came home* with another *before* clause;
  – *until her arms ached* with another *until* clause.
- Point out that when an adverb clause comes at the beginning of a sentence, it is separated from the main clause by a comma.
- Do the activity orally.

Answers

Adverb clause = bold; verb = circled

1 (Put) up your umbrella **because it is beginning to rain**.
2 **Although it was a draw**, we didn't (play) extra time.
3 I (cleaned) the hamster's cage **when I came home from school**.
4 **After it had snowed**, we (made) a snowman.
5 We will (go camping) **if I can find the tent**.

Practice

- Children should work individually.

Answers

Ⓐ Individual answers

Ⓑ 1 **When the postman knocked at the door**, the dog began to bark.
   2 **Because I've lost a piece**, I can't finish the jigsaw.
   3 **Unless it starts to rain**, we will go to the park at one o'clock.

Extension

- Children should work individually.
- When complete, discuss answers.

Answers

Individual answers

Resource Book

Support PCM

- Activity A: Remind children that the adverb clause could be at the beginning of the sentence.
- Activity B: Remind children to use a comma after the adverb clause.

Answers

Ⓐ 1 **Although the audience clapped politely**, they didn't like the play.
   2 It didn't rain **even though the sky was very dark**.
   3 The fly was irritating **because it buzzed very loudly**.
   4 It was difficult to see **because my torch was fading**.

Ⓑ Individual answers

Extension PCM

- Some discussion may be necessary to stimulate children's ideas for sentences.

Answers

Individual answers

Extra

Make conjunction cards, e.g.

until	so that
after	as though

Children pick a card and use the conjunction as the beginning of an adverbial clause in a sentence. Encourage children to put the adverbial clause first in the sentence.

BOOK 4 UNIT 24 Nouns

Singular possessive

Nouns are usually explained as 'naming' words. Nouns are the most common part of speech that children of this age will encounter. Children's first words are usually nouns as they make sense of the world by naming things.

Throughout the course, children will encounter common, proper, collective, compound, abstract and possessive nouns, together with noun phrases.

This unit revises the concept of singular possessive nouns, and introduces plural possessive nouns that do not and do end in *s*.

Pupil Book

Focus
- Revise/discuss the term *noun* and ask for examples of:
  – common nouns
  – proper nouns
  – collective nouns
  – compound nouns
  – abstract nouns
- Revise/discuss the uses of the *apostrophe* that children have encountered, i.e. apostrophe of contraction/apostrophe of possession for singular nouns.
- Read the information box on page 52.
- The Activity should be done orally.
- If children are having difficulty in locating the *owner*, say *the spire belonging to the church/the gloves belonging to the man*, etc.

Answers
1. the **church's** spire
2. the **man's** gloves
3. the **bird's** nest
4. the **clock's** hands
5. **Barry's** shed
6. the **girl's** idea
7. **Susan's** face
8. the **teapot's** spout
9. the **bucket's** handle
10. the **CD's** box

Practice
- Children should work individually.

Answers
1. the **parents'** meeting
2. the **children's** homework
3. the **newspapers'** headlines
4. the **girls'** mothers
5. the **trees'** trunks

Extension
- Read and discuss the information box on page 53.
- Children should work individually.

Answers
1. The **twins'** birthday is in January.
2. The **policeman's** helmet fell on the ground.
3. The **flashes'** brightness hurt our eyes.
4. The **ladies'** changing room was full.
5. The **knives'** edges were blunt.

Resource Book

Support PCM
- Point out to the children that the *owners* could be singular or plural.
- Children should work individually.

Answers
(A)
1. The **policemen's** uniforms were blue.
2. **Mr Taylor's** house is being decorated.
3. The **children's** school was broken into.
4. My three **sisters'** bedroom is always a mess.
5. The **coats'** belts are on the floor.

(B)
1. a the ferry's passengers
   b the ferries' passengers
2. a the shelf's brackets
   b the shelves' brackets
3. a the watch's hands
   b the watches' hands

(C) Individual answers

Extension PCM
- Activity A: discuss the first answer so children understand what is required.
- Activity B can be done in pairs.

Answers
(A) Individual answers
(B)
1. teeth
2. diaries
3. salmon
4. wishes
Sentences = individual answers

Extra
Make singular and plural possession cards, e.g.

| the dog belonging to the children |

| the bats belonging to the boys |

| the idea belonging to the teacher |

| the presents belonging to the girl |

Children pick a card and then write the phrase on the board using an apostrophe.

BOOK 4 UNIT 2 Sentences

Split direct speech

The concept of a sentence as a unit of language that 'makes sense' can be a difficult concept for some children to grasp. The course builds children's confidence in this area through giving them the opportunity to look at punctuation of statements, questions and exclamations to familiarise themselves with what a 'sentence' looks and sounds like.

Throughout the course, children will encounter: sentence punctuation; the concept of 'making sense'; direct and indirect speech; clauses which combine to make multi-clause sentences; parts of sentences – subject/object, subject/predicate; focusing on the sentence as a unit of language that can be improved; and Standard English constructions.

Children often find correctly punctuating direct speech sentences problematic. Several units in the course focus on direct speech so that the various rules can be built up gradually. Speech marks (inverted commas), beginning a new line when a different person speaks, punctuation before the final speech marks and punctuation when the non-spoken words come before the spoken words have been introduced.

This unit focuses on split direct speech: two sentences split by non-spoken words and one sentence split by non-spoken words.

Pupil Book

Focus
- Begin by asking the children why direct speech (characters having a conversation) looks 'different' on the page.
- Revise the terms statement – *full stop*/question – *question mark*/exclamation – *exclamation mark*/speech marks *(inverted commas)*.
- Read the information box on page 54.
- Do several more examples on the board of each type of split speech for children to punctuate.
- The activity can be done orally.
- When the spoken words have been identified, ask which are two sentences and which are one sentence.

Answers
1. "**I won this medal**," said Lesley, "**for coming first in the high jump.**"
2. "**Where did you find that fossil**?" asked Pam.
3. "**You can ring me at work**," explained Nick, "**if you need to get in touch with me.**"
4. The climber shouted, "**Get away from the edge!**"
5. "**I'm not very musical**," mumbled Grace. "**I prefer art.**"
6. "**I'm not sure**," explained Mark, "**how you do these sums.**"

Practice
- Children can work independently or in pairs.
- Tell the children to decide which are one sentence and which are two sentences before they begin to copy and punctuate.

Answers
1. "That was a good goal," shouted Sandy, "but we've got to score another one!"
2. "**G**o to the shop and buy some bread," said Helen. "The money is in my purse."
3. "**T**his photograph was taken last year," said Rory. "**W**e were on holiday at the seaside."
4. "**W**e must be very quiet," whispered Monica, "or we'll wake the baby."
5. "**I**'m very tired," moaned Chris. "**I** stayed up too late last night!"
6. "**C**an you find my blue shoes," asked Mum, "and give them a polish?"

Extension
- Read and discuss the information box that continues work on synonyms for *said*.
- Discuss what sort of spoken words might be followed by *cried/yelled/muttered*, etc.
- Children work independently.

Answers
Individual answers

Resource Book

Support PCM
- Activity A: Discuss what *Nathan may shriek/Daisy may mutter,* etc. before children write.
- Using no.1 as an example, remind children of punctuation rules when the non-spoken words come between two sentences.
- Children work independently.
- Activity B: Discuss what *Carol may whisper/Nina may laugh about,* etc. before children write.
- Using no. 1 as an example, remind children of punctuation rules when the non-spoken words split a single sentence.
- Children work independently.

Answers
(A) Individual answers
(B) Individual answers

Extension PCM
- Children work independently.

Answers
"It's very dark in here," said Steve.
"Yes," said Liam, "and spooky!"
"I suppose we can't go back now," said Steve. "We've come this far so we have to see if we can find the treasure map."
"I know," said Liam, "but I don't like it!"
"What was that?" said Steve.
"What?" said Liam.
"The noise. Didn't you hear it?" said Steve.
"You are imagining things," said Liam.
"Imagining or not," said Steve, "I'm getting out of here!"
Synonyms = individual answers

Extra
- In pairs, children continue the conversation from the Extension PCM.

BOOK 4 UNIT 26 Nouns

Possessive and plural

Nouns are usually explained as 'naming' words. Nouns are the most common part of speech that children of this age will encounter. Children's first words are usually nouns as they make sense of the world by naming things.

Throughout the course, children will encounter common, proper, collective, compound, abstract and possessive nouns, together with noun phrases.

This unit revises the concept of singular and plural possessive nouns, and gives children the opportunity to differentiate between simple plural nouns and possessive plural nouns. This is important as, once the possessive apostrophe has been taught, some children see an *s* and automatically add an apostrophe!

Pupil Book

Focus

- Revise/discuss the term *noun* and ask for examples of:
  - common nouns
  - proper nouns
  - collective nouns
  - compound nouns
  - abstract nouns
- Revise/discuss the uses of the *apostrophe* that children have encountered, i.e. apostrophe of contraction/apostrophe of possession for singular nouns.
- Revise/discuss the terms *singular* and *plural*.
- Read the information box on page 56.
- The Activity should be done orally.

Answers

1	possessive noun	= Harry's
2	plural nouns	= coats/pegs
3	possessive noun	= boys'
	plural noun	= shoes
4	plural noun	= lights
5	possessive noun	= teacher's

Practice

Children should work individually.

Answers

1. The <u>horses'</u> (hooves) could be heard coming down the lane.
2. My <u>brother's</u> football (boots) are always so dirty!
3. Have you seen the <u>baby's</u> (toys)?
4. Can you find the <u>children's</u> (wellingtons)?
5. The <u>geese's</u> (hisses) were alarming!
6. <u>People's</u> (opinions) should be heard.

Extension

- Children should work individually.

Answers

1. The journeys were made in **John's** car.
2. **Sally's** cousins are visiting at the weekend.
3. All of the **tree's** leaves had blown off.
4. The **owl's** eyes shone in the moonlight.
5. **Tim's** stories were always about pirates!
6. The **children's** toothbrushes need replacing.

Resource Book

Support PCM

- Activity A: Children can work in pairs.
- When complete, discuss answers.
- Activity B: Children should work individually.

Answers

(A)
1	I saw the <u>meteor's</u> tail as it fell to earth.	S
2	The <u>cave's</u> walls were wet and slimy.	S
3	<u>Elephants'</u> tusks are made of ivory.	P
4	You could hear the <u>audience's</u> clapping in the street.	S
5	The <u>flowers'</u> petals had fallen off.	P

(B) Individual answers

Extension PCM

- Children should work individually.
- When complete, discuss answers.

Answers

1. girls' books
2. children's hats
3. lions' tails
4. houses' roofs
5. watches' straps

sentences = individual answers

Extra

Make singular noun cards, e.g.

boy	baby
knife	woman

Children pick a card and write sentences:
- one where the word on the card is a simple plural
- one where the word on the card is a plural possessive.

73

BOOK 4 UNIT 27 Adverbs

Fronted phrases and clauses

Adverbs are usually explained as words which 'add' to a verb giving the detail of how, where or when an action is done.

Throughout the course, children will encounter single adverbs (manner/time/place), comparative and superlative adverbs, adverbial phrases, adverb pairs and adverbial clauses.

Children have encountered the concepts of main and subordinate clauses earlier in the course. A main clause is a sentence in itself whereas a subordinate clause (beginning with a conjunction) is of less importance. Both main clauses and subordinate clauses contain a finite verb, i.e. a verb that makes a tense.

Adverbial clauses are one type of subordinate clause. Along with adverb phrases, they do the same job as a single adverb, answering the basic questions how, when or where. Adverb clauses also express *reason* with conjunctions such as 'because', 'since', 'as'; *purpose* with conjunctions such as 'so that', 'in order to'; *contrast* with conjunctions such as 'although', 'as though'; and *comparison* with conjunctions such as 'as if', 'as though'.

This unit revises the use of adverb phrases and clauses coming after the main clause, and gives children practice in using them as fronted adverbials.

Pupil Book

Focus

- Revise/discuss the terms *phrase, sentence, conjunction, main clause, subordinate clause, finite verb*.
- Write sentences with a main and subordinate clause on the board.
- Children identify:
  – the main clause
  – the subordinate clause
  – the conjunction which begins the subordinate clause
  – the verb in the main clause
  – the verb in the subordinate clause.
- Read the information box on page 58.
- Explain that one type of subordinate clause is an adverb clause.
- Ask children to substitute:
  – after he had lost his footing on the mountain path with another *after* clause;
- Point out that when an adverb phrase or clause comes at the beginning of a sentence, it is separated from the main clause by a comma.
- Do the activities orally.

Answers

(A) 1 He played the piano **surprisingly well**.
2 We have fish and chips **every Friday evening**.
3 The cat slept **in the sunniest spot**.

(B) 1 I put the books on the shelf **after I had sorted them**.
2 Horse riders wear hard hats **so that they don't get hurt**.
3 The snowman melted **although the sun wasn't shining**.

Practice

- Activity A: Remind children they are looking for a phrase. A phrase:
  – does not have a finite verb
  – cannot make sense on its own.

- Activity B: Remind the children to look for the conjunction that signals the beginning of the adverb clause that has a finite verb.

Answers

(A) 1 **Later in the day,** the rain fell in torrents.
2 **With great speed,** the sprinter crossed the finishing line.
3 **A few weeks ago,** we moved into the new house.

(B) 1 **After it is harvested,** the fruit is sold in the market.
2 **So that she could get a better job,** she worked very hard.
3 **Before you go to the shops,** you should make a shopping list.

Extension

- Children should work individually on the activities.

Answers

(A) 1 You should not swim **after/before** having a heavy meal.
2 Put fertilizer in the soil **because** plants need it to grow.
3 I knew the house had been broken into **because** the door was smashed.
4 This doesn't look like a Roman coin **because** it has an emperor's head on it.
5 I will be able to pass the test **if** I work very hard.

(B) 1 **After/Before having a heavy meal,** you should not swim.
2 **Because plants need it to grow,** put fertilizer on the soil.
3 **Because the door was smashed,** I knew the house had been broken into.
4 **Although/Even though it has an emperor's head on it,** this doesn't look like a Roman coin.
5 **If I work very hard,** I will be able to pass the test.

Resource Book

Support PCM

- Activity A: Children should work individually.
- Activities B and C: Monitor the children's work to ensure they understand the difference between a phrase and a clause.

Answers

(A) 1 As carefully as possible, I carried the tray of glasses.
2 So that he would not hurt his hands, he wore his thick gloves.
3 Even though the batsman played well, he did not score enough runs.
4 Although the bird was quite tame, it would not feed from my hand.
5 Because of the bad weather, we have to postpone our trip.

(B) Individual answers

(C) Individual answers

Extension PCM

- If necessary, model the first question so children understand what is required.

Answers

Individual answers

Extra

- Write adverb phrases on the board and ask children to turn them into adverb clauses, e.g.
  adverb phrase = after lunch
  adverb clause = when we had finished our lunch

BOOK 4 UNIT 28 Paragraphs

Aspects of a topic in non-fiction writing

A paragraph is a group of sentences within a piece of writing. It is usually signalled by:

– indenting in handwritten work and fiction (all paragraphs but the first)

– leaving a full line space (block paragraphing) in typing and non-fiction work.

The mechanics of paragraphing can be taught as a concept, but the 'reasons' for paragraphing are many and varied, and must be attached to a particular style of writing.

Throughout the course, children will encounter paragraphing in narrative writing – time, place and for the inclusion of direct speech; paragraphing for aspects of a topic in non-fiction information writing; and paragraphing to present for and against arguments in discursive writing.

This unit deals with paragraphing in non-fiction information writing based on various aspects of a given topic.

Pupil Book

Focus
- Revise/discuss the term *paragraph*.
- Ask children what they have learned about paragraphing in stories.
- Explain that there are different reasons for paragraphing in non-fiction writing.
- Use the non-fiction passage in the information box on page 60 to show children what a paragraph looks like on the page.
- Introduce the term *indenting* and discuss not indenting for the first paragraph.
- Read and discuss the information box on page 60 and work through the Focus questions with the children.

Answers
1. Individual answers
2. 4
3. Individual answers
4. Individual answers

Practice
- *Children can work in pairs with your support.*

Answers
First paragraph: individual answers
The animals should be grouped as follows:
Mammals: zebra/grizzly bear/lion
Reptiles: crocodile/gecko/tortoise
Fish: trout/catfish/herring
Birds: red kite/eagle/owl

Extension
- Factor in time for research and discussion before the children write.

Answers
Individual answers

Resource Book

Support PCM
- Children can work in pairs with your support.

Answers

Information for paragraph 1
George is ten years old. He likes swimming and football. George has one brother called Edward. George lives in a cottage. George has a dog called Rex. George has one more year in his primary school. George wears a blue and grey uniform at his school.

Information for paragraph 2
Leah is eleven and she likes riding her bicycle and playing netball. Leah has a sister called Rachel. Leah lives in a semi-detached house. Leah doesn't like animals but her sister has some tropical fish. Leah is going to secondary school in September. Leah's new school has a black and grey uniform.
Improvements = Individual answers

Extension PCM
- Children should work individually with your support.

Answers
Individual answers

Extra
Make topic cards, e.g.

| mountains | sports | music |

Children should work in small groups. Each group picks a card and discusses what aspects of the topic they could write about and makes a paragraph plan.

Book 4 Check-up answers

Check-up 1 (Units 1–6)

Verbs

verb family name	past simple tense	past progressive tense	perfect tense
to arrive	I arrived	I was arriving	I have arrived
to carry	It carried	It was carrying	It has carried
to paint	You painted	You were painting	You have painted

verb family name	present simple tense	present progressive tense	future tense
to arrive	They arrive	They are arriving	They will arrive
to carry	She carries	She is carrying	She will carry
to paint	We carry	We are carrying	We shall carry

Sentences

(A) 1 It's necessary to water the plants although it has rained today.
2 We must find our way out of the wood before the sun sets.
3 A dictionary is very useful because it tells you the meaning of words.

(B) 1 "We must find our key," said Dad.
2 "I don't want to swim in that dirty river!" shouted Ali.
3 She suggested, "Go early to get a good seat."

Nouns

(A) 1 sadness 2 weakness
3 brilliance 4 violence
(B) 1 imagination 2 collection
3 division 4 navigation

Suffixes

(A) 1 useful 2 painful 3 thoughtful
(B) 1 manageable 2 laughable 3 likeable

Adverbs

(A) 1 I visited my aunt two days ago.
2 The boy kicked the ball hard and straight.
3 The fox made its den in the middle of the wood.

(B) Individual answers

Adjectives

(A) 1 Eight large, hissing geese crossed the road.
2 The sea, calm and blue, sparkled in the sunlight.
3 The elephant with the longest tusks is the oldest.

(B) Individual answers

Check-up 2 (Units 7–12)

Singular and plural

1 tomatoes 2 potatoes 3 cellos
4 bamboos 5 photos 6 pianos
7 volcanoes 8 piccolos

Pronouns

(A) 1 This towel is mine.
2 That dog is theirs.
3 I'm taking this book back to the library. Do you want me to take yours?
4 I like his painting better.

(B) Individual answers

Verbs

(A)

verb family name	past simple tense	past progressive tense	perfect tense
to buy	I **bought**	I **was buying**	I **have bought**
to teach	You **taught**	You **were teaching**	You **have taught**
to bring	He **brought**	He **was bringing**	He **has brought**
to feel	It **felt**	It **was feeling**	It **has felt**
to catch	We **caught**	We **were catching**	We **have caught**
to speak	She **spoke**	She **was speaking**	She **has spoken**
to break	It **broke**	It **was breaking**	It **has broken**
to grow	They **grew**	They **were growing**	They **have grown**
to draw	I **drew**	I **was drawing**	I **have drawn**
to see	We **saw**	We **were seeing**	We **have seen**

(B) 1 The climbers had reached the summit before the storm broke.
2 I had completed the jigsaw after finding the lost piece.
3 If you had listened carefully, you would know what to do.

Adverbs

(A) 1 I read the instructions very carefully.
2 He laughed rather loudly at the comedian.
3 We talked extremely quietly so we would not be overheard.

(B) Individual answers

Sentences

(A) 1 The goat ate the grass.
2 We like to ride our bicycles.
3 The circus came to town.

(B) 1 Mrs Potter cleaned the windows.
2 Freda ate the ice cream.
3 I like oranges.

Check-up 3 (Units 13–18)

Adjectives

(A) 1 Can you find her other shoes?
2 Your coat is very muddy.
3 Their journey was long and difficult.

(B) Individual answers

Sentences

1 Mike asked where they were going.
2 The bus driver shouted that there were too many people on the bus.
3 Nina moaned that it was too early to go to bed.

Verbs

A
1. The dog **had bitten** the postman!
2. I **had finished** the crossword in ten minutes.
3. We **had found** the treasure map at last!

B
1. I **eat** toast for breakfast.
2. They **caught** the ball.
3. We **were** late for school.

C
1. May I **borrow** a rubber?
2. I haven't got one to **lend** you.

D
1. Will you **teach** me the piano?
2. I can't. I **learn** the violin.

Adverbs

A
1. The car stopped <u>because it ran out of petrol.</u>
2. The fields were flooded <u>when the river burst its banks</u>.
3. I am going to the match <u>even if it rains</u>.

B Individual answers

Nouns

A
1. Does <u>that fluffy kitten</u> belong to you?
2. I am playing <u>an exciting computer game</u>.
3. Tom told us that he had seen <u>an enormous snake</u>.

B Individual answers

Check-up 4 (Units 19–24)

Paragraphs
Individual answers

Sentences

A
1. I will <u>not</u> eat these sprouts!
2. You <u>never</u> listen to a word I say.
3. I've <u>nothing</u> to do.

B
1. Hamish did not get any lunch today.
2. Can't I go out today?
3. The boys couldn't find anywhere to play.

Pronouns
e.g.
1. "Your mum is at the shops, Beth" she said.
 "Beth, my mum is at the shops," she said.
2. Use an electric vacuum cleaner to clean the floor.
3. I dropped the basket as I was getting the cat out of it.

Verbs
Individual answers

Adverbs
1. **Although the sun was shining**, it was very cold outside.
2. **When I came home from school**, there was a parcel on the doorstep.
3. **After the party had finished**, Mum picked me up.

Nouns

A
1. the **pupils'** bags
2. the **children's** bags
3. the **ladies'** hats
4. the **women's** hats

B
1. The thieves' den was in the mountains.
2. My sisters' birthdays are in June and December.
3. The babies' blankets were on the washing line.

Check-up 5 (Units 25–28)

Sentences

A
1. "Can you get the bread," said Helen, "and some butter?"
2. "Why does it always rain," moaned Chris, "when I want to go out?"
3. "One of the cedar trees fell down!" cried Isaac. "It hit the car!"

B Individual answers

Nouns

1	b	the **bicycle's** wheels
2	a	a **cat's** whiskers
3	a	the **boy's** (boys') parents
4	b	the **children's** parents
5	b	the **babies'** toys

Adverbs
1. So that we can go out this afternoon, we must finish our work this morning.
2. Swiftly and quietly, the hunter stalked his prey.

Paragraphs
5 paragraphs in all

paragraph:	fruit	– orange/apple/banana/pear
paragraph:	vegetables	– broccoli/cabbage/potato/carrot
paragraph:	salad	– cucumber/tomato/lettuce/radish
paragraph:	fish	– salmon/cod/haddock/mackerel
paragraph:	meat	– beef/lamb/chicken

77

Book 5 Scope and Sequence

Unit	Pupil Book	Pupil Book Focus	Pupil Book Practice	Pupil Book Extension	Resource Book Support	Resource Book Extension
1	**singular and plural**: irregular plurals*	making singular nouns plural/writing sentences with plural nouns	completing sentences to show noun–verb agreement	singular and plural with same forms/ nouns always plural	classifying nouns according to plural formation	forming plurals/ sentence writing for noun–verb agreement
2	**pronouns and adjectives**: possessives*	identifying possessive pronouns and possessive adjectives in sentences	completing sentences with possessive pronouns and possessive adjectives	using possessive adjectives instead of possessive pronouns/ using possessive pronouns instead of possessive adjectives	identifying possessive pronouns and possessive adjectives in sentences/ writing sentences with possessive adjectives	rewriting sentences to use possessive adjectives instead of possessive pronouns/ writing sentences with pairs of possessive pronouns/adjectives
3	**verbs**: round-up	forming verb tenses for given infinitives/ identifying verb and tense in sentences	changing tenses in sentences	writing sentences with two actions	changing tenses in sentences	writing sentences about a given topic to include a given tense
4	**sentences**: direct speech*	identifying spoken words in sentences	completing and punctuating direct speech sentences	using speech bubbles to write a direct speech conversation and an indirect speech passage	punctuating various forms of direct speech sentences/completing and punctuating direct speech sentences/writing sentences with given phrases	rewriting and punctuating a narrative with direct speech
5	**adverbs**: clauses	identifying adverb clauses in sentences/ linking adverb clause to verb	completing sentences with adverb clauses/ rewriting sentences with frontal adverb clauses	joining sentences to make main clause + adverb clause	identifying adverb clauses/ writing sentences with main clause + adverb clause and adverb clause + main clause	writing sentences with adverb clauses from given subordinating conjunctions
6	**nouns**: singular and plural possessive*	forming possessive nouns by adding apostrophes to singular and plural owners	rewriting given phrases using possessive nouns	correcting UK landmarks with apostrophes	identifying possessive nouns in sentences/ forming singular and plural possessive phrases/ sentence writing	correcting newspaper headlines with apostrophes
7	**sentences**: direct and indirect speech*	identifying direct and indirect speech and noting changes	converting direct speech sentences to indirect speech sentences/ converting indirect speech sentences to direct speech sentences	writing conversation in direct speech/ converting conversation to indirect speech	punctuating direct speech and indirect speech sentences/ converting speech bubbles to direct speech and indirect speech sentences	writing direct and indirect speech sentences from picture stimuli
8	**sentences**: subject and predicate*	identifying sentence subjects and predicates	joining given subjects and predicates to make sensible sentences	completing sentences with interesting subjects and predicates	identifying subjects and predicates in sentences/ adding interesting predicates to given subjects	writing pairs of sentences where a given noun is used as the subject and in the predicate
9	**homophones***	completing sentences with the correct homophone	choosing correct homophones to solve clues/using homophones in sentences	using unusual homophones in sentences to show understanding of meaning	choosing the correct homophone/writing sentences including pairs of homophones	homophone crossword
10	**verbs**: formed with en, ate, ify and ise suffixes	identifying verbs in sentences from noun and adjective root	forming verbs from nouns and adjectives to complete sentences	forming verbs from given adjectives/ writing sentences	identifying verbs in sentences/forming verbs from given words to complete sentences/ using given verbs in own sentences	forming verbs from more unusual nouns and adjectives/writing own sentences
11	**adjectives**: synonyms*	synonyms for given adjectives	rewriting sentences using more interesting adjectives	using unusual adjectives in sentence writing	classifying adjectives in synonym groups	writing synonym groups/using in sentence writing
12	**pronouns**: relative	completing sentences with relative pronouns	joining sentences with relative pronouns	completing sentences with *whose* and *whom*	joining sentences with relative pronouns/ completing sentences	writing sentences using *who*, *which* and *that*
13	**homonyms***	identifying part of speech for homonyms	finding one word as the answer to two clues/ sentence writing to show different meanings	identifying parts of speech within sentences/sentence writing to show different meanings	identifying parts of speech in sentences/solving clues/ sentence writing to show different meanings	using pairs of homonyms as different parts of speech in sentences
14	**punctuation**: apostrophes*	identifying possession and contraction apostrophes in sentences	writing contractions and possessive nouns /adding missing apostrophes	identifying plurals, contractions and possessive nouns in sentences/adding missing apostrophes	identifying contractions and possessive nouns/ writing contractions and possessive nouns	using given pairs of contractions and possessive nouns in sentences

* denotes content that is not specified in the National Curriculum for England (2014) but which will support children's wider knowledge and understanding of grammar.

Unit	Pupil Book	Pupil Book Focus	Pupil Book Practice	Pupil Book Extension	Resource Book Support	Resource Book Extension
15	**sentences**: subject and predicate*	dividing sentences into subject and predicate	identifying subjects and predicates/adding to subjects and predicates for interest	completing sentences with *I* or *me*	adding adjectives to subjects for interest/ adding adjectives and adverbs to predicates for interest	adding adjectives to given nouns and forming sentences with interesting predicates
16	**pronouns** repetition and clarity	listing nouns, pronouns and proper nouns in sentences	joining pairs of sentences and using pronouns/rewriting sentences for clarity	rewriting sentences – substituting pronouns for nouns to avoid repetition	joining pairs of sentences and using pronouns/ rewriting sentences to avoid repetition	constructing sentences from given sets of nouns and pronouns
17	**sentences**: relative clauses	identifying relative clauses and related nouns in sentences	completing sentences with *who* or *which*	adding relative clauses to given main clauses/adding main clauses to given relative clauses	completing sentences with relative clauses/writing a description to include relative clauses	rewriting sentences with misplaced relative clauses
18	**verbs**: auxiliary*	identifying auxiliary verbs in sentences	completing sentences with *will* and *shall*; *have* and *has*; *was* and *were*	writing sentences with given verbs	choosing correct auxiliary verbs to complete sentences/changing auxiliary verbs to change the tense of sentences	adding auxiliary verbs to given verbs and using in sentences
19	**punctuation**: comma round-up*	explaining various uses of commas in sentences	adding missing commas to sentences	writing sentences with direct speech, frontal adverbial phrases and clauses from given stimuli	adding commas to sentences with direct speech, lists, frontal adverbials	writing conversation to include list, direct speech, split direct speech and frontal adverbials
20	**paragraphs**: adverbials	identifying adverbs, adverb phrases and adverb clauses in extended writing	descriptive writing using given adverbs and adverbial phrases	descriptive writing using own adverbials	identifying adverbials in descriptive writing/ continuing description	writing description from picture stimulus
21	**verbs**: prefixes	identifying prefix part of verbs	solving clues with prefix + verb	adding different prefixes to infinitive to form different verbs/using *co* + verb words in sentences	completing sentences with correct prefix + verb words/replacing phrases in sentences with one prefix + verb word/sentence writing	using unusual prefix + verb words in sentence writing
22	**confusing words***	correcting mistakes in sentences	correcting mistakes: *of – have, win – beat, it's – its*	sentence writing to show understanding	completing sentences with confusing words	sentence writing to show understanding: *accept – except, beside – besides, among – between* and *advice – advise*
23	**adverbs**: sequence words and phrases	identifying adverbs of sequence in sentences	completing sentences with given sequence adverbs	writing given groups of action in sentences with sequence adverbs and adverb phrases	identifying sequence adverbs in sentences/ rewriting sentences to avoid repeating *and then*/ sequencing actions done after school	converting recipe instructions into personal recount
24	**verbs**: auxiliary – modals	identifying modal verbs in sentences	completing sentences with *can* and *may*; *might* and *must*; *could, would* and *should*	writing sentences with given verbs	Identifying sentences that give permission or indicate ability to do something/ writing sentences with given verbs	writing sentences to show understanding of the various modal verbs
25	**sentences**: main, adverb and relative clauses	identifying main clauses in sentences	identifying adverb and relative clauses in sentences	adding relative clause to given main clauses/adding adverb clauses to given main clauses	extending given sentences in two ways with adverb and relative clauses	writing descriptive account to include adverb and relative clauses
26	**punctuation**: commas to avoid ambiguity	using commas to avoid ambiguity	adding commas to sentences to change meaning	explaining differences in meaning between pairs of sentences	adding commas to sentences to change meaning/adding commas so that adjective–noun + noun phrases become three nouns/writing silly sentences	explaining differences in meaning between pairs of sentences
27	**punctuation**: commas, brackets and dashes	identifying extra information in commas, brackets and dashes in sentences	adding punctuation for parenthesis in sentences	combining pairs of sentences by using parenthesis	identifying information in parenthesis in sentences/ adding given extra information to given sentences	combining pairs of sentences by using parenthesis/ incorporating given extra information into own sentences
28	**sentences**: improving writing	rewriting sentences to improve vocabulary	adding detail to simple sentences	using interesting vocabulary and adding detail to simple sentences	improving sentences with interesting vocabulary and detail	rewriting given passage to improve with vocabulary and detail

BOOK 5 UNIT 1 Singular and plural

Irregular plurals

Most nouns have a singular form (one) and a plural form (more than one). The vast majority of nouns form their plural by adding *s*.

Throughout the course, children will encounter plurals with *s* and *es*, pluralisation for words ending in *y/f/fe/o/oo*, and irregular plurals.

This unit revises the work on singular and plural with nouns that form their plurals by adding s or *es*, nouns ending in *y*, nouns ending *f/fe*, and nouns ending in *o/oo*. It extends the work to irregular plurals.

Pupil Book

Focus

- Revise/discuss *more than one (noun)* and ask for examples with *s* and *es*.
- Revise/discuss the terms *vowel* and *consonant*.
- Revise the terms:
  - *singular* = one
  - *plural* = more than one
- Read the information box on page 6.
- Do the activity on the board, explaining that all these words have irregular plurals.

Answers

(A) 1 women 2 teeth 3 oxen
    4 feet   5 mice   6 postmen

(B) Individual answers

Practice

- These activities revise noun/verb agreement.
- Children should work individually.

Answers

(A) 1 The mice **are** chewing through the rope.
    2 The ox **is** working in the field.
    3 The people **are** having a good time.

(B) 1 The children **were** having tea.
    2 The geese **were** swimming on the pond.
    3 My tooth **was** hurting.

Extension

- Children should work individually.
- When complete, discuss answers.

Answers

(A) All the words are the same in the plural as the singular.

(B) 1 trousers   2 clothes
    3 glasses/spectacles 4 scissors

Resource Book

Support PCM

- Children should work individually.

Answers

Add s	Add es
pandas	tomatoes
bookcases	watches
hippos	dingoes
girls	crashes
videos	volcanoes

Different word	Same in singular and plural
children	trout
teeth	cod
geese	salmon
men	sheep
feet	deer

Extension PCM

- Children should work individually.

Answers

(A) 1 cacti
    2 fungi
    3 nuclei
    4 aircraft
    5 species

(B) Individual answers

(C) Individual answers

Extra

Make plural ending cards, e.g.

| s | es | ies | ves |

Children pick a card and give a plural word corresponding to the ending on the card.

BOOK 5 UNIT 2: Adjectives and pronouns

Possessive

Adjectives are usually explained as 'describing' words. They pinpoint a quality or a feature of a noun or pronoun. Throughout the course, children will encounter single adjectives, comparative and superlative adjectives, adjective phrases, possessive adjectives and adjective (relative) clauses.

Pronouns are words that take the place of nouns and noun phrases. Throughout the course, children will encounter: personal pronouns (as subject and object); possessive pronouns; reflexive pronouns; and relative pronouns. Demonstrative pronouns are introduced in the work on noun phrases. Interrogative pronouns are not specifically labelled as such but children encounter them in work on relative pronouns. It is up to individual teachers if indefinite pronouns, e.g. each/many/few/some, are specifically labelled as such and taught as another group of pronouns.

This unit revises possessive adjectives and possessive pronouns. Possessive adjectives differ from possessive pronouns in that they are followed by a noun, but do not stand in place of a noun.

Pupil Book

Focus
- Revise/discuss the terms *adjective* and *pronoun*.
- Recap on the types of adjectives and pronouns the children have encountered.
- Read and discuss the information box on page 8.
- Do the activity orally.

Answers

(A)
1. I think this jumper is **hers**. — possessive pronoun
   This is **her** jumper. — possessive adjective
2. **Our** house is painted white. — possessive adjective
   The white house is **ours**. — possessive pronoun
3. Is this **their** address? — possessive adjective
   This address is **theirs**. — possessive pronoun
4. That's **my** book. — possessive adjective
   That book is **mine**. — possessive pronoun
5. That lunchbox is **hers**. — possessive pronoun
   She is eating **her** lunch. — possessive adjective

Practice
- If necessary, model the first one from each of the activities so children understand what is required.
- Children should work individually.

Answers

(A)
1. My brother is older than **yours**.
2. She has a blue bag. It must be **hers**.
3. I think these are **ours**.

(B)
1. The front tyre of the bicycle is flat but **its** back tyre is OK.
2. "Put **your** coats in the cloakroom," the teacher said to the class.
3. "I have forgotten **my** gloves and **my** hands are cold," complained Sam.

Extension
- If necessary, model the first one from each of the activities so children understand what is required.
- Children should work individually.

Answers

(A)
1. This is **his** boat.
2. That is **our** dog.
3. It is **my** black cat.
4. It is **their** horse.
5. Is this **your** football?

(B)
1. The mistake is **mine**.
2. Are those shoes **hers**?
3. These tickets are **ours**.
4. That horse is **theirs**.
5. Is this bicycle **yours**?

Resource Book

Support PCM
- Children should work individually.

Answers

(A)
1. "These photographs are <u>mine</u>," said Ned.
2. "Where are <u>yours</u>?" asked the teacher.
3. Sam had put <u>his</u> on the desk.
4. Sonu had <u>hers</u> in an envelope.
5. I brought <u>ours</u> to school yesterday.

(B)
1. <u>Her</u> brother is very upset.
2. <u>His</u> dog is lost.
3. <u>Its</u> lead snapped and the dog ran off.
4. <u>Their</u> parents are out looking for the dog.
5. <u>Our</u> parents are helping.

(C) Individual answers

Extension PCM
- Activities B and C: If children struggle to write one sentence containing the pair of adjectives/pronouns, they can write two related sentences.

Answers

(A)
1. This is **my** clarinet.
2. This is **your** book.
3. These are **her** shoes.
4. These are **our** pencils.
5. This is **their** dog.

(B) Individual answers

(C) Individual answers

Extra

Make possessive adjective and possessive pronoun cards, e.g.

| our | ours | their | theirs |

Children pick a card and put the pronoun/adjective into a sentence.
What do the children notice about *his*?
It is not important that children can say which is a pronoun and which an adjective at this stage. Far more important is that they can use the words correctly in sentences.

BOOK 5 UNIT 3 Verbs

Round-up of tenses

Throughout the course, children will encounter the present simple, present progressive (also known as continuous), past simple, past progressive, present perfect (labelled simply *perfect* throughout the course), past perfect, future, infinitive (labelled *verb family name* in the early parts of the course), auxiliary verbs, modals, active and passive verbs and subjunctive verbs (a construction very rarely used except in extremely formal writing).

Participles are referred to as '*ing* words' and 'regular past simple tense words'; finite verbs are referred to as 'main' or 'proper verbs', and it is for the teacher to decide the appropriate time to introduce the terms *participle* and *finite verb*.

This unit recaps on all the verb tenses the children have learned so far:

- present simple
- present progressive
- past simple
- past progressive
- present perfect (Technically, the present perfect tense is constructed with *has/have* + past participle. It is simpler to say that it is constructed with *has/have* + the past simple tense (regular or irregular)).
- past perfect (Technically, the past perfect tense is constructed with *had* + past participle. It is simpler to say that it is constructed with *had* + the past simple tense (regular or irregular). Mistakes where the past simple tense and the past participle are NOT the same can be dealt with on an individual basis.
- future

Pupil Book

Focus

- Revise/discuss the term verb and ask for examples of:
  - present simple
  - past simple
  - perfect
  - future
  - present progressive
  - past progressive
  - past perfect
- Read and discuss the information box on page 10.
- Do the activity orally.

Answers

(A) 1 I climbed/I was climbing/I have climbed/I had climbed/I climb/I am climbing/I shall climb
2 I ate/I was eating/I have eaten/I had eaten/I eat/I am eating/I shall eat
3 I spoke/I was speaking/I have spoken/I had spoken/I speak/I am speaking/I shall speak
4 I drew/I was drawing/I have drawn/I had drawn/I draw/I am drawing/I shall draw
5 I thought/I was thinking/I have thought/I had thought/I think/I am thinking/I shall think
6 I swam/I was swimming/I have swum/I had swum/I swim/I am swimming/I shall swim

(B) 1 The cat **was walking** on the narrow wall. — past progressive
2 The ladder **fell** with a crash. — past simple
3 He **had forgotten** his car keys. — past perfect
4 We **shall visit** at the weekend. — future
5 I **have seen** that film before. — perfect

Practice

- Children should work individually.

Answers

(A) Present progressive tense = I am going for a walk.
They are riding their horses.
We are swimming.

Past progressive tense = I was going for a walk.
They were riding their horses.
We were swimming.

(B) Perfect tense = The birds have flown away.
My strap has broken.
They have eaten.

Past perfect tense = The birds had flown away.
My strap had broken.
They had eaten.

(C) Present simple tense = I leave.
The sun sets.
You go.

Past simple tense = I left.
The sun set.
You went.

Extension

- Read and discuss the first answers so children understand what is required.
  When complete, discuss answers.

Answers

(A) Suggested answers
1 I went to the park and shall go again tomorrow.
2 He has finished the loaf of bread so he will buy more tomorrow.
3 They dug the garden and will plant seeds next week.
4 We washed our clothes and shall iron them later.

Resource Book

Support PCM

- Children can work individually or in pairs.
- When complete, discuss answers.

Answers

(A) 1 **I was feeding** the dog and then **I packed** my school bag.
2 **I have returned** my book to the library.
3 **I had gone** to bed when the telephone **rang**.
4 The rain **will pour** down on Saturday.

Extension PCM

- Children should work individually.

Answers

Individual answers

Extra

Make infinitive and tense cards, e.g.

infinitive cards: | to explore | to dig | to answer |

tense cards: | past perfect | future |

Children pick an infinitive card and a tense card and make a sentence.

82

BOOK 5 UNIT 4 Sentences

Direct speech

The concept of a sentence as a unit of language that 'makes sense' can be a difficult concept for some children to grasp. The course builds children's confidence in this area through giving them the opportunity to look at punctuation of statements, questions and exclamations to familiarise themselves with what a 'sentence' looks and sounds like.

Throughout the course, children will encounter: sentence punctuation; the concept of 'making sense'; direct and indirect speech; clauses which combine to make multi-clause sentences; parts of sentences – subject/object, subject/predicate; focusing on the sentence as a unit of language that can be improved; and Standard English constructions.

Children often find correctly punctuating direct speech sentences problematic. Several units in the course focus on direct speech so that the various rules can be built up gradually. Speech marks (inverted commas), beginning a new line when a different person speaks, punctuation before the final speech marks and punctuation when the non-spoken words come before the spoken words have been introduced. This unit focuses on split direct speech: two sentences split by non-spoken words and one sentence split by non-spoken words.

Pupil Book

Focus
- Begin by asking the children why direct speech (characters having a conversation) looks 'different' on the page.
- Revise the terms *statement* – full stop/*question* – question mark/*exclamation* – exclamation mark/*speech marks* (inverted commas).
- Read and discuss the information box on page 12.
- Do the activity orally, asking children to read only the spoken words. Ask: *Is the teacher saying one or two sentences? How can you tell?* etc.

Answers
1. "**Finish your paintings**," instructed the teacher, "**and then tidy up.**"
2. "**My cousin is coming at the weekend**," said Amy, "**and we are going to fly my kite.**"
3. "**The car was parked outside the house**," explained Mr Webb to the policeman. "**It must have been stolen in the early hours of the morning.**"
4. "**I really like apples and oranges**," said Abigail, "**but I don't like bananas!**"

Practice
- Read the incomplete direct speech sentences and ask: *How do you know that each speaker only says one sentence?*
- Children can work in pairs.

Answers
1. "I've made a apple pie," said Harry, "so _____ (. /? /!)"
2. "I took the dog to the vet," said Rob, "because _____ (. /? /!)"
3. "When you have finished your homework," said Mum, "can _____ (. /? /!)"
4. "I'm staying in," said Dad, "until _____ (. /? /!)"
5. "I'll meet you at one o'clock," said Joe, "outside _____ (. /? /!)"

Sentence completion = individual answers

Extension
- Activity A: Children can work in pairs. Remind them of synonyms for *said*.
- Activity B: Children should work individually.

Answers
(A) Suggested answer
"Which team do you think will win the league this year?" asked Sam.
"I don't care," replied Ben. "I don't like football."
"You don't like football?" exclaimed Sam. "Football is the greatest sport ever!"
"Not for me," said Ben. "I like cricket. It's a much more difficult and exciting game."

(B) Suggested answer
Sam asked Ben which team he thought would win the league this year. Ben said that he didn't care as he didn't like football. Sam was amazed as he thought football was the greatest sport ever. Ben didn't agree. He said that he liked cricket. He thought it was a much more difficult and exciting game.

Resource Book

Support PCM
- Children should work individually.

Answers
(A)
1. "What are you doing?" asked Mum.
2. Kim replied, "I'm looking for my bag."
3. "If we hurry up," said John, "we will catch the bus."
4. "This milkshake is delicious!" exclaimed Helen. "You must let me know how you made it."

(B)
1. "Get the big case out," said Dan, "so _____
2. "I have looked for the passports," said Polly. "but _____
3. "My passport is in the drawer," said Dan. "I think _____

Sentence completion = individual answers

(C) Individual answers

Extension PCM
- Tell children to read through the whole passage before they begin to write to help them get the sense of it.

Answers
- "If we are going to the cinema...
- It was ten minutes to seven...
- "I'm nearly ready!" called Tamsin. "I'll be down...
- Andy was already...
- "Are you two coming?"
- "We will be there in a minute,"
- Tamsin came running down the stairs...
- Mum locked the front door...
- "We'll just make it in time,"

Extra
- In pairs, children can create a cartoon-type story with frames and speech bubbles.
- Pairs swap their cartoons and change them into a direct speech conversation.

83

BOOK 5 UNIT 5 Adverbs

Clauses

Adverbs are usually explained as words which 'add' to a verb giving the detail of how, where or when an action is done.

Throughout the course, children will encounter single adverbs (manner/time/place), comparative and superlative adverbs, adverbial phrases, adverb pairs and adverbial clauses.

Children have encountered the concepts of main and subordinate clauses earlier in the course. A main clause is a sentence in itself whereas a subordinate clause (beginning with a conjunction) is of less importance. Both main clauses and subordinate clauses contain a finite verb, i.e. a verb that makes a tense.

This unit revises adverbial clauses, and the concept of adverbial clauses coming at the beginning of a sentence. As with adverbial phrases, an adverbial clause does the same job as a single adverb, answering the basic questions 'how', 'when' or 'where'. It also expresses *reason* with conjunctions such as 'because', 'since', 'as'; *purpose* with conjunctions such as 'so that', 'in order to'; *contrast* with conjunctions such as 'although', 'as though'; and *comparison* with conjunctions such as 'as if', 'as though'.

Pupil Book

Focus

- Revise/discuss the terms *phrase, sentence, conjunction, main clause, subordinate clause, finite verb*.
- Write sentences with a main clause and an adverbial subordinate clause on the board.
- Children identify:
  – the main clause
  – the adverbial subordinate clause
  – the conjunction which begins the subordinate clause
  – the verb in the main clause
  – the verb in the subordinate clause.
- Read the information box on page 14.
- Explain that one type of subordinate clause is an *adverb clause*.
- Ask children to substitute:
  – *because it was hit by lightning* with another *because* clause;
  – *after lightning struck it twice* with another *after* clause;
  – *as if it was made of paper* with another *as if* clause.
- Point out that when an adverb clause comes at the beginning of a sentence, it is separated from the main clause by a comma.
- Do the activity orally.

Answers

(bold = verb; underlining = adverbial clause)
1. The gardener **dug** a large hole <u>before he planted the tree</u>.
2. <u>Although she had followed the instructions carefully</u>, the model didn't **look** right.
3. **I played** on my computer game <u>after I had learned my spellings</u>.
4. <u>When you go into town</u>, will you **buy** some apples?
5. I will **see** the next patient <u>when I have washed my hands</u>.
6. <u>If we win today</u>, we **are** in the final!

Practice

- Children should work individually.

Answers

Ⓐ Individual answers
Ⓑ Individual answers

Extension

- Read and discuss the first answer so children understand what is required.

Answers

Individual answers

Resource Book

Support PCM

- Children should work individually.

Answers

Ⓐ
1. Heat the soup <u>before you make the toast</u>.
2. <u>Although I tried hard</u>, my writing was not very neat.
3. The plane cannot take off <u>until the fog has lifted</u>.
4. People left the cinema <u>as soon as the film ended</u>.
5. The prisoner escaped <u>even though the door was locked</u>!

Ⓑ Individual answers
Ⓒ Individual answers

Extension PCM

- Activity B: Remind children of the comma.

Answers

Individual answers

Extra

Make conjunction cards, e.g.

| since | whenever | even though | as long as |

Children pick a card and use the conjunction as the beginning of an adverbial clause in a sentence. Encourage children to put the adverbial clause first in the sentence.

84

BOOK 5 UNIT 6 Nouns

Possessive – singular and plural

Nouns are usually explained as 'naming' words. Nouns are the most common part of speech that children of this age will encounter. Children's first words are usually nouns as they make sense of the world by naming things.

Throughout the course, children will encounter common, proper, collective, compound, abstract and possessive nouns, together with noun phrases.

This unit revises the concept of singular and plural possessive nouns.

Pupil Book

Focus
- Revise/discuss the term noun and ask for examples of:
  - common nouns
  - proper nouns
  - collective nouns
  - compound nouns
  - abstract nouns
- Revise/discuss the uses of the *apostrophe* that children have encountered, i.e. apostrophe of contraction/apostrophe of possession for singular and plural nouns.
- Read the information box on page 16.
- The activity should be done orally.
- If children are having difficulty in locating the owner, say the stalk belonging to the leaf/the stalks belonging to the leaves, etc.

Answers
1. the leaf's stalk
2. the leaves' stalks
3. the ox's tail
4. the oxen's tails
5. the lady's house
6. the ladies' houses
7. the volcano's eruptions
8. the volcanoes' eruptions
9. the country's flag
10. the countries' flags

Practice
- Activity A: If necessary, model the first answer so children understand what is required.
- Children should work individually.

Answers
(A)
1. the elephants' journey
2. the brushes' handles
3. the knives' block
4. the teeth's fillings
5. the foxes' tails

(B) Individual answers

Extension
- Children can work in pairs.
- When complete, discuss answers.

Answers
1. Cleopatra's Needle
2. Fingal's Cave
3. Poets' Corner
4. St Catherine's Point
5. The Giant's Causeway
6. St Paul's Cathedral

Resource Book

Support PCM
- Activity A: Remind children that the apostrophe is always attached to the owner.
- Activity B: If necessary, model the first answer so children understand what is required.
- Children should work individually.

Answers
(A)
1. The princesses' father loved his daughters.
2. There was a wasps' nest outside the window.
3. The ladies' hairdresser was very busy.
4. Pets' Corner was very popular with the children.
5. We enjoyed Grandmother's visit

(B)
1.
  a. the fly's wings
  b. the flies' wings
2.
  a. the farmer's fields
  b. the farmers' fields
3.
  a. the pony's bridle
  b. the ponies' bridles

(C) Individual answers

Extension PCM
- Children can work in pairs against the clock!
- When complete, discuss answers.

Answers

| WEEK'S RAIN IN TWO DAYS |
| SHIP'S CREW RESCUED! |
| LORRY'S LOAD BLOCKS MOTORWAY |
| SATURDAY'S FOOTBALL RESULTS |
| FLOOD DESTROYS VILLAGERS' HOMES |
| LADIES' FASHION WEEK |
| CHILDREN'S AND PARENTS' SPORTS DAY GREAT SUCCESS |

Extra
Make singular noun cards, e.g.

| shelf | baby | child | brush |

Children pick a card. They write the plural of the word on the board.
They then write a sentence using that plural as a possessive noun.

BOOK 5 UNIT 7 Sentences

Indirect speech

The concept of a sentence as a unit of language that 'makes sense' can be a difficult concept for some children to grasp. The course builds children's confidence in this area through giving them the opportunity to look at punctuation of statements, questions and exclamations to familiarise themselves with what a 'sentence' looks and sounds like.

Throughout the course, children will encounter: sentence punctuation; the concept of 'making sense'; direct and indirect speech; clauses which combine to make multi-clause sentences; parts of sentences – subject/object, subject/predicate; focusing on the sentence as a unit of language that can be improved; and Standard English constructions.

Children often find correctly punctuating direct speech sentences problematic. Several units in the course focus on direct speech so that the various rules can be built up gradually. Previously, speech marks (inverted commas), beginning a new line when a different person speaks and punctuation before the final speech marks have been introduced. Children have also encountered 'indirect (reported) speech'.

In this unit the basic rules of direct and indirect speech are revised.

Pupil Book

Focus
- Begin by asking the children why direct speech (characters having a conversation) looks 'different' on the page.
- Revise the terms statement – *full stop*/question – *question mark*/exclamation – *exclamation mark*/speech marks *(inverted commas)* and *indirect (reported) speech*.
- Read the information box on page 18.
- Do the activity orally. Look at word changes, e.g. pronouns/verb tenses, etc. Discuss the addition of the word *that*.

Answers
| The first line of each question | = direct speech |
| The second line of each question | = indirect speech |

Practice
- Activities A and B: Explain that the children are going to change direct speech into indirect speech, and indirect speech into direct speech.
- Do the first question from each activity orally first.

Answers
(A) 1 The driver screamed that they needed an ambulance.
2 The Mayor welcomed everyone to their city.
3 The librarian explained that if they could wait just a minute, she/he would show them where to find the biography section.
4 The farmer groaned that the rain was a disaster and would ruin the crops.

(B) e.g.
1 "Is anyone thirsty?" asked Paul.
2 "I am good at map reading," said Sue.
3 "Will you come to my birthday party?" asked my friend.
4 "You have to do better in the second half," said the manager to the team.

Extension
- Activity A: Children can work in pairs to produce the conversation and read it as a duologue to the class.
- Remind them to include some synonyms for *said*.
- Activity B: Children should work individually.

Answers
Individual answers

Resource Book

Support PCM
- Children should work individually on the activities.

Answers
(A) 1 "One of the school buses has broken down," explained the head teacher.
2 We were told that one of the school buses had broken down.
3 "Why do we have to bring family photographs to school?" asked Ben.
4 Ben wanted to know why we had to bring family photographs to school.

(B) e.g
1 "Where is my sister?" asked John.
John wanted to know where his sister was.
2 "It is safe to cross now," said the lollipop lady.
The lollipop lady said it was safe to cross.
3 "My car has been stolen!" shouted the policeman.
The policeman shouted that his car had been stolen.

Extension PCM
- Remind children that a sentence can be a statement, question or exclamation.

Answers
Individual answers

Extra
Put children into pairs. Each pair comes to the front. One child says a direct speech sentence, e.g.
I don't like tomatoes.
The other child makes it into indirect speech, e.g.
She said that she doesn't like tomatoes.

BOOK 5 UNIT 8 Sentences

Subject and predicate

The concept of a sentence as a unit of language that 'makes sense' can be a difficult concept for some children to grasp. The course builds children's confidence in this area through giving them the opportunity to look at punctuation of statements, questions and exclamations to familiarise themselves with what a 'sentence' looks and sounds like.

Throughout the course, children will encounter: sentence punctuation; the concept of 'making sense'; direct and indirect speech; clauses which combine to make multi-clause sentences; parts of sentences – subject/object, subject/predicate; focusing on the sentence as a unit of language that can be improved; and Standard English constructions.

This unit introduces 'subject' and 'predicate' in sentences.

- The 'subject' is what the sentence is about and usually does the action expressed by the verb. The 'subject' can be a single noun, a noun phrase or pronoun – the latter being in the subject form.
- The predicate is the rest of the sentence and contains the verb.

Pupil Book

Focus
- Ask children what they understand by the term sentence.
- Revise/discuss the terms *noun* and *pronoun*.
- Revise/discuss the term *subject*.
- Introduce the term *predicate*.
- Read the information box on page 20.
- Ask children to identify the verb in each predicate in the table.
- Do more oral examples asking children to identify subject and predicate in simple sentences.
- Do the activities orally.

Answers
(A) 1 **I** have hurt my knee.
    2 **Sharks** live in the sea.
    3 **The Queen** lives in a palace.
    4 **The horses** are in the stables.
    5 **Roger** is travelling to India.

(B) 1 The bakery **opens at nine o'clock**.
    2 We **decided to go to the park**.
    3 The river **bursts its banks**.
    4 Our garage **is big enough for two cars**.
    5 My friends and I **like to play football**.

Practice
- Children can work in pairs.
- When complete, discuss answers.
- Can children give an alternative predicate for each subject?

Answers
1 The cottage was near the stream.
2 I am paddling a canoe.
3 The race was very exciting.
4 A large crowd watched the match.
5 Sam wrote the answers carefully.

Extension
- Activity A: Remind children that they can use adjectives to make their subjects more interesting.
- Model the first one in both activities so children understand what is required.
- Children should work individually.

Answers
(A) Individual answers
(B) Individual answers

Resource Book

Support PCM
- Children should work individually.

Answers
(A) 1 (The cows) were munching grass in the field.
    2 (The batsman) hit the ball for six runs.
    3 (A large audience) came to see the concert.
    4 (Our house) has a broken window.
    5 (These chips) are not cooked!
(B) Individual answers

Extension PCM
- Read and discuss the first answer so children understand what is required.

Answers
Individual answers

Extra
Make noun/verb cards, e.g.

| the cat/to eat | my friend/to call |

Children pick a card. They make a sentence using any tense of the verb where the noun on the card is the subject. They then make a sentence using any tense of the verb where the noun is part of the predicate.

BOOK 5 UNIT 9 Homophones

Words that are spelt the same and sound the same are homonyms.

Words that sound the same but are different in spelling and meaning are homophones. Homophones can often cause confusion. Children have encountered common homophones that frequently cause problems earlier in the course.

This unit looks at homophones in general and covers a variety of common words that children will need to differentiate.

Pupil Book

Focus
- Explain to the children that there are words that sound the same when we say them, but have different meanings and spellings.
- Introduce the term *homophone*.
- Read and discuss the information box on page 22.
- Do the Activity orally.

Answers
1. The train leaves in one **hour**.
2. I will **meet** you by the station clock.
3. Can you **buy** the tickets?
4. Make sure you get the **right** ones.
5. I **know** which tickets to get!
6. Sorry! I'm just **so** excited.
7. I can **hear** how excited you are!
8. **See** you there!

Practice
- Children can work in pairs against the clock!

Answers
(A)
1. paws
2. moat
3. beach
4. maize
5. stairs

(B) Individual answers

Extension
- Read and discuss the homophones before children write.

Answers
Individual answers

Resource book

Support PCM
- Activities A and B: Children can work in pairs.
- Encourage the use of dictionaries.
- Activity C: Children should work individually.

Answers
(A)
1. gate
2. soar
3. hare
4. jeans
5. manor

(B)
1. cereal
2. maize
3. plum
4. thyme
5. bread
6. meat
7. steak

(C) Individual answers

Extension PCM
- If children are unfamiliar with the crossword format, model the first across and first down answer so children understand what is required.

Answers

Across	Down
2 stares	1 vale
6 allowed	3 reed
8 mite	4 serial
9 paws	5 sleigh
11 hall	7 one
12 hare	9 plum
15 gate	10 sight
17 birth	13 rough
19 by	14 wring
21 manor	16 teem
22 cede	18 time
	19 bored
	20 knead

Extra
Remind children of the clue-solving they did in Practice Activity A.
In pairs, can they write clues for other pairs of homophones?

88

BOOK 5 UNIT 10 Verbs

Formed with *en/ate/ify/ise* suffixes

Verbs are often explained as 'doing words' or 'being words'. They are possibly the most complex part of speech for young children to grasp because of their many forms and tenses.

Throughout the course, children will encounter the present simple, present progressive (also known as continuous), past simple, past progressive, present perfect (labelled simply *perfect* throughout the course), past perfect, future, infinitive (labelled *verb family name* in the early parts of the course), auxiliary verbs, modals, active and passive verbs and subjunctive verbs (a construction very rarely used except in extremely formal writing).

Participles are referred to as '*ing* words' and 'regular past simple tense words'; finite verbs are referred to as 'main' or 'proper verbs', and it is for the teacher to decide the appropriate time to introduce the terms *participle* and *finite verb*.

Children have been introduced to forming adjectives and nouns with suffixes earlier in the course. This unit examines verbs formed from nouns and adjectives with specific suffixes.

Pupil Book

Focus
- Revise/discuss the terms verb, noun and adjective.
- Read and discuss the information box on page 24.
- Do the activity orally.

Answers
1. The moon **brightened** the cloudy sky.   adjective = bright
2. We **shall fertilise** the crops.   adjective = fertile
3. Europeans **colonised** America.   noun = colony
4. Parents **were notified** about the school closure.   noun = note
5. The cement **will harden** in a few hours.   adjective = hard

Practice
- Activities A and B: If appropriate, go through the words in the box asking, e.g.
  If you give someone an apology, you _____. etc.

Answers
(A)
1. Someone has **vandalised** the bus shelter.
2. If I take one of those bags, it will **lighten** the load.
3. The boy **apologised** for kicking his ball into the flowers.
4. The bandits **terrorized** the townspeople.
5. We will read the short story and then **dramatise** it.

(B)
1. The army commander had to **mobilise** his troops.
2. The magician **hypnotised** a member of the audience.
3. They will have to **widen** the road when the new houses are built.
4. **Tighten** the rope before the horse escapes!
5. Wild animals were **domesticated** by prehistoric people.

Extension
- Discuss the meaning of adjectives before children write.

Answers
1. straighten
2. deepen
3. sadden
4. brighten
5. glamorise
6. legalise

Sentences = individual answers

Resource Book

Support PCM
- Activity A: Remind children that a verb can be one word or two words.

Answers
- Children should work individually.

(A)
1. The librarian **categorised** the books on the shelves.
2. Roller coasters **terrify** me!
3. We **must deepen** the hole for that big plant.
4. The barking dog **maddened** the huge bull.
5. We **are computerising** our school records.

(B)
1. The sky **darkened** as the sun set.
2. They are **strengthening** the garden wall.
3. The bees are **pollinating** the flowers.
4. She was **horrified** by the news.
5. This is too hard. Can you **simplify** it?

(C) Individual answers

Extension PCM
- Some of the adjectives may be unfamiliar so encourage children to use dictionaries.

Answers
1. solidify
2. dignify
3. glorify
4. oxygenate
5. assassinate
6. authorise

Sentences = individual answers

Extra
- Children help you complete word family webs on the board.
- These can consist of any relevant parts of speech the children suggest.
- Begin the web with a noun or adjective, e.g.

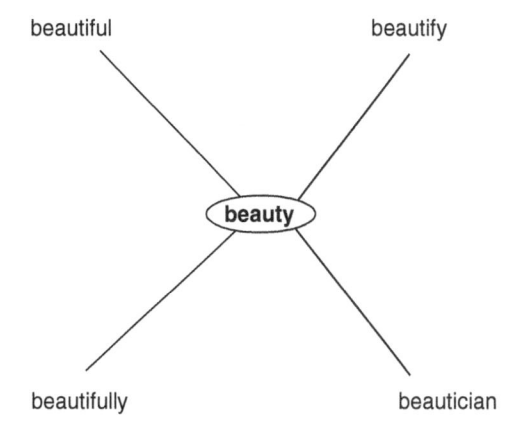

beautiful   beautify

(beauty)

beautifully   beautician

BOOK 5 UNIT 11 Adjectives

Synonyms

Adjectives are usually explained as 'describing' words. They pinpoint a quality or a feature of a noun or pronoun. Throughout the course, children will encounter single adjectives, comparative and superlative adjectives, adjective phrases, possessive adjectives and adjective (relative) clauses.

Children have encountered synonyms for 'said' and other verbs earlier in the course.

This unit continues work on improving writing with synonyms for common, overused adjectives.

Pupil Book

Focus
- Revise/discuss the term *adjective* and ask for examples.
- Revise/discuss the term *synonym*.
- Read and discuss the information box on page 26.
- Do the activity in teams as a timed game.
- When complete, make lists on the board from the children's suggestions and vote for the best synonym for each verb.

Answers
1. cross: angry/annoyed/displeased/furious/upset/enraged
2. bad: awful/nasty/dreadful/unpleasant/rank
3. boring: dull/tiring/tedious/unexciting/monotonous
4. broken: damaged/smashed/shattered/fractured
5. quiet: calm/peaceful/undisturbed/restful/tranquil/placid
6. happy: joyful/cheerful/merry/jolly/lively
7. cold: cool/chilly/frosty/icy/wintry/arctic
8. dirty: unclean/filthy/unwashed/foul/grimy/squalid
9. easy: simple/plain/obvious/effortless/uncomplicated
10. exciting: thrilling/stirring/startling/hair-raising/stimulating
11. kind: tender/gentle/mild/soothing/considerate
12. heavy: weighty/hefty/bulky/cumbersome

Practice
- Explain that certain adjectives go with certain nouns. You wouldn't have *delicious shoes* but you could have a *delicious meal*.

Answers
(A) Suggested answers
1. We had a delicious meal.
2. I had an interesting chat with my friend.
3. I like beautiful shoes.
4. She looked very sporty in her new clothes.
5. He scored an amazing goal.
6. We had a wonderful time.

(B) Suggested answers
1. The tiny mouse scurried across the floor.
2. You have small feet!
3. He collects miniature toy soldiers.
4. You can't see germs with your eyes because they are microscopic.

Extension
- Read and discuss the adjectives to ensure children understand meanings, or use this as an opportunity for dictionary work.

Answers
Individual answers

Resource Book

Support PCM
- Children should work individually.

Answers
(A)

Synonyms for pretty	Synonyms for clean
attractive	washed
lovely	unsoiled
pleasing	spotless
fair	fresh
beautiful	pure

Synonyms for funny	Synonyms for old
amusing	elderly
hilarious	ancient
witty	aged
comical	decrepit
humorous	venerable

(B) Individual answers

Extension PCM
- Model the first answer so that children understand what is required.

Answers
Individual answers

Extra
Make cards of common adjectives, e.g.

| big | hot | old | happy | little |

Put children into small groups.
Each group chooses a card and comes up with as many synonyms as they can in five minutes.
When complete, discuss answers and see if the class can add any more synonyms to the groups' lists.

BOOK 5 UNIT 12 Pronouns

Relative

Pronouns are words that take the place of nouns and noun phrases.

Throughout the course, children will encounter personal pronouns (as subject and object); possessive pronouns; reflexive pronouns; and relative pronouns.

Demonstrative pronouns are introduced in the work on noun phrases.

Interrogative pronouns are not specifically labelled as such but children encounter them in work on relative pronouns. It is up to individual teachers if indefinite pronouns, e.g. each/many/few/some, are specifically labelled as such and taught as another group of pronouns.

This unit introduces relative pronouns in preparation for relative (adjectival) clauses later in the course. For the purposes of this and other units dealing with relative pronouns and clauses, 'which' and 'that' are equally acceptable as the different uses are too complicated for primary school children.

Pupil Book

Focus
- Revise/discuss the terms *noun* and *conjunctions*.
- Revise/discuss the term *pronoun* and ask for examples.
- Introduce and discuss the term *relative pronoun*.
- Read the information box on page 28.
- Do the Activity orally.

Answers
1 That's the badger **which** comes into our garden.
2 This letter is from my pen friend **who** lives in America.
3 I want to go to the park **which** has a boating lake.
4 The doctor **who** visited me was very kind.
5 The topic, **which** we are doing at school, is very interesting.

Practice
- If necessary, go through the sentences orally before children write.

Answers
1 I found an old coin **which/that** was used in Roman times.
2 We have two cousins **who** live by the sea.
3 Sam bought a book **which/that** was about fishing.
4 He waved to his friend **who** was on the other side of the road.
5 Sally is a nurse **who** works with old people.

Extension
- Read and discuss the information box on page 29.
- Do more oral practice before the children write.

Answers
1 I know the man **whose** car was stolen.
2 From **whom** did you borrow this book?
3 **Whose** bag is this?
4 This is Fred, **whose** brother went to school with me.

Resource Book

Support PCM
- Children should work individually.

Answers
(A) 1 We replaced one of the windows **which/that** was broken.
2 Jane borrowed a bicycle **which/that** belonged to the girl next door.
3 The car splashed water on the man **who** was standing beside the road.
4 I took my books back to the library **which/that** was in the town centre.

(B) 1 **Whose** is this piece of work?
2 The woman, **whose** horse was lame, called the vet.
3 This is the footballer **whose** job it is to score goals.
4 **Whom** shall I say is calling?

Extension PCM
- Model the first answer so children understand what is required.

Answers
Individual answers

Extra
- Make relative pronoun cards, i.e.

| who | which | that | whose | whom |

Children pick a card and construct a sentence using the relative pronoun.

BOOK 5 UNIT 13 Homonyms

Homonyms

Words that are spelt the same and sound the same are homonyms. Homonyms do different jobs in language, i.e. they can be different parts of speech.

This unit introduces the concept of homonyms and gives children the opportunity to look at how they work as different parts of speech in sentences.

Pupil Book

Focus
- Revise/discuss the term *homophone* and ask for examples.
- Explain to the children that there are words that are spelt the same and sound the same when we say them, but do different jobs in sentences.
- Read and discuss the information box on page 30.
- Do the Activity orally.

Answers
1. a verb   b noun
2. a noun   b verb
3. a verb   b noun
4. a noun   b verb
5. a noun   b verb

Practice
- Activity A: Children can work in pairs against the clock!
  Activity B: Children should work individually.

Answers
(A)
1. mouse
2. chest
3. skip
4. pound
5. sole

(B) Individual answers

Extension
- Children should tackle Activities A and B individually if possible.

Answers
(A)
1. a adverb   b adjective
2. a noun   b verb
3. a verb   b noun

(B) Individual answers

Resource Book

Support PCM
- Children should work individually.

Answers
(A)
1. a verb   b noun
2. a verb   b noun
3. a adjective b noun
4. a verb   b noun
5. a noun   b verb

(B)
1. rose
2. tap
3. fix
4. hand
5. heart

(C) Individual answers

Extension PCM
- Model the first answer so children understand what is required.

Answers
Individual answers

Extra
Make homonym cards, e.g.

verb/noun: | book | command | iron |

adjective/noun: | flat | glass | right |

Children pick a card and make sentences to show the different parts of speech that the word on the card can be used as.

BOOK 5 UNIT 14 Punctuation

Contraction and possession

Children have so far encountered contractions of the verbs 'to be', 'to have', and 'not' contractions. Later in the course, contractions will be examined in Non-standard, as opposed to Standard English.

Nouns are usually explained as 'naming' words. Nouns are the most common part of speech that children of this age will encounter. Children's first words are usually nouns as they make sense of the world by naming things.

Throughout the course, children will encounter common, proper, collective, compound, abstract and possessive nouns, together with noun phrases.

This unit revises the two uses of the apostrophe and gives children the opportunity to differentiate between those two uses.

Pupil Book

Focus
- Revise/discuss the term *apostrophe* and ask for examples of its use.
- Read and discuss the information box on page 32.
- Look at each example carefully as apostrophes of both kinds can cause problems.
- Do the activity orally.

Answers
1. don't — contraction
2. puppies' — possession
3. I'm — contraction
4. can't — contraction
5. Everyone's — possession
6. geese's — possession

Practice
- Children should work individually on the activities.

Answers

A
1. don't
2. wouldn't
3. you're
4. it's
5. they've
6. isn't
7. let's
8. I'm

B
1. the boy's dog
2. the men's lorries
3. the ladies' scarves
4. the chimney's pot
5. the bears' cave
6. the tomato's skin

C
1. won't
2. can't
3. he's
4. you've
5. we're
6. I've
7. wouldn't
8. they're

D
1. the horse's hoof
2. the ship's captain
3. the magician's trick
4. the elephants' trunks
5. my aunt's flowers
6. the babies' mothers

Extension
- Children should work individually.

Answers
1. The **school's** football team won all the **matches** this term. — possessive noun/plural
2. **Nobody's** going anywhere until your **desks** are tidy. — contraction/plural
3. Many **people's** idea of a good time is visiting **theme parks**. — possessive noun/plural
4. The **explorer's** journeys took him to many **countries**. — possessive noun/plural
5. **It's** great to see that the **birds'** nests are safe. — contraction/possessive noun

Resource Book

Support PCM
- Children should work individually.

Answers

A
1. I <u>wouldn't</u> do that if I were you!
2. Are you sure <u>that's</u> right?
3. <u>What's</u> the matter?
4. <u>Where's</u> Harry gone?

B
1. I have found <u>Sam's</u> football boots.
2. The <u>postman's</u> van is on the lane.
3. The <u>children's</u> hands are freezing!
4. The <u>rabbits'</u> hutch needs cleaning out.

C
1. a the author's story
   b the author's stories.
2. a the chief's meeting
   b the chiefs' meeting
3. a the waltz's music
   b the waltzes' music

D
1. didn't
2. can't
3. she's
4. you'll
5. it's
6. mustn't

Extension PCM
- If necessary, model the first one so children understand what is required.

Answers
Individual answers

Extra
Write sentences on the board that contain a plural noun, a contraction and a possessive noun, e.g.
  Theyre Bens favourite books.
Individuals add the apostrophes.

BOOK 5: Sentences

Subject and predicate

The concept of a sentence as a unit of language that 'makes sense' can be a difficult concept for some children to grasp. The course builds children's confidence in this area through giving them the opportunity to look at punctuation of statements, questions and exclamations to familiarise themselves with what a 'sentence' looks and sounds like.

Throughout the course, children will encounter: sentence punctuation; the concept of 'making sense'; direct and indirect speech; clauses which combine to make multi-clause sentences; parts of sentences – subject/object, subject/predicate; focusing on the sentence as a unit of language that can be improved; and Standard English constructions.

This unit revises 'subject' and 'predicate' in sentences.

- The 'subject' is what the sentence is about and usually does the action expressed by the verb. The 'subject' can be a single noun, a noun phrase or pronoun – the latter being in the subject form.
- The predicate is the rest of the sentence and contains the verb.

The unit introduces the idea of adding to the subject and predicate to make writing more interesting.

Pupil Book

Focus
- Ask children what they understand by the term *sentence*.
- Revise/discuss the terms noun and pronoun.
- Revise/discuss the terms *subject* and *predicate*.
- Read the information box on page 34.
- Ask: *What words have been added to the subject to make it more interesting? What words have been added to the predicate to make it more interesting?*
- Do more oral examples. Write simple sentences on the board and ask children to
  – identify the subject and the predicate;
  – add to the subject and the predicate to make them more interesting.
- Do the activity orally.

Answers

	Subject	Predicate
1	The pillow	was on the bed.
2	I	like to go to the pictures.
3	The priest	wore a cloak.
4	This battery	is flat.
5	Rob	is cooking fish.

Practice
- Activities A and C: Children should work individually.
- Activities B and D: Some children may need support through discussion.

Answers
(A) 1 <u>The butterfly</u> sat on a leaf.
　　2 <u>Monkeys</u> live in the jungle.
　　3 <u>A package</u> was delivered.

(B) Individual answers

(C) 1 The flag <u>was hoisted up the pole</u>.
　　2 I <u>went to the shops</u>.
　　3 Ali <u>has a bicycle</u>.

(D) Individual answers

Extension
- Read the information box on page 35.
- This is a recap of the subject/object pronouns I and me within the context of subject and predicate.
- Children should work individually.

Answers
1 **I** saw a spider in the old, dark house.
2 Will you get **me** a drink?
3 Katy and **I** are going swimming.
4 The dog frightened Becky and **me**.

Resource Book

Support PCM
- Activities A and B: Children should work individually.
- Activity C: If necessary, recap on the use of adverbs. Ask: *How might Sam have walked/the plane landed?* etc.

Answers
(A) Individual answers
(B) Individual answers
(C) Individual answers

Extension PCM
- Read and discuss the first answer so children understand what is required.

Answers
Individual answers

Extra
- Make simple sentence cards, e.g.

| The car stopped. | Several people cheered. |

Children pick a card and:
　– identify the subject;
　– identify the predicate;
　– expand both subject and predicate to make a more interesting sentence.

BOOK 5 UNIT 16 Pronouns

Repetition and clarity

Pronouns are words that take the place of nouns and noun phrases.

Throughout the course, children will encounter personal pronouns (as subject and object); possessive pronouns; reflexive pronouns; and relative pronouns.

Demonstrative pronouns are introduced in the work on noun phrases.

Interrogative pronouns are not specifically labelled as such but children encounter them in work on relative pronouns. It is up to individual teachers if indefinite pronouns, e.g. each/many/few/some, are specifically labelled as such and taught as another group of pronouns.

Children have previously examined how the use of pronouns can cause ambiguity. This unit examines using pronouns to avoid repetition and how pronouns can make a sentence unclear if not used correctly in context.

Pupil Book

Focus
- Revise/discuss the terms *noun* and *proper noun* and ask for examples.
- Revise/discuss the term *pronoun* and ask for examples.
- Read the information box on page 36.
- Ask the children to identify the type of pronouns used in the second example.
- Do the Activity orally.

Answers

	nouns	proper nouns	pronouns
1	friend		I/my/me/her
2	shopkeeper	Mr Jones	he
3	ferry	Channel/Dover/Calais	
4	sunset		I/it
5	meteor shower		I

Practice
- Activity A: Model the first answer so children understand what is required.
- Activity B: Stress that there are no correct nouns. Children can decide the context themselves. Model the first answer with lots of variety so children understand what is required.

Answers

(A) 1 The robbers broke into the house **and they** stole the jewels.
2 I took my cat to the vet **because it** had been in a fight.
3 Alice caught the ball **and she** scored a goal.
4 We washed the baby's hands **before she** had her milk.
5 The leaves fell off the trees **and they** were bare.

(B) Individual answers, e.g.
1 Give the **ball** to the **boys**.
2 Can you wrap **the present** for me?
3 **Sam** needs **the puncture kit** to give to **his brother**.
4 Find the **sewing basket** and take it to **Mum**.
5 **The dog** took **the ball** and ran away with it in its mouth.

Extension
- Children should work individually

Answers

1 Bill went fishing so that **he** could catch a fish for **his** tea.
2 The girl went into the shop because **she** wanted to buy **herself** a new pen.
3 The scouts pitched **their** tents so **they** would be near the river.
4 Sally and I got up early so **we** could visit **her** aunt.
5 The tortoise raced the hare and **it** won because the hare went to sleep.

Resource Book

Support PCM
- Activity A: Model the first answer so children understand what is required.
- Activity B: Children should work individually.

Answers

(A) (Conjunctions will be individual choice)
1 The teacher put her books on the desk **before she** began to talk to the class.
2 My friends were off school **because they were** ill.
3 **The caretaker** switched off the lights **before he** swept the floor.
4 Dad and I weeded the garden **then we** planted the seeds.

(B) 1 If John comes in, tell **him** that **he** has to tidy **his** room.
2 In the evening, the blackbirds sit in **their** nest and sing **their** special song.
3 Sally put **her** homework in **her** bag before **she** left for school.

Extension PCM
- If necessary, model the first answer so children understand what is required.

Answers

Suggested answers

1 Kim took the duster and **she** dusted **her** room.
2 John took **his** hamster to school so **he** could show **it** to the class.
3 The squirrels dug up **their** nuts so they could eat **them**.
4 Meg and I made sandwiches **ourselves** and **we** had a picnic.
5 The dog hurt **its** paw and **it** howled because **it** was in pain.

Extra
- In pairs, children write sentences where no pronouns are used but nouns/proper nouns are repeated on paper.
Collect the sentences.

Individuals choose a sentence and write it on the board using pronouns to avoid repetition.

BOOK 5 UNIT 17 Sentences

Relative clauses

The concept of a sentence as a unit of language that 'makes sense' can be a difficult concept for some children to grasp. The course builds children's confidence in this area through giving them the opportunity to look at punctuation of statements, questions and exclamations to familiarise themselves with what a 'sentence' looks and sounds like.

Throughout the course, children will encounter: sentence punctuation; the concept of 'making sense'; direct and indirect speech; clauses which combine to make multi-clause sentences; parts of sentences – subject/object, subject/predicate; focusing on the sentence as a unit of language that can be improved; and Standard English constructions.

This unit introduces the concept of the relative clause introduced by a relative pronoun. For the purposes of this and other units dealing with relative pronouns and clauses, 'which' and 'that' are equally acceptable as the different uses are too complicated for primary school children.

As with adverbial clauses, relative clauses must contain a 'finite verb'. The best way of explaining a finite verb is one that makes a complete tense, so 'singing' is not finite but 'am singing' is. Both main and subordinate clauses need a finite verb.

Pupil Book

Focus
- Ask children what they understand by the term *sentence*.
- Revise/discuss the term relative pronoun and ask for examples.
- Revise/discuss the term clause and explain the difference between a phrase and a clause using the term finite verb.
- Read the information box on page 38.
- The activity can be done orally or children can write.

Answers
1. I delivered the (package) which my mother had given me.
2. Mark wrote to his (friend) who lives in Brazil.
3. This is the (badge) that I bought at the zoo.
4. I want to find the (boy) who owns this bicycle.
5. The lady thanked the young (girl) who had helped her across the road.

Practice
- Children should work individually.

Answers
1. They travelled by bus **which** took a long time.
2. I have thrown away the chair **which** had a broken arm.
3. Will you find someone **who** can take care of this dog?
4. There were several passengers **who** had lost their tickets.
5. Find the pencil **which** has a rubber on the end.

Extension
- Children can work individually but may need support.
- Discuss sentences in class.

Answers
(A) Individual answers
(B) Individual answers

Resource Book

Support PCM
- Activity A: Children should work individually.
- Activity B: Monitor the work in progress as children may need help in spotting where relative clauses could be added to what they write.

Answers
(A) Individual answers
(B) Individual answers

Extension PCM
- Read and discuss the information box on the PCM.
- Children can work in small groups.
- When complete, discuss answers.

Answers
1. We saw a man who was wearing a raincoat with a dog.
2. The robin that comes to the house for food lives in the tree.
3. The owl that has brown feathers hunted the mouse.
4. They have a house which is painted white near a stream.
5. We have a cabinet that is fifty years old for storing food.

Extra
This is a difficult concept for most children so plenty of practice is needed.
Ask children for simple sentences and write on the board.
Can they add a relative clause to expand the sentence?

BOOK 5 UNIT 18 Verbs

Auxiliary – to be/to have

Verbs are often explained as 'doing words' or 'being words'. They are possibly the most complex part of speech for young children to grasp because of their many forms and tenses.

Throughout the course, children will encounter the present simple, present progressive (also known as continuous), past simple, past progressive, present perfect (labelled simply *perfect* throughout the course), past perfect, future, infinitive (labelled *verb family name* in the early parts of the course), auxiliary verbs, modals, active and passive verbs and subjunctive verbs (a construction very rarely used except in extremely formal writing).

Participles are referred to as '*ing* words' and 'regular past simple tense words'; finite verbs are referred to as 'main' or 'proper verbs', and it is for the teacher to decide the appropriate time to introduce the terms *participle* and *finite verb*.

Children have encountered the verbs 'to be' and 'to have' earlier in the course and have used them in constructing verb tenses. This unit revises the construction of two-word verbs and introduces the term *auxiliary* verb in preparation for units on modals later in the course.

Pupil Book

Focus
- Revise/discuss the term *verb*.
- Ask children to name tenses where the verbs are made up of two words.
- Introduce and explain the term *auxiliary*.
- Read and discuss the information box on page 40.
- Do the activity orally.

Answers
1. The picture **was** hanging on the wall.
2. I **have** forgotten to do my homework!
3. The horse **is** galloping across the fields.
4. The shield **will** keep you safe.
5. I **am** making a cake for my brother's birthday.
6. The explorers **were** trekking through the mountains.
7. He **has** bought a new computer game.
8. We **shall** miss the bus!

Practice
- Discuss the use of shall and will before children write.

Answers
(A)
1. I **shall** write very neatly in my new exercise book.
2. You **will** need gloves because it is very cold.
3. He **will** find these sums difficult.
4. We **shall** pack our suitcases in the morning.

(B)
1. They **have** won the relay race.
2. She **has** painted a beautiful picture.
3. I **have** lost my dinner money!
4. Ben and Tim **have** built a snowman.

(C)
1. The car **was** stuck in the mud.
2. It **was** snowing in the night.
3. They **were** collecting eggs from the hens.
4. Kim and I **were** going to a friend's after school.

Extension
- Ensure children understand meanings.
- When complete, discuss answers.

Answers
Individual answers

Resource Book

Support PCM
- Activities B and C: If appropriate, help children to locate the two-word verb in each sentence before they write.

Answers
(A)
1. Cowslips **are** growing in the meadow.
2. I **am** spreading butter on my bread before I put on the jam.
3. She **is** going abroad for her holidays.

(B)
1. I **was** thinking about what I **was** going to do.
2. We **were** walking to the town and then we **were** going to catch the bus.

(C)
1. I **shall meet** a friend after lunch.
2. We **shall hope** for sunny weather.

Extension PCM
- Children should work individually.
- Encourage them to choose a different auxiliary each time.

Answers
Individual answers

Extra
Make auxiliary verb cards, e.g.

| shall | have | is | were |

Children choose a card and construct a sentence using the word on the card as an auxiliary.

BOOK 5 UNIT 19 Punctuation

Comma round-up

The comma is the commonest punctuation mark which does a variety of jobs. So far in the course, children have encountered the comma for:

– separating items in a list in sentences;

– use in direct speech;

– separating phrases and clauses from the main clause in sentences.

This unit gives children the opportunity to revise these uses of the comma before looking at commas to avoid ambiguity, and commas used in the same way as dashes and brackets later in the course.

Pupil Book

Focus

- Revise/discuss the term comma and ask for examples of its use.
- Read and discuss the information box on page 42.
- Look at each example carefully, asking children to provide other examples for each of the uses.
- Do the activity orally.

Answers

1. list
2. direct speech
3. adverbial phrase
4. adverbial clause
5. list
6. split direct speech

Practice

- Children should work individually on the activities.

Answers

1. "Will you go up into the loft," asked Mum, 'and bring down the cases?"
2. The box contained old books, a board game, a broken mobile phone and some comics.
3. Because I am very tired, I won't be staying late.
4. Early in the morning, the birds began their dawn chorus.
5. We saw sheep grazing, cows being milked, horses galloping and chickens scratching in the dirt.

Extension

Children should work individually but some may need support in constructing sentences.

Answers

(A) Individual answers
(B) Individual answers
(C) Individual answers

Resource Book

Support PCM

- Children should work individually so you can assess areas that are still problematic for some children.

Answers

(A)
1. The day was grey, misty and very cold.
2. We are doing a project on frogs, toads and tadpoles.
3. He walked into the building, queued at the desk, asked to see the manager and sat down to wait.

(B)
1. "I think the library is round the corner, " said the helpful passer-by.
2. Adam said, "I've been picked for the team!"
3. 'We'll go to the post office tomorrow," said Dad, "and collect the parcel."

(C)
1. By evening, all the animals fell silent.
2. Seeing the danger, she leapt over the fence.
3. Inside the old mill, a mysterious light had been seen.

(D)
1. So you will not be late, I'll lend you my watch.
2. If you feed the guinea pigs now, you won't have to go out in the dark.
3. Because the roof was leaking, we had to put buckets under the drips.

Extension PCM

- Discussion/preparation for the activity can be done in pairs or groups.
- Children should write individually.

Answers

Individual answers

Extra

- Write sentences on the board that need at least two different uses of the comma, e.g.
  Later that day Tom packed shorts football top socks and boots so he would be ready for the match.

Individuals add the commas.

BOOK 5 UNIT 20 Paragraphs

Using adverbs and adverbial phrases in descriptive paragraphs

A paragraph is a group of sentences within a piece of writing. It is usually signalled by:
- indenting in handwritten work and fiction (all paragraphs but the first)
- leaving a full line space (block paragraphing) in typing and non-fiction work.

The mechanics of paragraphing can be taught as a concept, but the 'reasons' for paragraphing are many and varied, and must be attached to a particular style of writing.

Throughout the course, children will encounter: paragraphing in narrative writing – time, place and for the inclusion of direct speech; paragraphing for aspects of a topic in non-fiction information writing; and paragraphing to present for and against arguments in discursive writing.

This unit deals with adverbials as a reason for paragraphing in the context of descriptive writing.

Pupil Book

Focus
- Revise/discuss the term *paragraph*.
- Revise/discuss the term *indenting* and not indenting for the first paragraph.
- Ask children what they have learned about paragraphing in stories and information writing
- Use the descriptive passage in the information box on page 44 to show children what a paragraph looks like on the page.
- Explain that this could be a non-fiction personal recount, or it could be part of a story.
- Read and discuss the information box on page 44 and work through the Focus questions with the children.
- When complete, look at the opening phrase of each paragraph and discuss the job each is doing in the passage. Children explain why the passage is paragraphed at these points.

Answers
1. upstairs
2. Beneath the window
3. Piled near the wall
4. Beyond the garden
5. above it
6. To the right
7. To the left
8. In the distance

Practice
- Children can work individually with your support.

Answers
Individual answers

Extension
- Children can work individually with your support.

Answers
Individual answers

Resource Book

Support PCM
- Activity A: Children should work individually.
- Activity B: Some initial discussion may be necessary to stimulate ideas.

Answers
(A) We needed to move because our house was too small so we went to see three houses <u>at the weekend</u>. The first house was <u>at the end of a long, narrow lane</u>. <u>At the front of the house</u> was a small garden, planted with flowers and shrubs. <u>Beyond the hedge</u>, we could see a pond. <u>Nearby,</u> there were farm buildings. <u>Downstairs</u>, the windows were large but <u>upstairs,</u> they were tiny. <u>On the roof</u> was a weather vane which creaked and groaned as the wind spun it <u>around</u>.

(B) Individual answers

Extension PCM
- Children should work individually but monitor work in progress, helping them to spot opportunities to use adverbials.

Answers
Individual answers

Extra
Individuals volunteer a sentence with adverbials to describe one aspect of the classroom.
Write the sentences on the board as they are suggested to build up a description of the classroom with adverbials.

BOOK 5 UNIT 21 Verbs

Prefixes

Verbs are often explained as 'doing words' or 'being words'. They are possibly the most complex part of speech for young children to grasp because of their many forms and tenses.

Throughout the course, children will encounter the present simple, present progressive (also known as continuous), past simple, past progressive, present perfect (labelled simply *perfect* throughout the course), past perfect, future, infinitive (labelled *verb family name* in the early parts of the course), auxiliary verbs, modals, active and passive verbs and subjunctive verbs (a construction very rarely used except in extremely formal writing).

Participles are referred to as '*ing* words' and 'regular past simple tense words'; finite verbs are referred to as 'main' or 'proper verbs', and it is for the teacher to decide the appropriate time to introduce the terms *participle* and *finite verb*.

A prefix is a group of letters added to the beginning of a word to adjust or qualify its meaning which does not alter the spelling of the word it is being added to.

So far in the course, children have encountered the prefix *un* to make opposite adjectives and verbs, and prefixes with special meanings.

This unit examines prefixes that change the meanings of verbs.

Pupil Book

Focus

- Revise/discuss the term *prefix*.
- Read and discuss the information box on page 46, ensuring children understand the meaning of the verbs before the prefix is added.
- For each section, can children think of other verbs beginning with that prefix?
- Children should work individually.

Answers

1 **dis**believe   2 **mis**judged   3 **over**come
4 **re**start   5 **co**-write   6 **out**live
7 **under**charge   8 **dis**like   9 **mis**place
10 **over**rate   11 **re**unite   12 **out**strip

Practice

- Children should work individually.

Answers

1 **dis**obey
2 **out**line
3 **under**charge
4 **over**take
5 **mis**inform
6 **re**start

Extension

- Read and discuss the information box on page 47.
- Children can work on the activities in pairs. When complete, discuss answers.

Answers

(A) 1 re**appear**/**dis**appear
2 **re**place/**mis**place
3 **over**rate/**under**rate
4 **over**pay/**under**pay
5 **re**cover/**dis**cover
6 **out**do/**re**do
Sentences = individual answers

(B) 1 to cooperate — work with others to achieve something
2 co-author — write a novel, play, etc. with one or more other writers
3 co-host — hold a party, event, etc. with one or more other people
4 co-pilot — to fly a plane, sail a ship, etc. with one other qualified person
5 co-ordinate — organise an activity with one or more other people
6 co-exist — to live in the same place as others (people/plants / animals, etc.)

Sentences = individual answers

Resource Book

Support PCM

- Activity A: Children can work in pairs.
- Activities B and C: Children should work individually.

Answers

(A) 1 If you judge people wrongly, you **misjudge** them.
2 If you go out of sight, you **disappear**.
3 If you work too much, you **overwork**.
4 If you put more power in a battery, you **recharge** it.
5 If you live longer than others, you **outlive** them.
6 If you are not paid enough, you are **underpaid**.

(B) 1 You have **misbehaved** today.
2 I have **misplaced** my book.
3 I **dislike** shepherd's pie!
4 We will have to **restart** the race.

(C) Individual answers

Extension PCM

- Children should work individually.

Answers

Individual answers

Extra

- Make prefix cards, e.g.

| mis | re | over | under |

Children choose a prefix card and say an appropriate verb.

BOOK 5 UNIT 22 Confusing words

Confusing words
Throughout the course, children have encountered homophones and common mistakes in verb choice.

This unit continues the work on words that children often find confusing.

Pupil Book

Focus
- Read and discuss the information box on page 48.
- For each section, read the examples and ask for further examples.
- Do the activity orally.

Answers
1. I could **have** cried when I heard what happened.
2. I **beat** you in that match.
3. The house had a leaky roof and **its** windows were broken.
4. If I **practise**, I will get better.
5. I came first and **won** the prize.
6. The netball **practice** went well.
7. **It's** difficult to know what to do.

Practice
- Children should work individually on the activities.

Answers
(A) 1. I **have** heard of your accident.
2. Of course, I should **have** said something.
3. If I had been at school, I could **have** helped you but I **have** been ill.

(B) 1. If I **win** the race, I win the cup.
2. I can **beat** you any day.
3. He **beat** his friend by five metres.

(C) 1. **It's** no good, **its** tyre is flat!
2. **It's** a long walk to the garage.
3. **It's** probably shut at this time of night!

Extension
- Read and discuss the first answer so children understand what is required.

Answers
Individual answers

Resource Book

Support PCM
- Children should work individually.

Answers
(A) 1. The dog is shedding **its** coat.
2. I think **it's** nearly time for tea.
3. **It's** possible that the taxi has lost **its** way.

(B) 1. I will **beat** you if I train hard.
2. He really wanted to **win** the competition.
3. To **win**, I have to **beat** a lot of good swimmers.

(C) 1. The cost **of** petrol is going up every week!
2. I could **have** tried harder.
3. If I **have** the time, the list **of** jobs will be done.

(D) 1. **Practice** makes perfect.
2. I have to **practise** for half an hour each day.
3. If you **practise** regularly, your **practice** session will become easier.

Extension PCM
- The Extension activity introduces more words which children often confuse.

Answers
Individual answers

Extra
Make cards of the confusing words covered in the unit, e.g.

| win | practice | between | advise |

Individuals pick a card and use the word in a sentence.

101

BOOK 5 — Adverbs

Words and phrases for sequence

Adverbs are usually explained as words which 'add' to a verb giving the detail of how, where or when an action is done.

Throughout the course, children will encounter single adverbs (manner/time/place), comparative and superlative adverbs, adverbial phrases, adverb pairs and adverbial clauses.

Children have encountered the concepts of main and subordinate clauses earlier in the course. A main clause is a sentence in itself whereas a subordinate clause (beginning with a conjunction) is of less importance. Both main clauses and subordinate clauses contain a finite verb, i.e. a verb that makes a tense.

This unit revises single adverbs and adverb phrases in the context of sequencing in writing.

Pupil Book

Focus
- Revise/discuss the term *adverb* and ask for examples of *how, when* and *where* adverbs.
- What do children understand by the term *adverb phrase*?
- Read and discuss the information box on page 50.
- Do children think the first passage or the second passage is better? Why?
- Do the activity orally. When children have identified the adverbs/adverb phrases, ask if each is an adverb phrase of manner, time or place.

Answers
1. I fed the rabbit **before** I went to school.
2. **Secondly**, you need to chop the carrots.
3. **Meanwhile**, the paint was drying.
4. I will go the supermarket **first** and the pet shop **last**.
5. **Next**, the soil needs digging.
6. **After that**, I walked home.
7. **In the end**, it was just as I expected.
8. **Until then**, I hadn't experienced a theme park.
9. **Just then**, we heard a terrible scream.
10. **Eventually**, it was time to go.

Practice
- Tell children to read the adverbs in the box and all of the incomplete sentences before they write.

Answers
1. **After** we had finished supper, we washed up.
2. You must wash your hands **before** you touch food.
3. I put the washing in the machine. **Next**, I put in the powder.
4. After many tries, she **finally** got the lid off the jar!
5. **Firstly**, I have to say that I am surprised at you.

Extension
- Read and discuss the first answer so children understand what is required.

Answers
Individual answers

Resource Book

Support PCM
- Activity A: Explain that the sequence adverb could be a single word or an adverb phrase.
- Activity B: Explain that children can divide the long sentence into shorter sentences which must include adverbs of sequence.
- Activity C: This can be done as a class or group discussion in preparation for Activity D, which should be done individually.

Answers
(A)
1. <u>Finally</u>, the match was over and we had won!
2. The potatoes were boiling. <u>Meanwhile</u>, I set the table.
3. <u>Thirdly</u>, check through your work for spelling mistakes.
4. We visited Gran <u>later</u> in the day.
5. I was so pleased when we <u>eventually</u> arrived.

(B) Suggested answers
Firstly, he went across the field **before** he jumped over the gate. **After that**, he picked the mushrooms and **finally** he went home.

(C) Individual answers

(D) Individual answers

Extension PCM
- Discuss the term recount. Explain that they are going to recount (describe) what they did to make the nut cookies.
- What tenses do children think they will use?
- Children can work in pairs or individually.

Answers
Individual answers

Extra
Make sequence adverb cards, e.g.

| next | later | after that | finally |

Children pick a card and use the sequence adverb in a sentence.

BOOK 5 UNIT 24 Verbs

Auxiliary – modals

Verbs are often explained as 'doing words' or 'being words'. They are possibly the most complex part of speech for young children to grasp because of their many forms and tenses.

Throughout the course, children will encounter the present simple, present progressive (also known as continuous), past simple, past progressive, present perfect (labelled simply *perfect* throughout the course), past perfect, future, infinitive (labelled *verb family name* in the early parts of the course), auxiliary verbs, modals, active and passive verbs and subjunctive verbs (a construction very rarely used except in extremely formal writing).

Participles are referred to as '*ing* words' and 'regular past simple tense words'; finite verbs are referred to as 'main' or 'proper verbs', and it is for the teacher to decide the appropriate time to introduce the terms *participle* and *finite verb*.

Children have encountered the verbs 'to be' and 'to have' earlier in the course and have used them in constructing verb tenses. They have encountered the term *auxiliary verb* used to indicate tense. This unit introduces modals – another form of auxiliary verb – used to differentiate shades of meaning, e.g.

- can   –   ability
- may   –   possibility/permission
- must   –   obligation/strong belief
- might   –   possibility
- should   –   possibility/advice
- could   –   possibility
- would   –   request/offer/conditional

Pupil Book

Focus

- Revise/discuss the term *verb*.
- Ask children to name tenses where the verbs are made up of two words.
- Revise/introduce and explain the term *auxiliary*.
- Introduce the term *modal verb*.
- Read and discuss the information box on page 52.
- Discuss the shades of meaning.
- Do the activity orally.

Answers

1. We **would** like to discuss the problem.
2. I **must** leave at six o'clock.
3. I **could** find the station on the map.
4. I **can** jump over the fence.
5. We **may** buy some sweets.
6. I **should** get ready for school.
7. There **might** be some biscuits in the tin.
8. There **might** be snow this winter.

Practice

- Discuss the use of each pair of verbs before children write.

Answers

(A)
1. This book is quite difficult but I am sure you **can** read it.
2. You **may** go out to play when you have changed your clothes.
3. He **can** get to the top of that tree without a ladder.
4. You **may** not cross the road by yourself.

(B)
1. I **must** get some sleep because I need to be up early tomorrow.
2. He **might** finish his book if he reads quickly.
3. She **might** have toast or porridge for breakfast.
4. We **must** feed the cat before we go to school.

(C)
1. I **could** write that letter in five minutes!
2. I **should** write the letter because he is waiting for a reply.
3. I **would** write that letter if my pen hadn't run out of ink.

Extension

- Children should work individually.

Answers

Individual answers

Resource Book

Support PCM

- Children should work individually.

Answers

(A)
1. A
2. P
3. P
4. A
5. P

(B) Individual answers

Extension PCM

- Initial discussion may be necessary to help children differentiate between things they must/can/might do, etc.

Answers

Individual answers

Extra

Make modal verb cards, e.g.

| can | might | could | should |

Children choose a card and construct a sentence using the word on the card as an auxiliary.

BOOK 5 UNIT 25 Sentences

Main clause/adverb clause/relative clause

The concept of a sentence as a unit of language that 'makes sense' can be a difficult concept for some children to grasp. The course builds children's confidence in this area through giving them the opportunity to look at punctuation of statements, questions and exclamations to familiarise themselves with what a 'sentence' looks and sounds like.

Throughout the course, children will encounter: sentence punctuation; the concept of 'making sense'; direct and indirect speech; clauses which combine to make multi-clause sentences; parts of sentences – subject/object, subject/predicate; focusing on the sentence as a unit of language that can be improved; and Standard English constructions.

This unit revises:

- main clauses – sentences in themselves;
- adverbial clauses – introduced by a conjunction;
- relative clauses – introduced by a relative pronoun. In British English, the use of the relative pronoun 'which' and the relative pronoun 'that' is, in many cases, equally correct. For the purposes of this and other units dealing with relative pronouns and clauses, 'which' and 'that' are equally acceptable as the different uses are too complicated for primary school children.

All clauses contain a finite verb. The best way of explaining a finite verb is one that makes a complete tense, so 'singing' is not finite but 'am singing' is.

Resource Book

Support PCM
- Read and discuss the first answer so children understand what is required.
- When complete, discuss sentences.

Answers
Individual answers

Extension PCM
- If necessary, have an initial discussion about the scenario.
- Monitor the children's work so that you can point out opportunities for adding clauses to the children's work.

Answers
Individual answers

Extra
This is a difficult concept for most children so plenty of practice is needed.
Ask children for simple sentences and write on the board. Can they add a relative clause and/or an adverb clause to expand the sentence?

Pupil Book

Focus
- Revise/discuss the terms *main clause/conjunction/adverb clause/relative pronoun/relative clause/finite verb*.
- Read and discuss the information box on page 54.
- The activity can be done orally, or children can write.

Answers
1. <u>I want to see the man</u> who won the race.
2. <u>The man won the race</u> because he ran so quickly.
3. <u>You must have something to eat</u> before you go out.
4. <u>The winners were presented with the cup</u> after the match had ended.
5. <u>I will write neatly</u> when I get a new pen.
6. <u>This is the ball</u> that broke the window.

Practice
- *Children should work individually.*

Answers
1. <u>Although it is a warm day</u>, you must take your coats.
2. I have to wash the football shirts <u>that are muddy</u>.
3. The trip was cancelled <u>because it had rained all night</u>.
4. We will invite the twins <u>who live on the farm</u>.
5. Look at that duck <u>whose beak is black</u>!
6. He was nervous about the test <u>even though he had worked hard</u>.

Extension
- *Children should work individually.*

Answers
Individual answers

BOOK 5 UNIT 26 Punctuation

Commas to avoid ambiguity

The comma is the commonest punctuation mark which does a variety of jobs. So far in the course, children have encountered the comma for:

– separating items in a list in sentences;
– use in direct speech;
– separating phrases and clauses from the main clause in sentences.

This unit examines how omitting commas can alter the meaning of a sentence so that it becomes ambiguous in the mind of the reader.

Pupil Book

Focus
- Revise/discuss the term *comma* and ask for examples of its use.
- Read and discuss the information box on page 56.
- Look at each example carefully, asking children what the difference in meaning is when a comma is used/not used.
- Do the activity orally.

Answers
1. a The writer is telling Tony that his/her brother is happy.
   b The writer's brother is called Tony and is happy.
2. a The writer is thankful that they applauded.
   b The audience is thankful and applauds because it was good/awful and they are glad it is over.
3. a It was strange that the dog would bark in the circumstances.
   b The sound the dog made when it barked was strange.
4. a Amy thought Pat was acting oddly.
   b Pat was of the opinion that Amy was acting oddly.
5. a asking permission from Dad to do some painting.
   b Writer asking permission from someone else to actually paint Dad.

Practice
- Children can work in pairs.
- When complete, discuss answers.

Answers
1. All the children sang, happily.
2. Sophie, the dog is eating my shoe!
3. Don't, stop!
4. Harry, imagined George, was cheating.
5. May we shower, Gran?

Extension
- Children can work in pairs.
- When complete, discuss answers.

Answers
1. a The writer has eaten pizza before but not in a restaurant.
   b The writer has never eaten pizza before.
2. a The man was carrying a walking stick but didn't necessarily use it to point the way.
   b The man used the walking stick to point the way.
3. a People who travel are usually on edge.
   b People who travel through time are usually on edge.
4. a The people provide two things: quality service and attention to detail.
   b The people provide three things; quality, service and attention to detail.
5. a Children walking very slowly are crossing.
   b Drivers are told to slow down because children are crossing.
6. a The writer cooks her animals.
   b The writer loves to cook and loves her horse and her dog.

Resource Book

Support PCM
- Children should work individually.

Answers
(A) 1 She likes Amy, who plays netball, better than Tina.
    2 Sam, suspected his friend, was unwell.
    3 Stop, deer crossing.
    4 I have just had my first flight, on a plane.
    5 May I finish, Mum?

(B) 1 Bob likes chocolate, cake and crisps.
    2 Mum collects silver, paper and stamps for charity.
    3 We saw the mountain, lake and forest.
    4 She put the coffee, cups and sugar on the table.
    5 I got the water, jug and glasses ready.

(C) Individual answers

Extension PCM
- Children should work individually.

Answers
1. a This indicates the lighthouse building, the man who keeps the lighthouse and his dog were very old.
   b This indicates that just the man who keeps the lighthouse and his dog were very old.
2. a This indicates that the whole village, the village green and the park were flooded.
   b This indicates that just the village green and the park were flooded.
3. a This indicates that the artist paints some flowers and then departs.
   b This indicates that the artist paints both flowers and leaves.
4. a This indicates that a glove has been left on the bus.
   b This indicates that a left glove has been found on the bus.

Extra
- Introduce and discuss the example 'Eats shoots and leaves.'

Can the children come up with similar ambiguous statements, using this as a model?

BOOK 5 UNIT 27 Punctuation

Commas, brackets and dashes for parenthesis

The comma is the commonest punctuation mark which does a variety of jobs. So far in the course, children have encountered the comma for:

- separating items in a list in sentences;
- use in direct speech;
- separating phrases and clauses from the main clause in sentences;
- avoiding ambiguity of meaning.

This unit examines the comma, along with dashes and brackets for parenthesis. Which of the three options to use depends on the circumstance. It is sufficient here that children appreciate the concept of 'extra information' and use one of the three choices.

Pupil Book

Focus

- Revise/discuss the term *comma* and ask for examples of its use.
- Introduce the terms *dashes* and *brackets*.
- Read and discuss the information box on page 58.
- Look at each example carefully, asking children where the extra information is in each case.
- Do the activity orally.

Answers

1. none of whom I knew
2. shown on page 25
3. minus some of their star players
4. which took place in 1969
5. now open to the public

Practice

- Children can work in pairs.
- When complete, discuss answers.

Answers

NB Any of the three punctuation marks can be used in any sentence.

1. Aruba, an island in the Caribbean Sea, is a popular holiday destination.
2. All of the family – except Aunt Susan – came for my birthday.
3. The old bridge (built in the 19th century) badly needed repair.
4. *The Chronicles of Narnia*, written by C. S. Lewis, is a wonderful collection of novels.
5. Fill in the form – use block capitals and black ink – and return it in the prepaid envelope.

Extension

- Read/discuss the first answer so children understand what is required.

Answers

NB Any of the three punctuation marks can be used in any sentence.

1. Lake Garda, situated in the north of Italy, is a beautiful place to visit.
2. King penguins – found in Antarctica – are amazing creatures.
3. Richard 1st (known as The Lionheart) lived in the 12th century.
4. The Great Fire of London – generally believed to have started in Pudding Lane –took place in 1666.
5. The *Lord of the Rings*, written by J. R. R. Tolkien, is about the fight between good and evil.

Resource Book

Support PCM

- Children should work individually.

Answers

(A) 1. The pupils, <u>all aged between ten and eleven</u>, enjoyed their visit to the castle.
2. Giant pandas – <u>native to China</u> – are an endangered species.
3. Five-a-day (<u>fruit and vegetables</u>) should be included in a healthy diet.
4. The local choir (<u>winner of many competitions</u>) is performing in the Town Hall tonight.
5. The doctor, <u>who has lived in the village for many years</u>, is retiring In March.

(B) NB Any of the three punctuation marks can be used in any sentence.
1. My dog Goldie, a labrador, has had five puppies.
2. Loch Ness – home of the legendary monster – is well worth a visit.
3. The cottage, old and desolate, stood on the edge of the desert.
4. He sorted the photographs (all of them of his family) and put them in the album.

Extension PCM

- Children should work individually.

Answers

NB Any of the three punctuation marks can be used in any sentence.

(A) 1. The carpet, stained with coffee, was ruined.
2. My sister – three years younger than me – starts school in September.
3. The lawn, covered in leaves, needed mowing.
4. The nurse (newly qualified) listened carefully to the doctor.

(B) Suggested answers
1. The rowing boat, drifting in the water, was sinking quickly.
2. A cricket team – made up of eleven players – has batsmen, bowlers and a wicketkeeper.
3. The robin (seen in the garden in winter) is often quite tame.

Extra

- Write simple sentences on the board.
- Discuss what extra information can be added.
- Individuals rewrite the sentence, adding the extra information with the relevant punctuation.

BOOK 5 UNIT 28 Sentences

Improving writing

The concept of a sentence as a unit of language that 'makes sense' can be a difficult concept for some children to grasp. The course builds children's confidence in this area through giving them the opportunity to look at punctuation of statements, questions and exclamations to familiarise themselves with what a 'sentence' looks and sounds like.

Throughout the course, children will encounter: sentence punctuation; the concept of 'making sense'; direct and indirect speech; clauses which combine to make multi-clause sentences; parts of sentences – subject/object, subject/predicate; focusing on the sentence as a unit of language that can be improved; and Standard English constructions.

This unit builds on work that children have done with synonyms, adverbs and adjectives with the emphasis on improving writing.

Pupil Book

Focus
- Revise/discuss the terms *synonym, adjective, adjective phrases, relative (adjective) clause, adverb, adverb phrase* and *adverb clause*.
- Read and discuss the information box on page 60.
- Children should work individually on the activity with your support.

Answers
Suggested answers
1. Our **beautiful** hedge has grown **enormously** this spring.
2. "I've got **a mountain** of work to do!" **groaned** Harry.
3. I **enjoy freezing** weather because I've **bought** a really warm coat.
4. "This book is **really interesting**," **enthused** Nancy.

Practice
- Children can work individually or in pairs.
- When complete, discuss answers.

Answers
Suggested answers
1. The **oak** trees are growing **in the meadow**.
2. The **excited** children played football **noisily in the muddy field**.
3. **Last Saturday**, the **champion** jockey won the **last** race **in a close finish**.
4. Can you see the **colourful** butterfly **that has landed on that orange flower**?
5. I walked **wearily** into the **gloomy** valley **at the end of my journey**.

Extension
- Children should work individually. Monitor the work in progress to assist with opportunities for synonyms and detail.

Answers
Individual answers

Resource Book

Support PCM
- Children can work individually or in pairs.

Answers
Ⓐ Individual answers
Ⓑ Individual answers

Extension PCM
- Children should work individually.

Answers
Individual answers

Extra
- Choose a piece of continuous prose that each child has completed in another area of their English work. This can be different for each child.
- Ask children to read it again and see where it could be improved.

Book 5 Check-up answers

Check-up 1 (Units 1–6)

Singular and plural
(A) 1 volcanoes 2 children
3 teeth 4 flashes
5 deer 6 cacti
(B) 1 cod 2 fungi
3 geese
Sentences = individual answers

Pronouns and adjectives
(A) 1 adjective 2 adjective
3 adjective 4 pronoun
5 pronoun
(B) Individual answer
(C) Individual answer

Verbs
(A) 1 Our newspaper <u>was delivered</u> late today.
2 The gardener <u>had cut</u> the hedges before the birds <u>built</u> their nests.
3 I <u>completed</u> the quiz in ten minutes.
4 He <u>has found</u> what he <u>was looking</u> for.

Sentences
(A) 1 "Copy the sums from the board," said the teacher, "and do them without a calculator."
2 "The birds nest here in the summer," said the farmer. "They go south for the winter."
3 "I'm not sure where it is," explained his friend, "although I have been there before."
(B) Individual answer
(C) Individual answer

Adverbs
Individual answer

Nouns
(A) 1 The travellers' hostel was very comfortable. P
2 My children's school is closed because of the weather. P
3 One twin's hair is blonde. S
4 The man's dog is missing. S
5 Lorries' tyres are huge. P
(B) 1 a the donkey's pack
   b the donkeys' packs
2 a the ruby's shine
   b the rubies' shine
3 a the calf's mother
   b the calves' mother

Check-up 2 (Units 7–12)

Sentences
(A) Rewrite these sentences as *indirect speech*.
1 The teacher explained that the exercise was very simple.
2 Sarah insisted that she had to leave by four o'clock.
3 Mum said I should go to the door and see who was there.

(B) Rewrite these sentences as *direct speech*.
1 "I have lost one of my oars," the rower moaned.
2 "I will show you how to make gingerbread men," said Mum.
3 "I have a package for you," said the postman.
(C) Individual answers

Homophones
1 knight 2 allowed
3 flower 4 might
5 course 6 grater
7 chord 8 alter

Verbs

add suffix *en*	add suffix *ate*
straighten	medicate
brighten	captivate
frighten	assassinate
sharpen	domesticate

add suffix *ify*	add suffix *ise*
purify	hypnotise
simplify	equalise
beautify	computerise
horrify	apologise

Adjectives
Individual answers

Pronouns
(A) 1 Fred watched a programme **which/that** was about whales.
2 I have an uncle **who** is a policeman.
3 Have you seen the kittens **which/that** were born on the farm?
(B) 1 This is the child **whose** arm is bleeding.
2 Is there anyone from **whom** I can borrow a pen?
3 Can you tell me **whose** is this jacket?

Check-up 3 (Units 13–18)

Homonyms
Individual answers

Punctuation
1 cann't ___ OR can't ✔
2 ladies' hats ✔ OR ladie's hats ___
3 would'nt ___ OR wouldn't ✔
4 Sams' bike ___ OR Sam's bike ✔
5 childrens' toys ___ OR children's toys ✔

Sentences
(A) Individual answers
(B) 1 I needed a new bag **which/that** I could take to school.
2 We have two mice **which/that** are white.
3 I visited a friend **who** lives by the sea.

Pronouns
(A) 1 My pen is leaking **because** it is broken.
2 The postman whistled **as he** delivered the letters.

3 I know that tree is an oak **because** it has acorns.

(B) e.g.
1 **Tim** put **the model** on the table and began to take it apart.
2 **The children** saw **the bus** and ran after it but they could not catch it.
3 My brother carefully mended **his football shirt** and hung it in his wardrobe

Verbs

(A) 1 I <u>am</u> drawing a flower and a tree.
2 The lions <u>have</u> drunk at the water hole.
3 We <u>shall</u> go to the park tomorrow.

(B) 1 I **was** writing a letter.
2 We **were** visiting our cousins.
3 You **were** running very quickly.

Check-up 4 (Units 19–24)

Punctuation
1 "This is a really interesting book," said Ben.
2 I have completed Level 1, Level 2, Level 3 and I've almost finished Level 4.
3 After the storm, we were without electricity for ten days!
4 The tents were pitched, the campfire lit, the burgers cooking and everyone looking forward to the evening meal.
5 "In a week," said Mum, "we will have new neighbours."

Paragraphs
Individual answers

Confusing words
1 The cat got **its** whiskers trapped.
2 I will never **win** that race.
3 My **practice** went very well.
4 I might **have** guessed!

Verbs
(A) 1 The children **may** have a dog if they look after it.
2 I **can** meet you at one o'clock.
3 You **can** write more neatly than that.

(B) 1 I **must** hurry or I will be late.
2 She **might** be lucky and win first prize!
3 The cat **must** see the vet.

(C) Individual answers

(D)

dis + verb	*mis* + verb
disobey	misbehave
disapprove	mistreat
dislike	misjudge
discontinue	misunderstand
***re* + verb**	***over* + verb**
reproduce	overdo
restart	overrule
reassemble	oversee
react	overhear

Adverbs
Individual answers

Check-up 5 (Units 25–28)

(Unit 26)

Punctuation
(A) NB Any of the three punctuation marks can be used in any sentence.
1 The goal, an amazing strike by the captain, won the match.
2 I'll need a suitcase (a big one) to take on holiday.
3 The house – flooded by water – will take months to repair.

(B) Individual answers

(C) 1 Slow, tortoise crossing.
2 Andy, thought Tina, was very good at football.
3 Polly, the parrot escaped from its cage.
4 The people left, thankfully.

Sentences
(A) Individual answers
(B) Individual answers
(C) Individual answers

109

Book 6 Scope and Sequence

Unit	Pupil Book	Pupil Book Focus	Pupil Book Practice	Pupil Book Extension	Resource Book Support	Resource Book Extension
1	**sentences**: subject and object	identifying the subject and object in given sentences	completing sentences with interesting objects	adding adjectives to subjects and objects to make interesting sentences/constructing sentences from given subject–object pairs	identifying subjects and objects in sentences/completing chart/writing sentences with given subjects	making given nouns the subject, then the object of own sentences
2	**sentences**: subject and predicate	identifying subjects and predicates in sentences	matching subjects and predicates to form sentences	writing interesting subjects to complete sentences/writing interesting predicates to complete sentences	identifying subject and predicate in sentences/completing sentences with interesting predicates	using given nouns as both subject and predicate in pairs of sentences
3	homophones and homonyms	completing sentences with correct homophone/identifying parts of speech – homonyms	solving clues with correct homophone – homonym/sentence writing	using unusual homophones in sentences	choosing the correct homophone/identifying parts of speech – homonyms/sentence writing	writing homophones for given words/using pairs of homonyms in sentences
4	**pronouns**: relative	completing sentence with relative pronouns	joining pairs of sentences with relative pronouns	completing sentences with *whose* and *whom*	joining pairs of sentences with relative pronouns/completing sentences with *whose* and *whom*	writing sentences with relative pronouns about given subjects
5	**verbs**: modals	identifying modal verbs in sentences	completing sentences with *may – can*; *might – must*; *could – would – should*	writing sentences with given modal verbs	using *could – would – should* in own writing/writing sentences with given modal verbs	using modal verbs in given scenarios
6	**sentences**: relative clauses	identifying relative clause and associated noun in sentences	completing sentences with *who* or *which*	adding relative clauses to main clauses/adding main clauses to relative clauses	completing sentences with relative clauses/writing description using relative clauses	positioning relative clauses to make sense
7	**verbs**: round-up	putting given verbs into a variety of tenses	changing sentences into a variety of other tenses	writing sentences with past simple and past perfect tenses	changing sentences into given tenses	writing sentences with given tenses about given subjects
8	**sentences**: single- and multi-clause	identifying main clauses and conjunctions in sentences	joining pairs of sentences with co-ordinating conjunctions	adding conjunctions and main clauses to given main clauses	identifying main clauses and conjunctions in sentences/joining pairs of sentences to make multi-clause sentences	writing single-clause sentences with given phrases/turning single-clause sentences into multi-clause sentences
9	confusing words	correcting mistakes in sentences using *all together – altogether*; *lie – lay*; *past – passed*	completing sentences with *all together – altogether*; *lie – lay*; *past – passed*	completing sentences with verb *to lie*	completing sentences with *all together – altogether*; *lie – lay*; *past – passed*/sentence writing with verb *to lie*	sentence writing with more unusual confusing words
10	**sentences**: single- and multi-clause	identifying main and subordinate clauses in sentences	joining pairs of sentences with subordinating conjunctions	adding subordinate clauses to main clauses	identifying subordinate clauses/joining single-clause sentences to make multi-clause sentences	writing single-clause sentences with given phrases/turning sentences into multi-clause sentences
11	**Improving writing**: vocabulary and detail	replacing overused words in sentences	expanding simple sentences/rewriting sentences to avoid repetition	improving sentences with vocabulary and detail	rewriting simple passage to improve vocabulary	rewriting sentences to avoid beginning with *I*
12	**nouns**: phrases	identifying noun phrases in sentences/forming noun phrases	identifying and expanding noun phrases	identifying noun phrases with infinitives/sentence writing with given noun phrases	identifying noun phrases in sentences/expanding noun phrases and using them in sentences	completing sentences with noun phrases as indicated/writing sentences with given infinitives
13	**improving writing**: presenting information	answering questions about structure of extended writing	completing a chart from given information	researching and presenting information	using information given in continuous prose about *Henry VIII's wives* to create a chart	researching information about the *Solar System* and creating a chart
14	**confusing words**	correcting mistakes in sentences	completing sentences with *who's* or *whose*	writing sentences with pairs of often confused words	choosing correct word to complete sentences	completing traditional poem/writing sentences
15	**punctuation**: hyphens in compound words	adding hyphens where appropriate	adding hyphens where appropriate	correcting ambiguous headlines with hyphens	contracting phrases into compound adjectives/writing numbers and fractions as words/making hyphenated and non-hyphenated compound words from given root words	explaining meaning of hyphenated and non-hyphenated phrases/contracting phrases into hyphenated compound adjectives

* denotes content that is not specified in the National Curriculum for England (2014) but which will support children's wider knowledge and understanding of grammar.

Unit	Pupil Book	Pupil Book Focus	Pupil Book Practice	Pupil Book Extension	Resource Book Support	Resource Book Extension
16	**sentences**: direct speech round-up*	punctuating direct speech sentences/setting out as conversation	completing and punctuating direct speech sentences	writing conversation in direct and indirect speech	writing a conversation with speech marks from speech bubbles	writing a conversation from picture stimulus
17	**verbs**: modal/auxiliary verbs*	identifying auxiliary verbs	completing sentences with *must – ought to/have to, has to* or *had better*	writing sentences with modal and auxiliary verbs	ranking statements with auxiliary verbs in order of strength of purpose/sentence writing with auxiliary verbs	writing a conversation about a given situation to include auxiliary verbs
18	**verbs**: active and passive	identifying active and passive verbs in sentences	changing sentences from active to passive/passive to active	writing active sentences with given verbs/changing sentences to passive	identifying active and passive verbs in sentences/changing active sentences to passive sentences	completing sentences with active and passive verbs/writing active and passive sentences with given verbs
19	**Standard English**: slang	identifying how Non-standard English sentences would be written in Standard English	changing words into Standard English in sentences	interpreting Cockney rhyming slang	changing slang words and phrases in sentences to Standard English/rewriting sentences in Standard English/interpreting Cockney rhyming slang	rewriting a slang conversation in Standard English
20	**sentences**: conditional clauses*	identifying conditional clauses in sentences	completing sentences with conditional clauses	completing sentences with frontal conditional clauses	completing sentences with conditional clauses/writing about the weekend including conditional clauses	writing sentences with given conditional conjunctions
21	**punctuation**: semicolon and colon	explaining use of semicolon and colon in sentences	punctuating sentences	writing sentences about given topics with semicolons and colons	adding missing semicolons and colons to sentences/writing sentences with semicolons and colons	constructing sentences from given situations using semicolons and colons
22	**paragraphs**: discursive writing	answering questions about structure in extended writing	supported writing for a discursive piece on given subject	writing a discursive piece on choice of subject	writing discursive piece with given paragraph plan and arguments	researching and writing discursive piece
23	**verbs**: active and passive	identifying active and passive verbs in sentences	completing passive sentences with agents/with actions	writing active and passive sentences from given pairs of subjects and objects	identifying active and passive sentences/changing active sentences to passive sentences	completing sentences with active and passive verbs/writing active and passive sentences with given verbs/supplying agents for passive sentences
24	**Standard English**: grammatical constructions	changing Non-standard English sentences into Standard English	choosing correct word to complete sentences/rewriting sentences in Standard English	writing Non-standard English conversation/changing it to Standard English	identifying Non-standard words and phrases in sentences/correcting Non-standard English in sentences/rewriting double negative sentences	correcting Non-standard English sentences/writing sentences in Standard English
25	**punctuation**: hyphens with prefixes	adding hyphens	writing hyphenated words with given prefixes/using hyphenated words in sentences	writing sentences with *re* words unhyphenated and hyphenated	identify and correcting words needing a hyphen/matching hyphenated words to correct definition/sentence writing	sentence writing with hyphenated/non-hyphenated words
26	**sentences**: clause round-up*	identifying main clauses in sentences	completing sentences with given type of clause	extending sentences with adverb, relative and conditional clauses	writing story opening from picture stimulus and given clauses	writing story opening from picture stimulus to include given clauses
27	**verbs**: active/passive/subjunctives	identifying subjunctive verbs in sentences	rewriting active sentences as passive sentences/rewriting sentences to use the subjunctive form	changing informal sentences into formal sentences using the subjunctive *were*	writing active and passive sentences for each pair of nouns	forming the subjunctive from infinitives/writing sentences with subjunctives from word equations
28	**Standard English**: vocabulary	discussing different forms of writing for different purposes and audiences	translating and writing text messages/translating and writing emails/identifying formal English expressions in letter	writing text message, email and letter on chosen subject	rewriting a Non-standard English email for a non-native speaker	creating a Non-standard English email to a classmate/correcting an email

BOOK 6 UNIT 1 Sentences

Subject and object

The concept of a sentence as a unit of language that 'makes sense' can be a difficult concept for some children to grasp. The course builds children's confidence in this area through giving them the opportunity to look at punctuation of statements, questions and exclamations to familiarise themselves with what a 'sentence' looks and sounds like.

Throughout the course, children will encounter: sentence punctuation; the concept of 'making sense'; direct and indirect speech; clauses which combine to make multi-clause sentences; parts of sentences – subject/object, subject/predicate; focusing on the sentence as a unit of language that can be improved; and Standard English constructions.

This unit revises 'subject' and 'object' in sentences.

- The 'subject' is what the sentence is about and usually does the action expressed by the verb. The 'subject' can be a single noun, a noun phrase or pronoun – the latter being in the subject form.
- The object is what has been directly affected by the verb. The 'object' can be a single noun, a noun phrase or pronoun – the latter being in the object form.

Pupil Book

Focus
- Ask children what they understand by the term *sentence*.
- Revise/discuss the terms *noun* and *pronoun*.
- Revise/discuss the terms *subject* and *object*.
- Read and discuss the information box on page 6.
- Do more oral examples asking children to identify subject and object in simple sentences.
- Do the activities orally.

Answers
(A) 1 **Sam** concentrated on his reading.
2 **The horse** jumped the fence.
3 **The archers** shot at the targets.
4 **Nina** ate a biscuit.

(B) 1 Ali washed **the car**.
2 My friends bought me **a present**.
3 Policemen catch **robbers**.
4 The spider devoured **the fly**.

Practice
- Children can work in pairs. What are the most unusual objects they can come up with?

Answers
Individual answers

Extension
- Activity A : Children should work individually.
- Activity B: Model the first answer to help children who are finding the concept difficult.

Answers
Individual answers

Resource Book

Support PCM
- Activities A and C: Children should work individually.
- Activity B: Children can work in pairs.

Answers
(A) 1 <u>The racing driver</u> crashed the (car.)
2 <u>The nurse</u> bandaged (the boy's arm.)
3 <u>They</u> rowed (the boat.)
4 <u>Huge clouds</u> hid (the stars.)
5 <u>Ben</u> bought (the winning ticket.)

(B)

	Sentence 1	Sentence 2	Sentence 3
subject	The manager	Meg	Everyone
verb	closed	broke	loves
object	the shop	the plate	ice cream

(B) Individual answers

Extension PCM
- Model the first answer so children understand what is required.

Answers
Individual answers

Extra
- Make subject and object cards, e.g.
subject cards:

| That policeman | | He |

| The wind |

object cards:

| the robber | | a cake |

| a blackbird |

Individuals choose a subject card and an object card and make a sentence. This can result in some bizarre sentences which the children will find funny.

BOOK 6 UNIT 2 Sentences

Subject and predicate

The concept of a sentence as a unit of language that 'makes sense' can be a difficult concept for some children to grasp. The course builds children's confidence in this area through giving them the opportunity to look at punctuation of statements, questions and exclamations to familiarise themselves with what a 'sentence' looks and sounds like.

Throughout the course, children will encounter: sentence punctuation; the concept of 'making sense'; direct and indirect speech; clauses which combine to make multi-clause sentences; parts of sentences – subject/object, subject/predicate; focusing on the sentence as a unit of language that can be improved; and Standard English constructions.

This unit revises 'subject' and 'predicate' in sentences.

- The 'subject' is what the sentence is about and usually does the action expressed by the verb. The 'subject' can be a single noun, a noun phrase or pronoun – the latter being in the subject form.
- The predicate is the rest of the sentence and contains the verb.

The unit also revises the idea of adding to the subject and predicate, to make writing more interesting.

Pupil Book

Focus
- Ask children what they understand by the term *sentence*.
- Revise/discuss the terms *noun* and *pronoun*.
- Revise/discuss the terms *subject* and *predicate*.
- Read and discuss the information box on page 8.
- Ask: *What words have been added to the subject to make it more interesting? What words have been added to the predicate to make it more interesting?*
- Do more oral examples. Write simple sentences on the board and ask children to
  – identify the subject and the predicate;
  – add to the subject and the predicate to make them more interesting.
- Do the activity orally.

Answers
(A) 1 **That valuable book** has been left in the rain!
2 **A flock of geese** frightened the children.
3 **The enthusiastic audience** clapped wildly.

(B) 1 The mist **lingered in the bottom of the valley**.
2 Every old car **causes pollution**.
3 The gigantic tree **had fallen across the road**.

Practice
- Children should work individually.

Answers
1 An octopus has eight legs.
2 The tennis player served an ace.
3 The queue went all the way around the building.
4 My aunt is coming to visit.
5 Some people don't like flying.

Extension
- Children can work individually or in pairs on both activities.
- When complete, discuss and take a vote on the most interesting sentences.

Answers
(A) Individual answers
(B) Individual answers

Resource Book

Support PCM
- Children should work individually.

Answers
(A) 1 (The town centre) was crowded with tourists.
2 (Our cat) has had kittens.
3 (The bus) broke down on the bridge.
4 (This sandwich) is horrible!
5 (Everyone) joined in the cheering.

(B) Individual answers

Extension PCM
- Read and discuss the first answer so children understand what is required.

Answers
Individual answers

Extra
- Make simple sentence cards, e.g.

| The bird sang. | The plane took off. |

Individuals pick a card and:
– identify the subject;
– identify the predicate;
– expand both subject and predicate to make a more interesting sentence.

BOOK 6 UNIT 3 Homophones and homonyms

Homophones and homonyms

Words that sound the same but are different in spelling and meaning are homophones. Homophones can often cause confusion. Children have encountered common homophones earlier in the course that frequently cause problems.

Words that are spelt the same and sound the same are homonyms. Homonyms do different jobs in language, i.e. they can be different parts of speech.

This unit revises homophones and homonyms.

Pupil Book

Focus
- Revise/discuss the terms *homophone* and *homonym*, and ask for examples.
- Read and discuss the information box on page 10.
- Do the activities orally.

Answers
1. The cowboy **rode** into town.
2. The **knight** approached the castle.
3. I **knew** what I had to do.

(B) 1 **a** type = verb
    b type = noun
  2 **a** bowl = noun
    b bowl = verb
  3 **a** book = verb
    b book = noun

Practice
- Children can work in pairs against the clock!

Answers
(A) 1 wood
  2 plaice
  3 right
  4 tow
  5 nose

(B) Individual answers

(C) 1 grave
  2 bark
  3 rock
  4 port
  5 free

(D) Individual answers

Extension
- Read and discuss the homophones before children write, or use this as an opportunity for dictionary work.

Answers
Individual answers

Resource Book

Support PCM
- Children should work individually.

Answers
(A) 1 pear
  2 bean
  3 bread
  4 deer
  5 ewe

(B) 1 **a** race = noun
    b race = verb
  2 **a** ring = verb
    b ring = noun
  3 **a** tip = verb
    b tip = noun

(C) Individual answers

Extension PCM
- Activities A and B: Children can work in pairs.
- Activity C: Children should work individually.

Answers
(A) 1 bough
  2 court
  3 daze
  4 fir
  5 reed
  6 soul

(B) 1 scent/cent
  2 write/rite
  3 rein/reign
  4 pair/pare

(C) Individual answers

Extra
Make homonym cards, e.g.

verb/noun: block | dust | box

adjective/noun: history | ticket | race

Individuals pick a card and make sentences to show the different parts of speech that the word on the card can be used as.

114

BOOK 6 UNIT 4 Pronouns

Relative

Pronouns are words that take the place of nouns and noun phrases.

Throughout the course, children will encounter: personal pronouns (as subject and object); possessive pronouns; reflexive pronouns; and relative pronouns.

Demonstrative pronouns are introduced in the work on noun phrases.

Interrogative pronouns are not specifically labelled as such but children encounter them in work on relative pronouns. It is up to individual teachers if indefinite pronouns, e.g. each/many/few/some, are specifically labelled as such and taught as another group of pronouns.

This unit revises relative pronouns in preparation for relative (adjectival) clauses later in the course. In British English, the use of the relative pronoun 'which' and the relative pronoun 'that' are, in many cases, equally correct. For the purposes of this and other units dealing with relative pronouns and clauses, 'which' and 'that' are equally acceptable as the different uses are too complicated for primary school children.

Pupil Book

Focus
- Revise/discuss the terms *noun* and *conjunctions*.
- Revise/discuss the term *pronoun* and ask for examples.
- Revise/discuss the term *relative pronoun* and ask for examples.
- Read and discuss the information box on page 12.
- The activity can be done orally, or children can write.

Answers
1. She was on the bus **which/that** broke down.
2. I mowed the grass **which/that** had grown very tall.
3. We listened to the street musicians **who** played outside the town hall.
4. She likes poetry **which/that** tells a story.
5. The photographer, **who** takes wildlife pictures, is very talented.

Practice
- If necessary, go through the sentences orally before children write.

Answers
1. Mary blew out the candles **which/that** were on her cake.
2. The explorer found an island **which/that** was uninhabited.
3. Giraffes have long necks **which/that** enable them to feed from high branches.
4. This book is about astronauts **who** landed on the Moon.
5. The drawbridge crossed the moat **which/that** went around the castle.

Extension
- Read and discuss the information box on page 13.
- Do more oral practice before the children write.

Answers
1. Could you tell me to **whom** I should complain?
2. I think I know **whose** these shoes are.
3. **Whose** parents are coming to the play?
4. This is my sister **whom** I think you have met.

Resource Book

Support PCM
- Activity A: Children should work individually.
- Activity B: Some children may need support.

Answers
(A) 1. The farmer mended the fence **which/that** had come down in the gale.
2. We pulled up the weeds **which/that** had taken over the flowerbed.
3. The bus picked up the passengers **who** were waiting in the rain.
4. I drew a map for my friend **who** was coming to visit.

(A) 1. **Whose** homework is this?
2. The cyclist, **whose** tyre had a puncture, had to walk home.
3. This is the boy **whose** dog has gone missing.
4. With **whom** do you wish to speak?

Extension PCM
- Model the first answer so children understand what is required.

Answers
Individual answers

Extra
- Make relative pronoun cards, i.e.

who	which	that
whose	whom	

Individuals pick a card and construct a sentence using the relative pronoun.

BOOK 6 UNIT 5 Verbs

Modals

Verbs are often explained as 'doing words' or 'being words'. They are possibly the most complex part of speech for young children to grasp because of their many forms and tenses.

Throughout the course, children will encounter the present simple, present progressive (also known as continuous), past simple, past progressive, present perfect (labelled simply *perfect* throughout the course), past perfect, future, infinitive (labelled *verb family name* in the early parts of the course), auxiliary verbs, modals, active and passive verbs and subjunctive verbs (a construction very rarely used except in extremely formal writing).

Participles are referred to as '*ing* words' and 'regular past simple tense words'; finite verbs are referred to as 'main' or 'proper verbs', and it is for the teacher to decide the appropriate time to introduce the terms *participle* and *finite verb*.

Children have encountered the verbs 'to be' and 'to have' earlier in the course and have used them in constructing verb tenses. They have encountered the term *auxiliary verb* used to indicate tense, and *modal* – another form of auxiliary verb – used to differentiate shades of meaning, e.g.

- can – ability
- may – possibility/permission
- must – obligation/strong belief
- might – possibility
- should – possibility/advice
- could – possibility
- would – request/offer/conditional

This units revises the use of modals.

Pupil Book

Focus
- Revise/discuss the term *verb*.
- Ask children to name tenses where the verbs are made up of two words.
- Revise/discuss and explain the term *auxiliary*.
- Revise/discuss the term *modal verb*.
- Read and discuss the information box on page 14.
- Discuss the shades of meaning.
- Do the activity orally.

Answers
1. I **must** remember to take my homework to school.
2. I **should** warn you that the weather will get worse.
3. It **might** be a good idea to ring up and check what time it starts.
4. **Can** you reach the top shelf?
5. They **would** like to visit in the spring.
6. I **could** eat a horse!
7. You **may** leave at six o'clock.
8. **May** I borrow that CD?

Practice
- Discuss the use of each pair of verbs before children write.

Answers
(A) 1. **May** I have a cup of tea and a slice of toast?
    2. **Can** you find your way?
    3. You **may** go to the library if you **can** find your library card.

(B) 1. If you **must** sing along, do it quietly!
    2. The river **might** flood if it keeps on raining.
    3. She **must** set off now because the bus **might** be early.

(C) 1. We **could** easily climb that mountain.
    2. We **should** not attempt to climb that mountain.
    3. We **would** be foolish to climb that mountain.

Extension
- Children should work individually.

Answers
Individual answers

Resource Book

Support PCM
- Discuss the scenario before children write.

Answers
(A) Individual answers
(B) Individual answers

Extension PCM
- Initial discussion may be necessary to help children differentiate between things they must/can/might do, etc.

Answers
Individual answers

Extra
Make modal verb cards, e.g.

| can | might | could | should |

Individuals choose a card and construct a sentence using the word on the card as a modal verb.

BOOK 6 UNIT 6 Sentences

> **Relative clauses**
>
> The concept of a sentence as a unit of language that 'makes sense' can be a difficult concept for some children to grasp. The course builds children's confidence in this area through giving them the opportunity to look at punctuation of statements, questions and exclamations to familiarise themselves with what a 'sentence' looks and sounds like.
>
> Throughout the course, children will encounter: sentence punctuation; the concept of 'making sense'; direct and indirect speech; clauses which combine to make multi-clause sentences; parts of sentences – subject/object, subject/predicate; focusing on the sentence as a unit of language that can be improved; and Standard English constructions.
>
> This unit revises the concept of the relative clause introduced by a relative pronoun. For the purposes of this and other units dealing with relative pronouns and clauses, 'which' and 'that' are equally acceptable as the different uses are too complicated for primary school children.
>
> As with adverbial clauses, relative clauses must contain a 'finite verb'. The best way of explaining a finite verb is one that makes a complete tense, so 'singing' is not finite but 'am singing' is. Both main and subordinate clauses need a finite verb.

Pupil Book

Focus
- Ask children what they understand by the term *sentence*.
- Revise/discuss the term *relative pronoun* and ask for examples.
- Revise/discuss the term *clause* and explain the difference between a phrase and a clause using the term *finite verb*.
- Read and discuss the information box on page 16.
- Ask children to provide a different 'which' ending for *Grandad had some stamps*, and a different 'who' ending for *The audience applauded the actor*.
- The activity can be done orally or children can write.

Answers
1. Where is the (**sock**) that matches this one?
2. I received a postcard from my (**sister**) who is on holiday in Greece.
3. She watered the (**plant**) that had drooping leaves.
4. May I speak to the (**person**) who left this message?
5. The farmer made a (**scarecrow**) that frightened the birds.

Practice
- Children should work individually.

Answers
1. I found an old coin **which** had been buried for hundreds of years.
2. These people, **who** use the well, live in the village.
3. Is Saturn the planet **which** has the rings around it?
4. The plane, **which** flew faster than the speed of sound, was called Concorde.
5. I know the people **who** have moved in next door.

Extension
- Children can work individually but may need support.
- Discuss sentences in class.

Answers
- (A) Individual answers
- (B) Individual answers

Resource Book

Support
- Activity A: Children should work individually.
- Activity B: Monitor the work in progress as children may need help in spotting where relative clauses could be added to what they write.

Answers
- (A) Individual answers
- (B) Individual answers

Extension
- Read and discuss the information box on the PCM.
- Children can work in small groups.
- When complete, discuss answers.

Answers
1. The fish that has a yellow stripe lives in a tank.
2. The dog that has a red collar chewed the slipper.
3. There is a snake that is black and white in the garden.
4. We have a vase which is 100 years old on the shelf.

Extra
This is a difficult concept for most children so plenty of practice is needed.
Ask children for simple sentences and write on the board. Can they add a relative clause to expand the sentence?

BOOK 6 UNIT 7 Verbs

Tense round-up

Throughout the course, children will encounter the present simple, present progressive (also known as continuous), past simple, past progressive, present perfect (labelled simply *perfect* throughout the course), past perfect, future, infinitive (labelled *verb family name* in the early parts of the course), auxiliary verbs, modals, active and passive verbs and subjunctive verbs (a construction very rarely used except in extremely formal writing).

Participles are referred to as '*ing* words' and 'regular past simple tense words'; finite verbs are referred to as 'main' or 'proper verbs', and it is for the teacher to decide the appropriate time to introduce the terms *participle* and *finite verb*.

This unit recaps on all the verb tenses the children have learned so far:

- present simple
- present progressive
- past simple
- past progressive
- present perfect (Technically, the present perfect tense is constructed with *has/have* + past participle. It is simpler to say that it is constructed with *has/have* + the past simple tense (regular or irregular)).
- past perfect (Technically, the past perfect tense is constructed with *had* + past participle. It is simpler to say that it is constructed with *had* + the past simple tense (regular or irregular). Mistakes where the past simple tense and the past participle are NOT the same can be dealt with on an individual basis.
- future

Pupil Book

Focus

- Revise/discuss the term *verb* and ask for examples of:
  – present simple
  – present progressive
  – past simple
  – past progressive
  – perfect
  – past perfect
  – future
- Read and discuss the information box on page 18.
- Do the activity orally.

Answers

(A) past simple: it rained/it blew/it hailed/it shone/it drizzled
past progressive: it was raining/it was blowing/it was hailing/it was shining/it was drizzling
perfect: it has rained/it has blown/it has hailed/it has shone/it has drizzled
past perfect: it had rained/it had blown/it had hailed/it had shone/it had drizzled
present simple: it rains/it blows/it hails/it shines/it drizzles
present progressive: it is raining/it is blowing/it is hailing/it is shining/it is drizzling
future: it will rain/it will blow/it will hail/it will shine/it will drizzle

(B) 1 had gusted — past perfect
2 is battering — present progressive
3 swirled — past simple
4 has struck — perfect
5 will snow — future

Practice

- Children should work individually.

Answers

(A) 1 I **am sheltering** under a tree.
I **was sheltering** under a tree.
2 The thunder **is rumbling** in the distance.
The thunder **was rumbling** in the distance.
3 Flags **are fluttering** in the breeze.
Flags **were fluttering** in the breeze.

(B) 1 The wind **has blown** strongly.
The wind **had blown** strongly.
2 The sun **has shone** brightly.
The sun **had shone** brightly.
3 The clouds **have obscured** the sun.
The clouds **had obscured** the sun.

(C) 1 It **rains**.   It **rained**.
2 The wind **blows**.   The wind **blew**.
3 It **drizzles**.   It **drizzled**.

Extension

- Read and discuss the first example so children understand what is required.

Answers

Individual answers

Resource Book

Support PCM

- Children can work individually or in pairs.
- When complete, discuss answers.

Answers

1 I **had painted** the door and then I **washed** the brushes.
2 I **have seen** my friend in the street.
3 I **had heard** the thunder before I **went** to bed.
4 I **shall carry** the heaviest bag.

Extension PCM

- Children should work individually.

Answers

Individual answers

Extra

Make infinitive and tense cards, e.g.
infinitive cards:

| to worry | to know | to discover |

tense cards:

| past simple | present progressive |

Individuals pick an infinitive card and a tense card and make a sentence.

BOOK 6 UNIT 8 Sentences

Single- and multi-clause sentences

The concept of a sentence as a unit of language that 'makes sense' can be a difficult concept for some children to grasp. The course builds children's confidence in this area through giving them the opportunity to look at punctuation of statements, questions and exclamations to familiarise themselves with what a 'sentence' looks and sounds like.

Throughout the course, children will encounter: sentence punctuation; the concept of 'making sense'; direct and indirect speech; clauses which combine to make single- and multi-clause sentences; parts of sentences – subject/object, subject/predicate; focusing on the sentence as a unit of language that can be improved; and Standard English constructions.

This unit introduces the concept of single- and multi-clause sentences. The first type of multi-clause sentences are made up of two main clauses joined by *and*, *but*, or *or* (These are often known as compound sentences.). The sentence forms will be familiar to children so this unit revises these forms and gives children the proper terminology.

Pupil Book

Focus
- Ask children what they understand by the terms *conjunction*, *sentence* and *main clause*.
- Introduce the term *multi-clause sentence* and explain that these sentences are made up of two or more main clauses joined by *and, but,* or *or.*
- Read and discuss the information box on page 20.
- Ask children to provide a different 'and' ending for *The hawk soared into the sky;* a different 'but' ending for *We were caught in a traffic jam;* and a different 'or' ending for *It might rain tomorrow.*
- The activity can be done orally or children can write.

Answers
1. The famous explorer went to Africa (and) she stayed there for many months.
2. The volcano erupted (and) lava poured down its sides.
3. I enjoy basketball (but) I'm too tired to play it now.
4. Are you going shopping today (or) will you wait until tomorrow?
5. It's my birthday tomorrow (but) I'm not having a party.

Practice
- Children can work in pairs.
- Tell them to read both parts before they decide which conjunction to use.

Answers
1. My sandal is broken **but** I think I can mend it.
2. The library was busy **and** there was nowhere to sit.
3. I might have pizza for lunch **or** I might have soup.
4. I like this poem **but** I don't like that one.
5. The bird's feathers were blue **but** its beak was yellow.
6. The castle was ancient **and** its walls were in ruins.

Extension
- Children should work individually.

Answers
Individual answers

Resource Book

Support PCM
- Children should work individually.

Answers
(A)
1. I went to the leisure centre (and) swam fifty lengths.
2. Our neighbour is very quiet (but) his dog is noisy.
3. We could wait in the queue (or) we could go home.
4. He tried to persuade me (but) I wasn't convinced.
5. The sportsman could stay an amateur (or) he could turn professional.

(B)
1. I remembered my bag **but** I forgot my lunch.
2. Is this a sentence **or** is this a phrase?
3. It was an amazing experience **but** I wouldn't want to do it again.
4. Have you had enough **or** do you want some more?
5. The guard blew his whistle **and** the train pulled out of the station.

Extension PCM
- Model the first answer to A and B so children understand what is required.

Answers
Individual answers

Extra
Use the sentences in the Extension activity in the pupil book.
Ask children to finish each of them with main clauses beginning with *and, but,* or *or.*
NB *or* is not always possible.

BOOK 6 UNIT 9 Confusing words

Homophones
Throughout the course, children have encountered homophones and common mistakes in verb choice.

This unit continues the work on words that children often find confusing.

Pupil Book

Focus
- Read and discuss the information box on page 22.
- For each section, read the examples and ask for further examples.
- Do the activity orally.

Answers
1. We must walk to the library **all together**.
2. The cars zoomed **past**.
3. **Lie** down and have a rest.
4. **Lay** those sheets flat.
5. I am **altogether** sure I am right.
6. In the **past**, people travelled by horse and carriage.
7. He **passed** by unnoticed.

Practice
- Children should work individually on the activities.

Answers
(A)
1. It's **altogether** a bit of a mess!
2. Let's go **all together**.
3. **Altogether**, it is a difficult problem.

(B)
1. He **lies** down for a 10-minute nap every day.
2. Are you **laying** the table?
3. Why are you **lying** down?

(C)
1. The dog ran **past** me.
2. I **passed** my exam!
3. The tiger strolled **past** the water hole.

Extension
- Read and discuss the information box on page 23.

Answers
1. Last night, I **lay** on the sofa.
2. I am **lying** down for a little while.
3. I had **lain** awake last night.
4. He has **lain** in bed all day!

Resource Book

Support PCM
- Children should work individually.

Answers
(A)
1. It's **altogether** too much trouble.
2. If we work **all together** we should get it done.
3. Let's say the alphabet **all together**.

(B)
1. If you **lie**, you will always be found out.
2. **Lay** your coats on the chair.
3. If you **lie** down for a few minutes, you may feel better.

(C)
1. I have **passed** my driving test!
2. Do you go **past** the shops on your way to the station?
3. History is about what happened in the **past**.

(D) Individual answers

Extension PCM
- Read through the words so children understand their meaning, or use this as an opportunity for dictionary work.

Answers
Individual answers

Extra
Make cards of the confusing words covered in the unit, e.g.

| lay | passed | altogether | past |

Individuals pick a card and use the word in a sentence.

BOOK 6 UNIT 10 Sentences

Single- and multi-clause sentences

The concept of a sentence as a unit of language that 'makes sense' can be a difficult concept for some children to grasp. The course builds children's confidence in this area through giving them the opportunity to look at punctuation of statements, questions and exclamations to familiarise themselves with what a 'sentence' looks and sounds like.

Throughout the course, children will encounter: sentence punctuation; the concept of 'making sense'; direct and indirect speech; clauses which combine to make multi-clause sentences; parts of sentences – subject/object, subject/predicate; focusing on the sentence as a unit of language that can be improved; and Standard English constructions.

This unit revises the concept of single- and multi-clause sentences, and sentences made up of a main clause and subordinate clauses (These are often known as complex sentences.). The sentence forms will be familiar to children so this unit revises these forms and gives children the proper terminology.

Pupil Book

Focus
- Ask children what they understand by the terms *conjunction*, *sentence* and *main clause*.
- Revise/discuss the term *multi-clause sentence* and explain that these sentences are made up of two or more main clauses joined by *and, but,* or *or*.
- Ask children what they understand by the term *subordinate clause*. Can they name different types of clauses?
- Explain that some sentences are made up of a main clause and one or more subordinate clauses.
- Read and discuss the information box on page 24.
- Ask children to provide a different conjunction and ending for *The house had been empty for many years*.
- The activity can be done orally or children can write.

Answers
1. The guitar was broken = main clause
   before I borrowed it = subordinate clause
2. Although it was very steep, = subordinate clause
   we climbed the mountain. = main clause
3. My sister will come over = main clause
   when she has finished her work. = subordinate clause
4. The people next door have a noisy dog = main clause
   which barks all day long. = subordinate clause
5. If you remember to buy it, = subordinate clause
   we can post the card in the morning. = main clause

Practice
- Remind children they can use any conjunction other than *and, but* or *or*.

Answers
1. The microscope isn't working **although** I checked it this morning.
2. We are going on holiday **so** we have bought new suitcases.
3. The flowers died **even though** I watered them every day.
4. We saw the wrecked ship **which/where it** had crashed on the rocks.
5. That's the man with the dog **who** lives in the old cottage.

Extension
- Children should work individually.

Answers
(A) Individual answers
(B) Individual answers

Resource Book

Support PCM
- Children should work individually.

Answers
(A) 1. I couldn't answer the question <u>because my mind went blank</u>!
   2. The new business was doing well <u>even though it had only been open a month</u>.
   3. <u>Unless we tackle globing warming</u>, we will face real problems in the future.
   4. The police talked to the girl <u>whose bicycle was stolen</u>.
   5. <u>After the sun had set</u>, the air was filled with insects.

(B) Suggested answers
   1. I read my book **until** it was time to go to sleep.
   2. **When** the army surrounded the castle, the people surrendered.
      The people surrendered **after** the army surrounded the castle.
   3. The lead actor recovered **so** the play went on.
      The play went on **because** the lead actor recovered.
   4. It is difficult to judge **because** I don't have all the facts.
      If I don't have all the facts, it is difficult to judge.
   5. You made a promise **so** you have to stick to it
      If you made a promise, you have to stick to it.

Extension PCM
- Model the first answer to A and B so children understand what is required.

Answers
Individual answers

Extra
Make sentence cards and sentence type cards, e.g.

sentences: | The man walked his dog. |

| Our friends came to stay. |

types: | single-clause | | multi-clause |

Individuals choose a sentence card and a type card. They make the single-clause sentence into a sentence stipulated by the type card.

121

BOOK 6 UNIT 11 Improving writing

Vocabulary and detail

The concept of a sentence as a unit of language that 'makes sense' can be a difficult concept for some children to grasp. The course builds children's confidence in this area through giving them the opportunity to look at punctuation of statements, questions and exclamations to familiarise themselves with what a 'sentence' looks and sounds like.

Throughout the course, children will encounter: sentence punctuation; the concept of 'making sense'; direct and indirect speech; clauses which combine to make multi-clause sentences; parts of sentences – subject/object, subject/predicate; focusing on the sentence as a unit of language that can be improved; and Standard English constructions.

This unit revises the work on improving writing with synonyms and detail, and examines how to avoid repetition when using 'I' and the technique of ellipsis.

Pupil Book

Focus
- Revise/discuss the terms *synonym, adjective, adjective phrase, relative (adjective) clause, adverb, adverb phrase* and *adverb clause*.
- Read and discuss the information box on page 26.
- Children should work individually on the activity with your support.

Answers
Suggested answers
1. strolled/ambled
2. rushed/hurried
3. whispered/murmured
4. shouted/yelled
5. delicious/scrumptious
6. interesting/exciting
7. tiny/minuscule
8. huge/enormous
9. received
10. bought/acquired

Practice
- Children can work individually or in pairs.
- When complete, discuss answers.

Answers
(A) Individual answers

(B)
1. He drove to the shops and [then he drove] to the park.
2. I sat on the wall and [I] waited for the bus.
3. The tree was battered by the wind and eventually [the tree] fell over.
4. Dad is mending the car. Will you help him [mend the car]?

Extension
- Children should work individually with your support.

Answers
- individual answers

Resource Book

Support PCM
- Children can work individually or in pairs.
- Alternatively, this can be done as a class exercise, with individuals suggesting vocabulary changes, and the class discussing and choosing the vocabulary they think the best.

Answers
Individual answers

Extension PCM
- Model the first answer so children understand what is required.

Answers
Individual answers

Extra
Choose a piece of continuous prose that each child has completed in another area of their English work. This can be different for each child.

Ask children to read it again and see where it could be improved.

BOOK 6 UNIT 12 Nouns

Phrases

Nouns are usually explained as 'naming' words. Nouns are the most common part of speech that children of this age will encounter. Children's first words are usually nouns as they make sense of the world by naming things.

Throughout the course, children will encounter common, proper, collective, compound, abstract and possessive nouns, together with noun phrases.

This unit introduces the concept of noun phrases introduced by:
– articles
– demonstrative adjectives [also called demonstrative pronouns when not followed by a noun]
– adjectives including 'ing' participles
It introduces other word classes that begin noun phrases:
– possessive adjectives
– possessive nouns
   It introduces the concepts of 'specific' and 'general'.

Pupil Book

Focus
- Revise/discuss the term *noun* and ask for examples of:
  – common nouns
  – proper nouns
  – collective nouns
  – compound nouns
  – abstract nouns
  – possessive nouns
- Revise/discuss the term *phrase*.
- Introduce/discuss the term *noun phrase*.
- Read and discuss the information box on page 28.
- The activity should be done orally.

Answers
(A) 1 **The police officer's dog** caught **the thief**.
    2 **Their house** is on fire!
    3 **The long river** wound its way across **the plain**.
    4 **This sandwich** is made with **juicy tomatoes**.
    5 **The howling wind** damaged **the old chimney pot**.

(B) 1 **the** elephant
    2 **an** orange
    3 to 6 individual answers

Practice
- Read/discuss the first answer so children understand what is required.

Answers
Noun phrases:
1 **A tree** has fallen on **the garage**.
2 **The lighthouse** is on **the coast**.
3 **A lion** was prowling in **the grass**.
4 **A crowd** gathered at **the stadium**.
5 **The flag** fluttered in **the breeze**.
6 **The crows** are on **the lawn**.
7 **A car** broke down in **the lane**.
8 **The girl** passed **the test**.
Expanded noun phrases = individual answers

Extension
- Read and discuss the information box on page 29.
- Children should work individually.

Answers
(A) 1 That is the **correct attitude to adopt**.
    2 I haven't got a **warm coat to wear**.
    3 I need **somewhere to sleep**.
    4 Have you got **a book to read**?
    5 That's **the film to watch**.

(B) Individual answers

Resource Book

Support PCM
- Children should work individually.

Answers
(A) 1 The cold, weary boy trudged through the freezing fog.
    2 My sister's car is in the garage.
    3 Have you seen his new black shoes?
    4 The screeching owl could be heard in the wood.
    5 A blue car and a red van were parked outside the school.

(B) Individual answers

Extension PCM
- Activity A: Model a possible answer to question 1 so that children understand what is required.
- Activity B: Discuss the first answer so children understand what is required.

Answers
(A) Suggested answers
    1 **A lame** horse was in **the small** field.
    2 **My bleeding** finger really hurts!
    3 Where is **Sally's new** coat?
    4 **The long, winding** road stretched into **the distance**, passing **my friend's** house.

(B) Suggested answers
    1 I need a scarf to wear.
    2 Is this the train to catch?
    3 I think this is the right thing to do.
    4 Is this the place to pay?
    5 I need something to eat.

Extra
Make noun cards, e.g.

| mountain | ghost | experience | bird |

Individuals take a card and expand the noun into as long a noun phrase as they can.

123

BOOK 6 UNIT 13 Improving writing

Headings/subheadings/bullet points/columns/charts

Throughout the course, children will encounter: sentence punctuation; the concept of 'making sense'; direct and indirect speech; clauses which combine to make multi-clause sentences; parts of sentences – subject/object, subject/predicate; focusing on the sentence as a unit of language that can be improved; and Standard English constructions.

This unit revises the work on improving writing with synonyms, detail, and how to avoid repeatedly beginning sentences with 'I'. It extends this by looking at presentational devices that are used to make the meaning of non-fiction continuous prose easier for a reader to understand.

Pupil Book

Focus
- Read and discuss the information box on page 30.
- Ensure children are clear about the terms *main heading, subheading, bullet point, chart* and *column*.
- Do the activity orally.

Answers
1. a heading
2. subheadings/bullet points/charts
3. Individual answers suggesting that it makes it very clear to the reader what aspects of a topic you have written about.
4. devised by Sir Francis Beaufort
5. individual answers

Practice
- Children can work in pairs with your support.

Answers

Force	Type of wind	What you can see	Speed
0	calm	smoke rises straight up	0 km/h
1	light air	smoke drifts	1–5 km/h
2	light breeze	leaves rustle/weather vane moves	6–11 km/h
3	gentle breeze	twigs move/flags flap	12–19 km/h
4	moderate breeze	dust and paper blown about/small branches move	20–29 km/h
5	fresh breeze	small trees start to sway	30–39 km/h
6	strong breeze	large branches move	40–49 km/h
7	near gale	whole trees bend over	50–61 km/h
8	gale	twigs break off	62–74 km/h
9	strong gale	chimneys and slates fall	75–88 km/h
10	storm	trees uprooted/buildings badly damaged	89–102 km/h
11	violent storm	general destruction	103–117 km/h
12	hurricane	coast flooded/devastation	over 117 km/h

Extension
- Children should work individually.
- Give time for research and, if possible, have suitable materials in the classroom for children to use.

Answers
Individual answers

Resource Book

Support PCM
- Children can work individually or in pairs.
- Alternatively, this can be done as a class exercise, with individuals adding information in the correct columns.

Answers

Name	Date married	Children	Date no longer queen	What happened to them
Katherine of Aragon	1509	Mary	1533	divorced
Anne Boleyn	1533	Elizabeth	1536	beheaded
Jane Seymour	1536	Edward	1537	died
Anne of Cleves	1540	none	1540	divorced
Katherine Howard	1540	none	1542	beheaded
Katherine Parr	1543	none	1547	survived

Extension PCM
- Children should work individually.
- Give time for research and, if possible, have suitable materials in the classroom for children to use.

Answers

Name	Origin of name	Distance from Sun	Diameter	Main moons
Mercury	messenger god	57,910,000 km	4,880 km	No moons
Venus	goddess of love	108,200,000 km	12,103.6 km	No moons
Earth	Gaea	149,600,000 km	12,756.3 km	Moon (Luna)
Mars	god of war	227,940,000 km	6,794 km	Deimos/Phobos
Jupiter	king of the gods	778,330,000 km	142,984 km	Io/Europa/Ganymede/Callistro
Saturn	god of agriculture	1,429,400,000 km	120,536 km	Titan/Atlas/Calypso
Uranus	lord of the skies	2,870,990,000 km	51,118 km	Titania/Oberon
Neptune	god of the sea	4,504,000,000 km	49,532 km	Triton/Galatea

Extra
Choose a piece of continuous prose that each child has completed in another area of the curriculum. This can be different for each child.

Ask children to read it again and see if it could be improved by the use of the presentational devices they have learned.

BOOK 6 UNIT 14 Confusing words

Homophones
Throughout the course, children have encountered homophones and common mistakes in verb choice.

This unit continues the work on words that children often find confusing.

Pupil Book

Focus
- Read and discuss the information box on page 32.
- For each section, read the examples and ask for further examples.
- Do the activity orally.

Answers
1. **Who's** coming to play football?
2. **Your** story was very exciting.
3. There are **fewer** cars in the village now they have built the bypass.
4. I'm not sure **whether** I want to go or not.
5. There's **less** time than I thought.
6. I think **you're** going to be late!
7. We had very good **weather** on our holidays.
8. I don't know **whose** this book is.

Practice
- Children should work individually on the activities.

Answers
(A) 1. The man **whose** car was damaged is furious.
2. **Who's** taken the last biscuit?
3. I know **who's** responsible for the mess.

(B) 1. If **you're** very tired, go to bed.
2. What's **your** name?
3. If **you're** certain, I'll take **your** word for it.

(C) 1. That check-out says 'Five items or **fewer**'.
2. If you eat **less** sugar, you will be healthier.
3. If you spend **less** time you will sell **fewer** tickets.

(D) 1. The **weather** is unusual for this time of year.
2. I'm wondering **whether** to play tennis or not.
3. I don't know **whether** the **weather** will be good or not.

Extension
- If children struggle to write one sentence, they can write two related sentences.

Answers
Individual answers

Resource Book

Support PCM
- Children should work individually.

Answers
(A) 1. **Who's** making supper?
2. Do you know **who's** won the prize?
3. I have a friend **whose** mother is French.

(B) 1. Is this **your** first visit to a theme park?
2. **You're** sure you left **your** bag on the bus?
3. I'm sure **your** cat will come back home.

(C) 1. He got **fewer** votes so didn't win!
2. I'm **less** sure about the answer to number 2.
3. You need to keep **fewer** fish in that tank.

(D) 1. There's nothing we can do but **weather** the storm!
2. I'm not sure **whether** to go out or not.
3. I'll check **whether** the flight is landing on time.

Extension PCM
- Activity A: Children can work in pairs.
- Activity B: Children should work individually.

Answers
(A) **Whether** the **weather** be fine,
Or **whether** the **weather** be not,
Whether the **weather** be cold,
Or **whether** the **weather** be hot,
We'll **weather** the **weather**
Whatever the **weather**,
Whether we like it or not!

(B) Individual answers

Extra
Make cards of the confusing words covered in the unit, e.g.

| weather | fewer | whose | you're |

Individuals pick a card and use the word in a sentence.

125

BOOK 6 UNIT 15 Punctuation

Hyphens

Hyphens are small dashes that connect parts of words. Their specific use is not universally agreed, as a look at a variety of dictionaries will testify.

This unit introduces the hyphen to form:
– compound nouns
– compound verbs
– compound adjectives
– adverb phrases where the adverb does not end in *ly*
– numbers from 21 to 99
– fractions

Pupil Book

Focus

- Revise/discuss the term *punctuation* and ask children to list the punctuation marks they know.
- Introduce the term *hyphen*.
- Read and discuss the information box on page 34.
- Children can work in pairs and use a dictionary.
- When complete, discuss answers.

Answers

	a		b		c	
1	a	film clip	b	film-maker	c	filmset
2	a	sea anchor	b	sea-angel	c	seabed
3	a	land yacht	b	landslide	c	land-wind
4	a	raindrop	b	rain cloud	c	rain-worm

Practice

- Children should work individually with the aid of a dictionary.

Answers

1	a	light-fingered	b	light-hearted	c	lighthouse
2	a	wetsuit	b	wetland	c	wet-weather
3	a	team-mate	b	team-teaching	c	teamwork
4	a	drift-net	b	drift-ice	c	driftwood
5	a	cheeseburger	b	cheese-cutter	c	cheese cake

Extension

- Children can work in pairs or small groups.
- When complete, discuss answers.

Answers

1. Heavy Metal Detector Finds Treasure Trove
   No hyphen = the detector is made of metal and is heavy
   Heavy-Metal Detector Finds Treasure Trove
   Hyphen = the detector is designed to detect heavy metal
2. Small business men launch new superstore
   No hyphen = the business men are small
   Small-business men launch new superstore
   Hyphen = the business men own small businesses
3. Foreign car dealer goes under
   No hyphen = the car dealer is foreign
   Foreign-car dealer goes under
   Hyphen = the car dealer deals in foreign cars
4. Man eating snakes spotted in village
   No hyphen = a man eating some snakes has been spotted
   Man-eating snakes spotted in village
   Hyphen = snakes that eat men have been spotted

Resource Book

Support PCM

- Children should work individually.

Answers

A
1. a red-hot poker
2. a hard-working boy
3. a fire-proof box
4. a smooth-haired dog
5. an air-tight tin

B
1. forty-one
2. seven-tenths
3. eighty-five
4. three-fifths

C Suggested answers
1. dry-clean/dry-eyed — drystone/drywall
2. eye-catching/eye-shade — eyeshadow/eyepatch
3. gold-digger/gold-beater — goldfish/goldfinch
4. pipe-cleaner/pipe-rack — pipework/pipeline
5. cross-check/cross-eyed — crossbow/crossbar

Extension PCM

- Activity A should be done individually.
- Activity B: Read and discuss the information box on page 103.

Answers

A
1. five year-old children — the number of year-old children is five
2. five-year-old children — the children are five years of age
3. light-blue bag — the bag is light-blue in colour
4. light blue bag — the bag is both light (not heavy) and blue

B
1. a one-litre jug
2. a six-page booklet
3. a four-door car
4. a ten-pound bill
5. a five-mile race

Extra

Find common words that have hyphenated forms in the dictionary that the children use.

List the words on the board and see who can find a hyphenated word first.

Discuss meaning and usage of each example the children find.

BOOK 6 UNIT 16 Sentences

Direct/indirect speech round-up

The concept of a sentence as a unit of language that 'makes sense' can be a difficult concept for some children to grasp. The course builds children's confidence in this area through giving them the opportunity to look at punctuation of statements, questions and exclamations to familiarise themselves with what a 'sentence' looks and sounds like.

Throughout the course, children will encounter: sentence punctuation; the concept of 'making sense'; direct and indirect speech; clauses which combine to make multi-clause sentences; parts of sentences – subject/object, subject/predicate; focusing on the sentence as a unit of language that can be improved; and Standard English constructions.

Children often find correctly punctuating direct speech sentences problematic. Several units in the course focus on direct speech so that the various rules can be built up gradually. Children have encountered: speech marks (inverted commas); beginning a new line (paragraph) when a different person speaks; punctuation before the final speech marks; split direct speech; and word changes in indirect speech.

This unit revises all of the above.

Pupil Book

Focus

- Begin by asking the children why *direct speech* (characters having a conversation) looks 'different' on the page.
- Revise the terms *statement – full stop/question – question mark/exclamation – exclamation mark/speech marks (inverted commas)*.
- Read and discuss the information box on page 36.
- Read and discuss the sentences in the activity, asking children which spoken words are:
  – one complete sentence
  – two complete sentences
  – one split sentence
- Children should work individually.

Answers

1. "Have you visited Australia before?" asked the travel agent.
2. Harry replied, "I was there when I was three."
3. "So," said the travel agent, "I don't suppose you remember much about it."
4. "Not much," agreed Harry. "I do remember it was very hot."
5. "Where did you stay?" the travel agent inquired.
6. "We stayed in Sydney," said Harry, "and I think we went on to Melbourne."
7. "Where to this time?" asked the travel agent.
8. "Ayers Rock and Alice Springs," said Harry. "I'm really looking forward to travelling across the desert."

Practice

- Read the incomplete direct speech sentences and ask: *How do you know that each speaker only says one sentence?*
- Children can work individually.

Answers

Individual answers

Extension

- Read and discuss the information box on page 37 which revises indirect (reported) speech.
- Activity A: Children can work in pairs. Remind them of synonyms for *said*.
- Activity B: Children should work individually.

Answers

Individual answers

Resource Book

Support PCM

- Children can work in pairs.

Answers

Individual answers

Extension PCM

- Children should work individually.

Answers

Individual answers

Extra

- In pairs, children can create a cartoon-type story with frames and speech bubbles.
- Pairs swap their cartoons and change them into a direct speech conversation.

BOOK 6 UNIT 17 Verbs

Modals

Verbs are often explained as 'doing words' or 'being words'. They are possibly the most complex part of speech for young children to grasp because of their many forms and tenses.

Throughout the course, children will encounter the present simple, present progressive (also known as continuous), past simple, past progressive, present perfect (labelled simply *perfect* throughout the course), past perfect, future, infinitive (labelled *verb family name* in the early parts of the course), auxiliary verbs, modals, active and passive verbs and subjunctive verbs (a construction very rarely used except in extremely formal writing).

Participles are referred to as '*ing* words' and 'regular past simple tense words'; finite verbs are referred to as 'main' or 'proper verbs', and it is for the teacher to decide the appropriate time to introduce the terms *participle* and *finite verb*.

Children have encountered the verbs 'to be' and 'to have' earlier in the course and have used them in constructing verb tenses. They have encountered the term *auxiliary verb* used to indicate tense, and 'modal' – another form of auxiliary verb – used to differentiate shades of meaning, e.g.

- can – ability
- may – possibility/permission
- must – obligation/strong belief
- might – possibility
- should – possibility/advice
- could – possibility
- would – request/offer/conditional

This unit revises the use of true modals with the addition of auxiliary phrases which perform the same function as modals.

Pupil Book

Focus

- Revise/discuss the term *verb*.
- Ask children to name tenses where the verbs are made up of two words.
- Revise/discuss and explain the term *auxiliary*.
- Revise/discuss the term *modal verb*.
- Read and discuss the information box on page 38.
- Discuss the shades of meaning.
- Do the activity orally.

Answers

1. I **had better** water the plants before they all die!
2. You **ought to** take more care of yourself.
3. I **have got to** warn him before it is too late.
4. He **had better** do as he is told this time!
5. It **has got to** stop raining soon!
6. She **has to** go to the dentist.
7. They **ought to** keep to the footpath.
8. We **have to** win this match.

Practice

- Discuss the use of each pair of verbs before children write.

Answers

(A)
1. They **ought to** look at the map but I don't think they will!
2. I'm so hungry I **must** have something to eat.
3. You can play in the garden but you **must** not go into the lane.
4. Do you think we **ought to** phone an ambulance?

(B)
1. He **has to** meet his friends at one o'clock.
2. The neighbours **had better** turn the music down or I will phone the police!
3. She **had better** hurry or the coach will go without her.
4. Nurses **have to** work at the weekend.

Extension

- Initial discussion may be necessary to help children differentiate between things they should do/ought to do/have got to do, etc.

Answers

Individual answers

Resource Book

Support PCM

- Activities A and B: Children should work in pairs.
- Have an initial discussion about the urgency of the statements and what is implied if the call is not made.

Answers

(A) Individual reading
(B) 6 1 4 5 2 3
(C) Individual answers

Extension PCM

- Children should work in small groups.

Answers

Individual answers

Extra

Make modal/auxiliary verb cards, e.g.

| ought to | have to | had better |

Individuals choose a card and construct a sentence using the word on the card as a modal verb.

BOOK 6 UNIT 18 Verbs

Active and passive

Verbs are often explained as 'doing words' or 'being words'. They are possibly the most complex part of speech for young children to grasp because of their many forms and tenses.

Throughout the course, children will encounter the present simple, present progressive (also known as continuous), past simple, past progressive, present perfect (labelled simply *perfect* throughout the course), past perfect, future, infinitive (labelled *verb family name* in the early parts of the course), auxiliary verbs, modals, active and passive verbs and subjunctive verbs (a construction very rarely used except in extremely formal writing).

Participles are referred to as '*ing* words' and 'regular past simple tense words'; finite verbs are referred to as 'main' or 'proper verbs', and it is for the teacher to decide the appropriate time to introduce the terms *participle* and *finite verb*.

This unit introduces the 'active' and 'passive' mood of verbs. In the active mood, the subject does the action. In the passive mood, the subject receives/is affected by the action. The subject of an active sentence becomes the 'agent' in a passive sentence.

Pupil Book

Focus

- Revise/discuss the term *verb* and ask for examples of:
  – present simple
  – present progressive
  – past simple
  – past progressive
  – perfect
  – past perfect
  – future
- Introduce the terms *active verb* and *passive verb*.
- Read and discuss the information box on page 40.
- Do the activity orally.

Answers

1	The judge **banged** the table.	active
2	A sailor **was hit** by the rigging.	passive
3	A few regular customers **went** into the shop every day.	active
4	The monster **attacked** the town.	active
5	One of the escalators **was stopped** by the shop manager.	passive
6	The bridge **fell** into the river.	active
7	The library **was broken into** by a thief.	passive
8	I **have lost** my dictionary.	active

Practice

- If appropriate, discuss the answers before children write.
- Activity B: When completed, discuss what/who is the agent in each sentence.

Answers

(A)
1. A story was read to the class by a teacher.
2. A famous victory was won by the captain.
3. Thunder was heard by the hikers in the afternoon.
4. The room was tidied by Lucy yesterday.
5. A goal was scored by the striker.

(B)
1. The boy cracked the new vase.
2. My dad cleaned the windows this morning.
3. The audience disliked the play.
4. The trees shaded the house.
5. Some farmers shoot rabbits.

Extension

- Children can use any verb tense they wish.

Answers

(A) Individual answers

(B) Individual answers

Resource Book

Support PCM

- Children can work in pairs on the activities.

Answers

(A)
1	The cliff-face was battered by the sea.	P
2	The sea battered the cliff-face.	A
3	The manager served the customer.	A
4	The customer was served by the manager.	P
5	The computer file was destroyed by a virus.	P
6	A virus destroyed the computer file.	A

(B)
1. The trip was organised by our teacher.
2. The tree was chopped down by the woodcutter.
3. The fields were flooded by the river.
4. Our school was visited by the Mayor.
5. The window was fixed by the workman.

Extension PCM

- Children should work individually.

Answers

(A) Individual answers

(B) Individual answers

(C) Individual answers

(D) Individual answers

Extra

Make subject/agent cards, e.g.

| the wind | my friend | our cousin |

Individuals pick a card and give an active and a passive sentence using the words on the card as the subject, then the agent.

129

BOOK 6 UNIT 19 Standard and Non-standard English

> **Slang**
> This is the first of three units that examine Standard and Non-standard English with the aim of helping children to appreciate the use of appropriate registers.
> This unit examines the concept of 'slang'.

Pupil Book

Focus
- Ask what the children understand by the term *slang*. Can they give you examples?
- Read and discuss the information box on page 42.
- The activity can be done orally or the children can write.

Answers
1. We're **going to** be late for school.
2. That goal was **amazing/marvellous/really good**.
3. The park keeper told us to **go away**.
4. You do talk **nonsense**!
5. I think these shoes are **amazing/fantastic/fashionable**.
6. He is **full**.
7. You're always **telling me off/blaming me**.
8. The thief **hid the money** in his garage.
9. That's **amazing/fantastic/marvellous**!
10. I'm really **unhappy/bored/miserable**.

Practice
- Children can work in pairs.
- When complete, discuss answers.

Answers
(A)
1. May I have some more **potatoes**?
2. That cost me five **pounds**!
3. Who was that **man** you were talking to?
4. Our neighbours have seven **children**.
5. The old **people** like the park.
6. This is my favourite **food**!
7. He wants to be a **policeman** when he grows up.
8. The **men/boys** in the football team are really good.

(B)
1. I'm sure that **isn't** right.
2. We had a **very** good time.
3. He's tired **because** he didn't sleep very well.
4. They **have got to** win the match.
5. She's **going to** have a party at the weekend.
6. Are you **telling** me the truth?

Extension
- Read and discuss the information box on page 43.
- This can be done as a class activity or in teams against the clock!

Answers
1	mince pies	eyes
2	clothes pegs	legs
3	loaf of bread	head
4	north and south	mouth
5	brass bands	hands
6	plates of meat	feet
7	biscuits and cheese	knees
8	Chevy Chase	face
9	Hampstead Heath	teeth

Resource Book

Support PCM
- Children should work individually.

Answers
(A)
1. What are you **going to** wear for the party?
2. We had a **great/fantastic** time!
3. He was busy so he told me to **go away**.
4. I **am not** happy about this.
5. I'm **very/really** pleased with my test mark.

(B)
1. I bought **potatoes** for **my** tea.
2. The **children** next door go to bed **very** early!
3. We **have got to** save **two pounds** for the school trip.
4. That **policeman** has been talking to that **man** for a long time.

(C)
1. You've got lovely, blue **eyes**.
2. My **hands** are freezing without gloves!
3. His **feet** were sore after the long walk.
4. I banged my **head** on the beam.

Extension PCM
- Children should work individually.

Answers
Suggested answers
"What **are** you **doing**'? asked Ben.
"**Going** for a walk," Sean replied.
" **Do you** want some company? asked Ben.
" **Yes**, why not," said Sean. "I've **got to** be back by five, so we can't go far."
" No **problem**," said Ben. "Have you got any **money** in case we want some **food**?"
"**No**, not a **penny**," sighed Sean.
" That **isn't** much good. Never mind. You come back to mine and we'll have a **really** good **meal** after the walk," suggested Ben.
"**Great**!" said Sean. " That's a **brilliant** idea."

Extra
Can children compile a list of other slang terms in common usage? Best to advise them that they cannot be rude!

BOOK 6 UNIT 20 Sentences

Conditional clauses

The concept of a sentence as a unit of language that 'makes sense' can be a difficult concept for some children to grasp. The course builds children's confidence in this area through giving them the opportunity to look at punctuation of statements, questions and exclamations to familiarise themselves with what a 'sentence' looks and sounds like.

Throughout the course, children will encounter: sentence punctuation; the concept of 'making sense'; direct and indirect speech; clauses which combine to make multi-clause sentences; parts of sentences – subject/object, subject/predicate; focusing on the sentence as a unit of language that can be improved; and Standard English constructions.

This unit introduces the concept of the conditional clause introduced by a conjunction. In conditional clauses, the action in the main clause is dependent on the possibility/probability/condition stated in the conditional clause.

As with all clauses, conditional clauses must contain a 'finite verb'. The best way of explaining a finite verb is one that makes a complete tense, so 'singing' is not finite but 'am singing' is. Both main and subordinate clauses need a finite verb.

Pupil Book

Focus
- Ask children what they understand by the term *sentence*.
- Revise/discuss the term *clause* and elicit the difference between a phrase and a clause. Use the term *finite verb*.
- Introduce the term *conditional clause*.
- Read and discuss the information box on page 44.
- Ask children to provide a different 'if' ending for *The swallows will nest here,* and a different 'depends on' ending for *The swallows nesting here.*
- Ask children to provide a different 'unless' ending for *Pandas will die out,* and a different 'depends on' ending for *Pandas not dying out.*
- The activity can be done orally or children can write.

Answers
1. The old man will go fishing **as long as the weather remains fine**.
2. I'm going into town **assuming I can get a bus**.
3. The house will not be finished this month **unless the builders work more quickly**.
4. I will call in the morning **only if I have news**.
5. The concert will go ahead **provided that no more of the cast becomes ill**.
6. You can watch the film on condition that you go to bed **as soon as it has finished**.
7. Sports day will be great fun **if it doesn't rain**!
8. She doesn't like carrots **unless they are roasted**.

Practice
- Remind the children of the conjunctions in the information box on page 44.
- Children can work in pairs or individually.

Answers
Individual answers

Extension
- Read and discuss the information box on page 45.
- Look at children's answers to the Focus questions. Ask them to read the sentences, putting the conditional clause first.
- Children should work individually on the activity.

Answers
Suggested answers
1. **If the lighthouse isn't working**, the ships will crash onto the rocks.
2. **Unless we pack the cases**, we cannot go on holiday!
3. **Only if the tickets are not too expensive**, can we go to the concert?
4. **As long as you return it this afternoon**, you can borrow my bicycle.
5. **Assuming that the bridge is clear**, we will leave this afternoon.

Resource Book

Support PCM
- Activity A: Children should work individually.
- Activity B: Monitor the work in progress as children may need help in spotting where conditional clauses could be added to what they write.

Answers
(A) Individual answers
(B) Individual answers

Extension PCM
- Children should work individually.

Answers
Individual answers

Extra
This is a difficult concept for most children so plenty of practice is needed.
Ask children for simple sentences and write on the board. Can they add a conditional clause to expand the sentence?

BOOK 6 UNIT 21 Punctuation

Semicolon and colon
These can be tricky punctuation marks for primary school children.

A semicolon usually separates clauses and can be thought of as the punctuation equivalent of the conjunction 'and'.

A colon can introduce a list in a sentence; introduce a result or an example; and balance one statement against another.

The approach in this unit is to get children to use the models in the information box as the first step to introducing these punctuation marks into their own writing. The explanation of the uses of these punctuation marks is not comprehensive, as young children may find very complex explanations confusing.

Pupil Book

Focus
- Revise/discuss the term *punctuation* and ask children to list the punctuation marks they know.
- Introduce the terms *semicolon* and *colon*.
- Read and discuss the information box on page 46.
- Do the activity orally.

Answers
(A) 1 two related statements
 2 items in a list where the items are more than one word

(B) 1 to introduce a list
 2 to introduce a result
 3 to balance two statements

Practice
- Children can work in pairs.
- When complete, discuss answers.

Answers
1 Young men play football: older men play golf.
2 The park looked beautiful; gardeners worked tirelessly through the seasons.
3 We need a good striker: someone from the Premier League.
4 Kim looked down the high street: many well-known shops had closed; litter blew about the once tidy streets; graffiti scarred the walls.
5 The fire alarm went off: the fire brigade was quickly on the scene.

Extension
- Model the first answer so the children understand what is required.

Answers
Individual answers

Resource Book

Support PCM
- Activities A and B: Children can work in pairs.
- When complete, discuss answers.
- Activity C: Children can work individually.

Answers
(A) 1 Today I must buy the paint and wallpaper; clean the brushes; clear the room; put down dustsheets.
 2 The rabbit was frightened; the fox was on the prowl.
 3 The concert hall filled up rapidly; the audience was looking forward to the music.
 4 Now that it's autumn we must prune the shrubs; dig up the summer plants; put the garden chairs away; put the pots in the shed.

(B) 1 Write these on the list: paint, wallpaper, brush cleaner and dustsheets.
 2 The rabbit was frightened of the fox: the fox didn't bother the badger.
 3 The head teacher made a decision: the school would close because of the snow.
 4 The forest was full of strange sounds: rustling in the undergrowth; hooting from the trees; screeching from the shadows.

(C) Individual answers

Extension PCM
Read and discuss the first answer in each activity so children understand what is required.

Answers
(A) Suggested answers
 1 Everyone likes her; she is so kind.
 2 Ben hates dogs; he was badly bitten as a child.
 3 Nelson was not feeling well; he had eaten too much.

(B) Suggested answers
 1 Sophie had a beautiful voice: her sister didn't.
 2 We needed a large house: we bought a small one.
 3 The twins love Indian food: I don't.

Extra
Do more oral practice on the board.
Write sentences that require a colon/semicolon for individuals to punctuate.

BOOK 6 UNIT 22 Paragraphs

Discursive writing

A paragraph is a group of sentences within a piece of writing. It is usually signalled by:
- indenting in handwritten work and fiction (all paragraphs but the first)
- leaving a full line space (block paragraphing) in typing and non-fiction work.

The mechanics of paragraphing can be taught as a concept, but the 'reasons' for paragraphing are many and varied, and must be attached to a particular style of writing.

Throughout the course, children have encountered paragraphing in narrative writing – time, place and for the inclusion of direct speech; paragraphing for aspects of a topic in non-fiction information writing; and adverbials as a signal for paragraphing.

This unit examines paragraphing to present for and against arguments in discursive writing.

Pupil Book

Focus
- Revise/discuss the term *paragraph*.
- Revise/discuss the term *indenting* and not indenting for the first paragraph.
- Ask children what they have learned about paragraphing in stories and information writing.
- Introduce/discuss the term *discursive writing*.
- Use the discursive passage in the information box on page 48 to show children what a paragraph looks like on the page.
- Read and discuss the information box on page 48 and work through the Focus questions with the children.
- When complete, look at the opening phrase of each paragraph and discuss the *job* each is doing in the passage. Children explain why the passage is paragraphed at these points.

Answers
1. embolden word/phrase
2. introduction/points for/points against/conclusion
3. two
4. two

Practice
- Children can work in small groups for the discussion stage of this activity.
- They should then produce individual discursive pieces.

Answers
Individual answers

Extension
- Children should work individually with your support.

Answers
Individual answers

Resource Book

Support PCM
- Children should work individually with your support.

Answers
Individual answers

Extension PCM
- Children can work in small groups for the discussion stage of this activity.
- They should then produce individual discursive pieces.

Answers
Individual answers

Extra
Discuss with the class a topic they are interested in which would lend itself to discursive writing.

Set up a debate with proposers and seconders. The class can question the speakers and take a vote.

BOOK 6 UNIT 23 Verbs

Active and passive

Verbs are often explained as 'doing words' or 'being words'. They are possibly the most complex part of speech for young children to grasp because of their many forms and tenses.

Throughout the course, children will encounter the present simple, present progressive (continuous), past simple, past progressive, present perfect (labelled simply *perfect* throughout the course), past perfect, future, infinitive (labelled *verb family name* in the early parts of the course), auxiliary verbs, modals, active and passive verbs and subjunctive verbs (a construction very rarely used except in extremely formal writing).

Participles are referred to as '*ing* words' and 'regular past simple tense words'; finite verbs are referred to as 'main' or 'proper verbs', and it is for the teacher to decide the appropriate time to introduce the terms *participle* and *finite verb*.

This unit revises the 'active' and 'passive' mood of verbs. In the active mood, the subject does the action. In the passive mood, the subject receives/is affected by the action. The subject of an active sentence becomes the 'agent' in a passive sentence. It also introduces the 'invisible agent', i.e. when the agent in a sentence is implied or known by the reader because of the context.

Pupil Book

Focus
- Revise/discuss the term *verb* and ask for examples of:
  - present simple
  - present progressive
  - past simple
  - past progressive
  - perfect
  - past perfect
  - future
- Revise/discuss the terms *active verb* and *passive verb*.
- Read and discuss the information box on page 50.
- Do the activity orally.

Answers
1. The soldier **was hidden** by the bushes. — passive
2. The yacht **sailed** into the harbour. — active
3. The booking **was taken** by the restaurant manager. — passive
4. Competitors **were given** a number by the organiser. — passive
5. My neighbour **keeps** bees. — active
6. The birds **are** frequently **chased** by the cat. — passive

Practice
- Discuss the sentences before children write to stimulate ideas of who might have completed the picture/milked the cows, etc.

Answers
(A) Individual answers
(B) Individual answers

Extension
- Remind the children that, in a passive sentence, the subject of the active sentence becomes the agent.
- Demonstrate with the first pair.

Answers
Individual answers

Resource Book

Support PCM
- Children should work individually.

Answers
(A)
1. The waiter spilled the coffee. — A
2. The coffee was spilled by the waiter. — P
3. The elephant was stalked by the hunter. — P
4. The hunter stalked the elephant. — A
5. The old barn was struck by lightning. — P
6. Lightning struck the old barn. — A

(B)
1. The car was mended by the mechanic.
2. His foot was bandaged by the nurse.
3. The city centre was destroyed by fire.
4. Books are lent by public libraries.
5. The beanstalk was planted by Jack.

Extension PCM
- Children should work individually.

Answers
(A) Individual answers
(B) Individual answers
(C) Individual answers
(D) Individual answers
(E) Individual answers

Extra
Make subject/agent cards, e.g.

| the soldier | his friend | the snow |

Individuals pick a card and give an active and a passive sentence using the words on the card as the subject, then the agent.

BOOK 6 UNIT 24 Standard and Non-standard English

Grammatical constructions
This is the second of three units that examine Standard and Non-standard English with the aim of helping children to appreciate the use of appropriate registers.

Children have encountered the concept of 'slang'.

This unit introduces standard and non-standard grammatical constructions, many of which children will have encountered in noun–verb agreement and confusing words.

Pupil Book

Focus
- Read and discuss the information box on page 52.
- The activity can be done orally or the children can write.

Answers
1. I don't want **anything** to eat.
2. Would you **lend** me a pencil?
3. He **taught** me to speak French.
4. We should **have** left earlier.
5. **My brother and I** like cricket.
6. Give me the key **that** you found.
7. The tigers **were** hungry.
8. You **were** so noisy!
9. We **are** the best team.
10. **Those** are beautiful flowers.
11. They **have** gone on holiday.
12. I need **my** glasses.

Practice
- Children should work individually.

Answers
(A)
1. I **borrow** books from the library.
2. Will you put **those** flowers in a vase?
3. We should **have** brought an umbrella.
4. Can you tell me **what** time it is?
5. I would like a packet **of** biscuits.
6. Give me the plate **that** you broke.
7. Will you **lend** me that DVD?
8. I saw **them** outside the shop.

(B)
1. **Mum and I** go shopping on Saturday.
2. Sam never goes **anywhere**.
3. The elephants **are** huge!
4. I would **have** been on time but the bus broke down.
5. She **goes** to her friend's house after school.

Extension
- Children can work in pairs.
- The pairs can present their Non-Standard and Standard English duologues to the class.

Answers
Individual answers

Resource Book

Support PCM
- Children should work individually.

Answers
(A)
1. Mum said <u>me and my sister</u> could watch a DVD.
2. I <u>borrowed</u> my pen to Lizzie.
3. We could <u>of</u> won the match if one of our players hadn't been sent off.
4. I think <u>them</u> books are mine.
5. We <u>was</u> sure we <u>was</u> going to be late.

(B)
1. Mum said **my sister and I** could watch a DVD.
2. I **lent** my pen to Lizzie.
3. We could **have** won the match if one of our players hadn't been sent off.
4. I think **those** books are mine.
5. We **were** sure we **were** going to be late.

(C)
1. We didn't go **anywhere** at the weekend.
2. I haven't got **anything** to say to you.
3. I can't see **any** keys **anywhere**.
4. He **never** hid the book **anywhere**.

Extension PCM
- Children should work individually.

Answers
(A)
1. She **doesn't** care whether she goes or not.
2. Do you **want to** listen to my new CD?
3. Did you see him jump **off** the wall?
4. I **saw/have seen** that before!
5. Sam **did/had done** his jobs before he went to meet his friends.

(B) Individual answers

Extra
Make Non-standard English grammatical cards, e.g.

| we was | me and my friend |

| Can you borrow me that? |

Individuals pick a card and say the Standard English equivalent of the phrase/sentence on the card.

BOOK 6 UNIT 25 Punctuation

Hyphens with prefixes

Hyphens are small dashes that connect parts of words. Their specific use is not universally agreed, as a look at a variety of dictionaries will testify.

Children have encountered the hyphen to form:
– compound nouns
– compound verbs
– compound adjectives
– adverb phrases where the adverb does not end in *ly*
– numbers from 21 to 99
– fractions

This unit examines hyphens with prefixes.

Pupil Book

Focus
- Revise/discuss the term *punctuation* and ask children to list the punctuation marks they know.
- Revise/discuss the term *hyphen* and the uses that the children are familiar with.
- Read and discuss the information box on page 54.
- Do the activity orally.

Answers
1 ex-president
2 co-own
3 ex-service
4 pre-establish
5 self-adhesive
6 semi-detached
7 anti-inflammatory
8 re-roof
9 ex-con
10 semi-final
11 anti-British
12 self-aware

Practice
- Children should work individually with the aid of a dictionary.

Answers
(A) Individual answers
(B) Individual answers

Extension
- Read and discuss the information box on page 55.
- Children can work in pairs.
- When complete, discuss answers.

Answers
Individual answers

Resource Book

Support PCM
- Children should work individually.

Answers

(A)
1 undemanding
   unEnglish ✔
   unVictorian ✔
2 preexist ✔
   prefix
   preelect ✔
3 semiindependent ✔
   semibreve
   semiinvalid ✔
4 selfish
   selfcentred ✔
   selfdrive ✔
5 exmember ✔
   exchange
   extreasurer ✔

(B) un-English   un-Victorian
    pre-exist   pre-elect
    semi-independent   semi-invalid
    self-centred   self-drive
    ex-member   ex-treasurer

(C) 1 re-collect
      a to remember
      b to collect something again
    2 re-count
      a to count again
      b to tell/narrate
    3 re-sign
      a to leave one's job
      b to sign something again
    4 re-dress
      a to put something right
      b to get dressed again
    5 re-press
      a to iron something again
      b to keep hidden

(D) Individual answers

Extension PCM
- Read and discuss the information box on page 123.
- Children should work individually with the aid of a dictionary.

Answers
1 pre-owned
2 pre-establish
3 preamble
4 pre-adolescent
5 preoccupy
Sentences = individual answers

Extra
Make prefix cards, e.g.

| pre | anti | re |

Individuals pick a card and say a hyphenated word with that prefix.
The class look up the word in the dictionary to see if it is correct.

136

BOOK 6 UNIT 26 Sentences

Clause round-up

The concept of a sentence as a unit of language that 'makes sense' can be a difficult concept for some children to grasp. The course builds children's confidence in this area through giving them the opportunity to look at punctuation of statements, questions and exclamations to familiarise themselves with what a 'sentence' looks and sounds like.

Throughout the course, children have encountered:
- main clauses
- subordinate clauses
- adverbial clauses
- relative (adjectival) clauses
- conditional clauses

This unit revises these clauses.

All clauses must contain a 'finite verb'. The best way of explaining a finite verb is one that makes a complete tense, so 'singing' is not finite but 'am singing' is. Both main and subordinate clauses need a finite verb.

Pupil Book

Focus
- Revise/discuss the term clause and ask for examples in sentences.
- Read and discuss the information box on page 56.
- Children should work individually.

Answers
1. <u>That boat won the race</u> although the sail was damaged.
2. <u>She read the book</u> that had been recommended.
3. <u>We can fly the kite</u> unless the wind drops.
4. <u>The twins could go on the trip</u> provided they saved their pocket money.
5. <u>The gardener</u> who pruned the roses <u>works hard</u>.

Practice
- Model the first answer so children understand what is required.

Answers
Suggested answers
1. **Even though I own the car**, I don't know the registration number.
2. I will never get this finished **unless you help me**.
3. The pirate buried the treasure **that had come from the sunken ship**.
4. **If you finish all your work**, you can leave early.
5. I must learn to swim **so I can go in the deep end**.
6. Our new head teacher is a woman **who has been teaching for many years**.

Extension
- Read/discuss the first answer so children understand what is required.

Answers

A Suggested answers

1. The dog chased the rabbit.
   - adverb clause: The dog chased the rabbit after it popped up from its burrow.
   - relative clause: The dog chased the rabbit that lived in the garden.
2. People went to the concert.
   - adverb clause: People went to the concert even though they had no tickets.
   - relative clause: People went to the concert that had been advertised on television.
3. Adventurers climb mountains.
   - adverb clause: Adventurers climb mountains because they are there.
   - relative clause: Adventurers climb mountains which put them in danger.
4. He met his brother.
   - adverb clause: We met his brother after the match.
   - relative clause: He met his brother who is a famous footballer.
5. An iceberg sank the Titanic.
   - adverb clause: An iceberg sank the Titanic before help could reach it.
   - relative clause: An iceberg sank the Titanic which was on its maiden voyage.

B Individual answers

Resource Book

Support PCM
- Encourage children to add other clauses, if possible.
- Children should work individually.

Answers
Individual answers

Extension PCM
- Children should work individually.

Answers
Individual answers

Extra
Make simple sentence cards and clause cards, e.g.

sentences:
| My dad does the shopping. |
| She will cook the dinner. |

clauses:
| adverb clause |
| relative clause |
| conditional clause |

Individuals pick a sentence card and a clause card. They add a clause to expand the sentences.

BOOK 6 UNIT 27 Verbs

Passive and subjunctive forms

Verbs are often explained as 'doing words' or 'being words'. They are possibly the most complex part of speech for young children to grasp because of their many forms and tenses.

Throughout the course, children will encounter the present simple, present progressive (also known as continuous), past simple, past progressive, present perfect (labelled simply *perfect* throughout the course), past perfect, future, infinitive (labelled *verb family name* in the early parts of the course), auxiliary verbs, modals, active and passive verbs and subjunctive verbs (a construction very rarely used except in extremely formal writing).

Participles are referred to as '*ing* words' and 'regular past simple tense words'; finite verbs are referred to as 'main' or 'proper verbs', and it is for the teacher to decide the appropriate time to introduce the terms *participle* and *finite verb*.

This unit revises the 'active' and 'passive' mood of verbs. In the active mood, the subject does the action. In the passive mood, the subject receives/is affected by the action. The subject of an active sentence becomes the 'agent' in a passive sentence. It introduces the subjunctive form which is rarely used except in very formal situations.

Pupil Book

Focus
- Revise/discuss the term *verb* and ask for examples of:
  – present simple
  – present progressive
  – past simple
  – past progressive
  – perfect
  – past perfect
  – future
- Revise the terms *active verb* and *passive verb*.
- Introduce the term *subjunctive*.
- Read and discuss the information box on page 58.
- Do the activity orally.

Answers
Subjunctive:
1. I insist that you go home.
2. It was important that you finish the test.
3. It is a good idea that she send the letter.
4. Jill requested that we attend her party.
5. I suggest that you stop eating chocolate.
6. It is recommended that you don't swim the sea today.

Practice
- Children can work individually or in pairs.

Answers
(A)
1. Life jackets were worn by everyone on board.
2. An interesting talk was delivered by the speaker.
3. The boat was swamped by the rough sea.
4. Several buildings were damaged by fire.
5. A new Mayor was elected by voters.

(B)
1. He is recommending that there **be** great changes.
2. She suggested that she **need** an assistant.
3. The doctor suggested they **swim** every day.
4. I insisted he **leave** immediately.
5. They proposed there **be** longer working days.

Extension
- Read and discuss the information box on page 59.
- Do the activity as a class.

Answers
1. If I **were** the Head Teacher, **I would** let Sports Day go ahead.
2. I wish I **were** more successful.
3. If he **were** you, **he would** do the same.
4. If it **were** only that simple, everyone **could** do it.
5. She wished it **were** the weekend.

Resource Book

Support PCM
- Children should work individually with your support.

Answers
Suggested answers
1. A = The clouds hung low over the mountain.
   P = The mountain was covered by clouds.
2. A = The storm whipped up the sea.
   P = The sea was whipped up by the storm.
3. A = The fisherman did not catch the fish.
   P = The fish was not caught by the fisherman.
4. A = The crowd watched the hot-air balloon.
   P = The hot-air balloon was watched by the crowd.

Extension PCM
- Activity A: Children can work in pairs.
- When complete, discuss answers.
- Activity B: Read and discuss the first answer so children understand what is required.

Answers

(A)
	verb family name (infinitive)	subjunctive
1	to interrupt	interrupt
2	to sacrifice	sacrifice
3	to recommend	recommend
4	to queue	queue
5	to persuade	persuade

(B) Suggested answers
1. I ask that you choose quickly.
2. The teacher demanded that she tell the truth.
3. He insisted that I speak more clearly.
4. We propose that people volunteer in groups of three.
5. The chairman requested that we attend another meeting.
6. I suggest that applicants enclose a self-addressed envelope.

Extra
Make subject/agent cards, e.g.

| the snow | our cat | that bus |

Individuals pick a card and give an active and a passive sentence using the words on the card as the subject, then the agent.

BOOK 6 UNIT 28 Standard English

Vocabulary

This is the third of three units that examine Standard and Non-standard English with the aim of helping children to appreciate the use of appropriate registers.

Children have encountered the concept of 'slang' and 'non-standard grammatical constructions'.

This unit examines the use of 'sloppy' vocabulary, and appropriate register for the intended audience.

Pupil Book

Focus
- Read and discuss the information box on page 60.
- The activity can be done orally as a class or in groups.
- If children work in groups, discuss their findings as a class.

Answers
Recap on the use of slang and incorrect grammar.
Focus on the vocabulary in the letter.

Practice
- Children should work individually

Answers

(A) 1 How are you? I'm great.
    2 Individual answers
    3 Individual answers

(B) 1 Suggested answer
       Dear (name of sister) How are things with you? It is quite dull here. I am going shopping with Mum later today. I hope she will buy me something! Would you like to Skype later on?
       Beth
    2 Individual answers
    3 Individual answers

(C) 1 It's in the envelope   Please find enclosed
    2 the job   the post
    3 I've always wanted to   It has always been my ambition
    4 I think   I trust
    5 what I've done before   previous experience
    6 if you want to meet up   Should you wish to meet me
    7 it would be OK   I would be delighted
    8 when it suits   at your convenience
    9 there's some references   I also enclose references
    10 the people I work for now   my current employers

Extension
- Children should work individually with your support.

Answers
Individual answer

Resource Book

Support PCM
- Children should work individually with your support.

Answers
Suggested answer

Hello Aisha,

How are you doing? We are having a really great time here on our holidays. There are so many exciting things to do. We went windsurfing which was fantastic. The instructor said I was really good because I can keep my balance. You can really go fast on those things as they really get up some speed!
I was thinking you could come and stay next year and sample our English food.
Please write to me soon. You must have a lot of news to tell me.
Claire XX

Extension PCM
- Children should work individually with your support.

Answers
Individual answers

Extra
- Use the children's emails from the Extension as the basis of a discussion about choosing the appropriate way in which to write for a given audience.

Book-6 Check-up answers

Check-up 1 (Units 1–6)

Sentences

(A) 1 The baby was playing with the teddy.
2 The sea battered the rocks.
3 Fireworks lit up the sky.

(B) Individual answers
(C) Individual answers
(D) Individual answers

Homophones and homonyms

(A) Individual answers
(B) 1 fleet   2 fly
    3 fell   4 foil

Pronouns

(A) 1 Tom lost the money **that** was for his lunch.
2 We have relatives **who** live in Australia.
3 Do you know Mrs Dodds **who** has moved in next door?

(B) 1 This is the story **whose** main character is a clown.
2 **Whose** jackets are these?
3 To **whom** are you referring?

Verbs

(A) 1 The firemen **can** put out the fire if they arrive in time.
2 You **may** invite a friend for tea.
3 The committee **can** extend the meeting if they want to.

(B) 1 You have a temperature so you **must** see a doctor.
2 I have lost my dictionary so I **must** get a new one.
3 I am not sure but this coin **might** be ancient.

(C) Individual answers

Check-up 2 (Units 7–12)

Verbs

(A) 1 The pilot had flown for six hours.
2 I wake up at seven o'clock every morning.
3 Shall we go for a walk?
4 The knight rode across the drawbridge.
5 I am flying my kite.
6 She has taken the dog for a walk.
7 The ships were battling the storm.

(B) 1 past perfect   2 present simple
    3 future   4 past simple
    5 present progressive 6 perfect
    7 past progressive

Confusing words

(A) 1 Repeat after me **all together**.
2 I **passed** three police cars on my way to work.
3 Carefully **lay** the vase in the box.

(B) Individual answers

Sentences

(A) 1 I need to go to the doctor **but** I don't have time.
2 Was that the phone **or** was it the doorbell?
3 The car's tyre was punctured **and** the bumper was bent.

(B) Individual answers

(C) 1 Be careful with that vase **because** you might break it.
2 The plants need some water **although** it rained last night.
3 Here is the book **that** I found in the library.

(D) Individual answers
(E) Individual answers
(F) Individual answers
(G) Suggested answers
1 So no one would hear me, I moved quietly.
2 Creeping up to the window, I looked in.
3 Even though the room was in darkness, I could see the dog asleep on the mat.

Nouns

(A) 1 Where are Mum's keys?
2 He asked me to buy a huge, orange pumpkin.
3 Our neighbour's barking dog is a nuisance!

(B) Individual answers

Check-up 3 (Units 13–18)

Improving writing

Individual answers

Confusing words

1 Do you ever wonder **whether** there is life in outer space?
2 We have **less** time than you think!
3 **You're** going to miss the bus!
4 **Who's** got the TV remote?
5 There are **fewer** apples on the tree this year.
6 We have been learning about **weather** and climate.
7 I like the singer **whose** voice is amazing.
8 All **your** spellings are correct.

Punctuation

(A) 1 left-handed   2 cold-blooded
    3 short-sighted   4 old-fashioned
    5 middle-aged

Sentences

1 "Where do your cousins live?" asked Greg.
2 Kim thought for a moment. "Well, I have a cousin in Australia," she replied, "and a cousin in America."
3 "I would love to go to Australia," enthused Greg. "I'd love to go to America, too!"

Verbs

(A) 1 He has to go to the doctor's this afternoon.
2 I have to finish this book by the weekend.
3 We ought to tidy this room.

(B) Individual answers

(C) 1 The explosion was heard for miles around.   P
2 The buses crawled slowly along the road.   A
3 The parcel was delivered by the courier.   P

(D) 1 The wind blew down the tree.
2 The giraffes ate the topmost leaves.
3 A stone broke the window.

Check-up 4 (Units 19–20)

Standard English

(A)
1. policeman
2. man
3. food
4. child
6. money
7. potato

(B)
1. We **were very** sorry about the broken window.
2. I **didn't** see **anything because** I was asleep.
3. I'm **going to leave** now **because** I'm **bored**.
4. They **are spending** three **pounds** on a magazine.

(C)
1. See you
2. It was so funny I laughed out loud.
3. How are you?
4. That sounds great!

Sentences

(A)
1. He will be here on time <u>provided that there are no delays on the motorway</u>.
2. <u>As long as there is moonlight</u>, we will be able to see where we are going.
3. <u>Assuming your calculation is correct</u>, there will be enough seats for everyone.

(B) Individual answers

Punctuation

(A)
1. I like creamy mashed potatoes; roasted carrots; big, juicy sprouts; loads and loads of gravy!
2. We were scared; the lights had gone out.

(B)
1. These are the things I need: two eggs, flour, butter and water.
2. Dubai is a modern city: Amman is ancient.
3. The train was very late: the people were angry.

Paragraphs

Individual answers

Verbs

(A)
1. The penguins <u>were diving</u> for fish. A
2. The field <u>was ploughed</u> by the farmer. P
3. The prisoners <u>were locked</u> up by the guard. P

(B)
1. The accident was witnessed by several people.
2. The headlines were read out by the newsreader.
3. Bamboo is eaten by pandas.

Check-up 5 (Units 25–28)

Punctuation

1. re-press
2. recount
3. recollect
4. re-sign
5. reserve

Sentences

Individual answers

Verbs

(A)
1. The pilot <u>landed</u> the plane. A
2. The city <u>was struck</u> by a hurricane. P
3. Everyone <u>was startled</u> by the explosion. P
4. New trees <u>are planted</u> every year. P
5. The sailors <u>battled</u> with the storm. A

(B)
1. It was recommended that he <u>walk</u> two miles a day.
2. I request that you <u>leave</u> the room.
3. If I <u>were</u> really brave, I should risk everything.

Standard English

How R U?	How are you?
Fancy a cuppa?	Would you like a cup of tea?
Where you going?	Where are you going?
That's OK.	That's fine.
That's wicked.	That's wonderful.

141

Revision Book answers

Adjectives

1

(A)
1. The <u>strong</u> wind moved the <u>enormous</u> clouds across the <u>dark</u> sky.
2. A <u>beautiful</u> bird nested in the <u>shady</u> tree.
3. The <u>old</u> lady used a <u>wooden</u> stick to help her to walk.

(B) Suggested answers
tiny/timid/terrifying/tall/trustworthy

(C) Individual answers

2

(A) Suggested answers
blue: navy/light/azure/cobalt/sapphire/turquoise/ultramarine
green: moss/jade/mint/grass/forest/teal/olive
yellow: mustard/saffron/buttermilk/canary/lemon

3

(A)
1. The <u>first</u> bus was full but <u>three</u> people got off.
2. I came <u>fifteenth</u> in the race out of <u>thirty</u>.
3. <u>Thirteen</u> is supposed to be unlucky but he succeeded on his <u>thirteenth</u> attempt.

(B) Individual answers

4

(A)
1. beautiful — ugly/unattractive
2. loose — tight
3. middle — first/last
4. miserable — happy/joyous

(B)
1. insane
2. unforgiving
3. dissatisfied
4. incapable

5

(A)
1. colder
2. rougher
3. calmer

(B) Individual answers

6

(A)
1. slowest
2. quickest
3. meanest

(B) Individual answers

7

(A)

adjective	comparative adjective	superlative adjective
fat	fatter	fattest
flat	flatter	flattest
fierce	fiercer	fiercest
terrifying	more terrifying	most terrifying
tame	tamer	tamest
creepy	creepier	creepiest
magnificent	more magnificent	most magnificent
stormy	stormier	stormiest

(B)
1. This is the **best** I've ever done in a spelling test!
2. I like bananas **least** of all types of fruit.
3. People gave **more** money to the charity than last time.

8

(A)
1. a **featureless** landscape
2. a **beautiful** view
3. a **jumping** bean
4. a **torn** page
5. a **talking** parrot
6. a **childish** prank
7. a **furious** gale

(B) Individual answers

9

(A)
1. The <u>carpet with the dirty stain</u> has to be cleaned.
2. My great-aunt, <u>an active and curious person</u>, is ninety today!
3. The <u>wide, rolling, sunlit</u> hills stretched out before us.

(B) Individual answers

10

(A)
1. We'll take <u>my</u> picnic basket, <u>your</u> tent, <u>his</u> map and <u>her</u> torch.
2. With <u>our</u> car and <u>their</u> car, we'll have enough room for everyone.

(B) Individual answers

Adverbs

1

(A)
1. Tess copied <u>carefully</u> from the board.
2. The dog followed <u>obediently</u> at his master's heels.
3. The winds blew <u>ferociously</u> across the moors.

(B) Suggested answers
slowly/sensibly/softly/silently/sorrowfully

(C) Individual answers

2

(A)
1. Ali went swimming <u>yesterday</u>.
2. Just leave the books <u>there</u>.
3. I'm going <u>nowhere</u> until the rain stops

(B) Individual answers

3

(A)
1. higher
2. more willingly
3. faster
4. more quietly
5. more successfully

(B)
1. more elegantly
2. faster
Sentences = individual answers

4

(A)
1. nearest
2. most fiercely
3. earliest
4. most rarely
4. most disastrously

(B)
1. most carefully
2. highest
Sentences = individual answers

142

(C)

adverb	comparative adverb	superlative adverb
badly	worse	worst
well	better	best
far	farther/further	farthest/furthest

5

(A) 1 She got up <u>early in the morning</u> to pack for her holiday.
2 The lioness sprang <u>powerfully and swiftly</u> onto its prey.
3 I lost my money <u>somewhere on the way to school</u>.

(B) Individual answers

6

1 Every Saturday evening, we visit our relatives.
2 Calmly and courteously, the manager dealt with the problem.
3 In the deepest part of the forest, the children huddled together.

7

(A) 1 The tiger crept <u>almost noiselessly</u> through the undergrowth.
2 We come to see you <u>so often</u>, it feels like home.
3 <u>Rather hesitantly</u>, she approached the spider.

(B) Individual answers

8

Individual answers

Antonyms and synonyms.

1

(A)
clean	dirty
fat	thin
little	big
long	short
wide	narrow
sharp	blunt
young	old
wet	dry

(A) 1 unhealthy
2 unkind
3 uncertain
4 unselfish
5 unwise

(A) Individual answers

2

(A) Individual answers
(B) Individual answers
(C) Individual answers
(D) Individual answers

Articles

1

1 **an** orchard
2 **an** apple orchard
3 **a** pear orchard
4 **a** book
5 **an** interesting book
6 **a** boring book
7 **a** large army
8 **a** small army
9 **an** army
10 **an** orange dress
11 **a** dress
12 **a** black dress

2

1 Mount Everest is **the** tallest mountain in **the** world.
2 I would like **a** cup of tea, please.
3 **A** family called **the** Robinsons have moved in next door.

Capital letters

A Visit **T**o **A M**useum
On **F**riday, 27th **A**pril, **Y**ear 6 went to the museum in **B**lackminster. **T**he coach came for us at 9 o'clock and we arrived at the museum at 9.30. **O**ur teacher, **M**rs **H**oward, bought a guide book called **T**he **M**arvellous **M**useum so she could tell us about the things we were looking at.
My favourite room in the museum was all about the theatre. **I** liked the miniature stage sets. One of the sets was for a production of **S**hakespeare's play **K**ing **L**ear.
The museum also had a huge collection of **R**oman artifacts – weapons, coins and cooking pots. You could sit and watch a film called **T**he **R**omans **I**n **B**ritain which was very interesting. **I** learned all about **H**adrian's **W**all.
In **A**ugust, the museum is having a special exhibition about explorers such as **C**hristopher **C**olumbus and **C**aptain **C**ook. **I** want to come back and see that.

Clauses

1

(A) 1 <u>The carpet was ruined</u> because the log had burnt a hole in it.
2 Even though she felt unwell, <u>she was going to meet her friend</u>.

(B) 1 The pitch was dry <u>although it had rained the previous night</u>.
2 <u>If you arrive early</u>, will you save me a seat?

(C) Individual answers
(D) Individual answers

2

(A) 1 The supermarket closes <u>before the car park does</u>.
2 The hedge was overgrown <u>because no one had cut it</u>.
3 <u>When she read the letter</u>, she was very excited.

(B) Individual answers
(C) Individual answers

3

(A) 1 That's the hedgehog <u>which lives under the shed</u>.
2 I like the story about the selfish giant <u>who saw the error of his ways</u>.
3 Neil Armstrong was the astronaut <u>who first walked on the Moon</u>.

(B) Individual answers
(C) Individual answers

4

(A) 1 I will help you <u>providing that I have the time</u>.
2 You can go to the park <u>as long as you are back in time for dinner</u>.
3 We will get tickets <u>only if we book them early</u>.

(B) Individual answers
(C) Individual answers

Confusing words

1

1. If I go **to** the shops I will have **to** buy some chocolate!
2. In **two** weeks' time, I will have enough money so I can come, **too**.
3. I'm **too** tired **to** walk the last **two** miles.

2

1. **They're** sure **their** boots were **there**.
2. **Their** friend said she would meet them over **there**.
3. **There** is the castle which **their** enemies attacked.

3

1. **We're** going **where** we can find some shade.
2. The birds **were** singing but we couldn't see **where** they **were**.
3. **We're** not sure about **where** we are going.

4

1. If **it's** messy, we will have to clean out **its** cage.
2. **Its** paw is sore and **it's** limping.

5

1. If you **win**, you **win** the prize.
2. To **win** the race, I have to **beat** Sam and Ben.

6

1. May I **have** two **of** those apples?
2. Five **of** the children **have** packed lunches.

7

Individual answers

8

Individual answers

9

verb	to lie = putting yourself in a horizontal position
present simple	I lie
present progressive	I am lying
past simple	I lay
past progressive	I was lying
perfect	I have lain
past perfect	I had lain

verb	to lie = telling untruths
present simple	I lie
present progressive	I am lying
past simple	I lied
past progressive	I was lying
perfect	I have lied
past perfect	I had lied

10

1. adjective
2. noun
3. preposition
4. adverb

11

Individual answers

12

1. When **you're** ready, read out **your** poem.
2. **Your** painting shows **you're** very good at art.

13

use with fewer	use with less
lorry	butter
coin	furniture
mile	news
orange	advice
suitcase	music

14

1. I don't mind **whether** the **weather** is cold or not.
2. People always complain about the **weather**, **whether** it's sunny or wet.

Conjunctions

1

1. We were lost **but** we didn't panic.
2. The jug was knocked off the table **and** glass went everywhere.
3. My idea didn't work **but** I'll think of another one.

2

Individual answers

3

1. I'll take an umbrella **so** I won't get wet.
2. I'll take an umbrella **because** it is going to rain.

4

1. Let's go to the market **when** it opens at eight o'clock.
2. Let's go to the market **before/after** we have had supper.
3. Let's go to the market **while** it is still light.
4. Let's go to the market **when** we have made a shopping list.

Direct and indirect speech

1

(A)
1. "Do you know anything about Mars?" asked David.
2. "A red flag means it is too dangerous to swim in the sea," explained the lifeguard.
3. Angie muttered, "It isn't my fault."

(B)
1. "Dinosaurs lived millions of years ago," explained the teacher.
2. The pirate captain bellowed, "We set sail in an hour!"

(C) "Today, we are going to learn about Sir Francis Chichester," explained Mr Evans.
"Who was he?" asked Gina.
"He was a sailor who sailed around the world on his own," said Mr Evans.

2

1. "The car has broken down!" moaned Dad. "I'll have to ring the garage."
2. "It is Sports Day tomorrow," announced the teacher, "and I would like everyone to take part."

3

(A)
1. muttered/mumbled/whispered
2. grumbled/snapped/snarled
3. yelled/shrieked/screamed

4 explained/suggested/advised
5 laughed/giggled/joked
6 cried/sobbed/wailed

(B) Individual answer

4

Suggested answer
Amir asked his friends what sport they would like to be good at. Karen wanted to be a champion swimmer but George wanted to be a jockey and win the Grand National. Ben said that horses scared him and he wanted to be a racing car driver. Tania was amazed that Ben was scared of horses but wanted to drive around at over a hundred miles an hour! Ben wanted to know which sport she would choose. Tania announced that she had always fancied the idea of ski jumping.

Homophones and homonyms

1

(A)
1	meat/meet	2	by/buy
3	right/write	4	no/know
5	so/sew	6	here/hear
7	see/sea	8	time/thyme
9	paws/pause	10	moat/mote
11	beach/beech	12	maze/maize
13	stairs/stares	14	knave/nave
15	slay/sleigh	16	vale/veil
17	chord/cord	18	hair/hare
19	be/bee	20	air/heir
21	break/brake	22	caught/court
23	deer/dear	24	days/daze
25	you/ewe	26	feet/feat
27	fair/fare	28	herd/heard
29	hole/whole	30	pale/pail

(B)
1	pride/pried	2	root/route
3	sent/scent	4	taught/taut
5	tear/tier	6	waste/waist
7	wave/waive	8	wine/whine
9	key/quay	10	horse/hoarse

2

(A) 1 play 2 cap 3 well

(B) 1a noun 1b verb 2a verb
    2b noun 2a verb 3b noun

(C) Individual answers

Improving writing

1 Individual answers

2 Individual answers

3 Individual answers

4 Individual answers

Nouns

1 Individual answers

2

(A) Individual answers
(B) **S**unday/**M**onday/**T**uesday/**W**ednesday/**T**hursday/**F**riday/**S**aturday
(C) **J**anuary/**F**ebruary/**M**arch/**A**pril/**M**ay/**J**une/**J**uly/**A**ugust/**S**eptember/**O**ctober/**N**ovember/**D**ecember
(D) Individual answers

3

1	a **pack** of cards	2	a **bunch** of grapes
3	a **flight** of stairs	4	a **flock** of sheep
5	a **constellation** of stars	6	a **herd** of cows
7	an **orchestra**/a band of musicians	8	a **gaggle** of geese
9	a **forest/wood** of trees	10	a **crowd/throng/queue** of people

4 Individual answers

5

1	robber	robbery
2	miserable	misery
3	to please	pleasure
4	to free	freedom
5	friend	friendship
6	hero	heroism
7	active	action
8	kind	kindness
9	silent	silence
10	weak	weakness
11	forgetful	forgetfulness
12	fragrant	fragrance
13	to collect	collection
14	to describe	description
15	envious	envy
16	slave	slavery
17	to imagine	imagination
18	wise	wisdom
19	happy	happiness
20	important	importance

6

(A)
1	Tom's book	2	the dog's collar
3	the girl's brush	4	the fox's lair
5	Harry's shoes	6	the farmer's dog
7	Ben's sister	8	the car's tyre
9	the cat's claws	10	the bird's feathers

(B)
1	the lions' cubs	2	the twins' cat
3	the thieves' den	4	the pirates' ship
5	the babies' toys	6	the badgers' hole
7	the children's room	8	the people's bus
9	the ladies' bags	10	the oxen's plough

7

1	swim	I am a **swimmer**.
2	sing	I am a **singer**.
3	run	I am a **runner**.
4	drive	I am a **driver**.
5	paint	I am a **painter**.
6	ride	I am a **rider**.

8

1 **the** library
2 **a** disaster
3 **my/your/his/her/its/our/their** brainwave
4 (individual answers) problem
5 (individual answers) experience
6 (individual answers) storm

145

Paragraphs

Individual answers

Prefixes

1

1. **ir**relevant
2. **il**legal
3. **dis**honest
4. **anti**clockwise
5. **in**elegant
6. **un**wise
7. **im**mature
8. **ab**normal

2

1. **out**do
2. **co**operate
3. **sub**marine
4. **bi**ped
5. **re**do
6. **super**hero
7. **auto**graph
8. **under**weight
9. **re**visit
10. **ex**clude

Individual answers

Prepositions

(A)
1. The horse cantered <u>across</u> the field.
2. The dog's lead was wound <u>around</u> the tree.
3. We put our chairs <u>under</u> the desks.

(B)
1. The bus will arrive <u>at</u> midday.
2. School begins <u>on</u> the 8th September.
3. The building will be completed <u>in</u> three years.

(C) Individual answers

Pronouns

1

(A)
1. <u>She</u> remembered where the watch was.
2. <u>It</u> is blowing a gale out there.
3. <u>You</u> must try harder!
4. <u>They</u> are very lucky.

(B) 1 They 2 We 3 He

2

(A)
1. Tell <u>them</u> that supper is ready.
2. Did Tom give <u>me</u> the right key?
3. Can the policeman help <u>us</u>?
4. The teacher spoke to <u>him</u> yesterday.

(B)
1. **They** walked **it**.
2. **We** played with **them**.

3

1. The cat cleaned **itself** very carefully.
2. He helped **himself** to a banana.
3. We arranged the party **ourselves**.
4. I want to finish this crossword **myself**.
5. They built the model **themselves**.

4

(A)
1. I think this pen is <u>hers</u>.
2. Those scissors are <u>ours</u>.
3. That idea was <u>mine</u>!
4. Look at <u>its</u> scruffy coat!

(B) Individual answers

5

1. The shopping was in the basket but now that shopping has disappeared.
   The shopping was in the basket but now the basket has disappeared.

2 Jude told Amy, "My mum wants me."
   Jude told Amy, "My mum wants you."
   Jude told Amy, "Your mum wants you."
   Jude told Amy, "Your mum wants me."

3 The boys saw their friends while the boys were on the bus.
   The boys saw their friends while their friends were on the bus.

6

(A)
1. I would like to see the film **which/that** got such good reviews.
2. Do you know **who** handed in my wallet?
3. I am interested in books **which/that** have an historical setting.

(B)
1. I have joined the swimming club **which/that** meets every Tuesday.
2. My mum is a teacher **who** works in a primary school.

7

(A)
1. I know the people <u>whose</u> house was broken into.
2. The people to <u>whom</u> this letter is addressed have moved away.
3. This is the man <u>whose</u> sister won the lottery.

(B) Individual answers

8

1. The explorer needed funding so **he** could buy **himself** the equipment **he** needed.
2. The footballers practised every day because **they** had an important match which **they** had to win.

Let's Write

The children went to the park so **they** could play football. Sally and Jack carried jumpers. **Her** jumper and **his** jumper were used as goalposts. Sean brought the ball **which** was a birthday present. Harry brought Tim **who** was **his** younger brother. Sean and Kim chose the teams. **They** were captains. Kim was excited when **her** team scored a goal **that** put them in the lead. Sean was furious when **his** team missed an open goal!

Punctuation

1
1. What is the question**?**
2. It is a difficult question**.**
3. I've got it right**!**
4. That's not the answer**!**

2

(A)
1. that's
2. didn't
3. how's
4. mightn't
5. there's
6. let's

(B)
1. we had/we would
2. where is/where has
3. who is/who has
4. must not
5. who shall/who will
6. I would/had

3

(A)
1. "The sprinter has completed an amazing race," shrieked the commentator, "and brought home the gold medal."
2. The heptathlon competition consists of 100 m hurdles, high jump, shot put, 200 metres, long jump, javelin and 800 metres.
3. Having come first in five out of the seven races, she won the gold medal.
4. The gold medallist, who only six months ago was out with an injury, did a victory lap around the stadium.

(B) Individual answers

4

(A) 1 The manager of the shop (recently transferred from a smaller branch) is enjoying her new job.
2 The team – a man down after twenty minutes – pulled off an amazing victory.

(B) Individual answers

5

Individual answers

6

(A) 1 The band walked onto the stage; the crowd cheered.
2 The explorer had located the cave on the map; calculated the distance; worked out his route; checked his equipment.

(B) Individual answers

7

(A) 1 The chairwoman made a suggestion: the decision should be delayed until the next meeting.
2 The equipment for the game consisted of: two dice, question cards, bonus cards and a timer.

(B) Individual answers

Sentences

1

Individual answers

2

(A) 1 The horse pulled the cart.
2 The old man planted the tree.
3 Several young birds pecked at the ground.

(B) Individual answers

(C) 1 The birds nested in the oak tree.
2 The twins fed the stray cat.
3 Ashram scored the winning goal.

(D) Individual answers

3

(A) 1 Everyone wished me happy birthday.
2 The Pyramids are an amazing sight.
3 I didn't understand the explanation.

(B) Individual answers
(C) Individual answers

4

(A) 1 Read each question (and) think carefully about your answers.
2 I've flown in a plane (but) I have not been in a helicopter.
3 You can join this group (or) you can join that group.

(B) 1 I believe you (but) many people wouldn't.
2 I'm certain I had my keys (or) did I give them to you?

(C) Individual answers

5

(A) 1 **The town will be flooded** if the river bursts its banks.
2 When they got back to the car, **they found a parking ticket.**
3 **I can't help you** unless you tell me the truth.

(B) Individual answers

Singular and plural

1 churches
2 waltzes
3 bodies
4 teeth
5 byways
6 monasteries
7 pianos
8 piccolos
9 dispatches
10 surveys
11 harnesses
12 benches
13 calves
14 wives
15 buses
16 halves
17 porches
18 dominoes
19 mountains
20 tragedies
21 monkeys
22 theatres
23 stories
24 cuckoos
25 enquiries
26 delays
27 echoes
28 families
29 loaves
30 sheaves
31 sopranos
32 censuses
33 mosquitoes
34 heroes
35 lorries
36 enemies
37 cliffs
38 bicycles
39 hutches
40 thieves
41 geese
42 thoraxes
43 gardens
44 altos
45 hunches
46 strays
47 chimneys
48 cargoes
49 banjos
50 yourselves
51 photos
52 carcasses
53 mangos
54 solos
55 scarves
56 witnesses
57 galleys
58 mice
59 varnishes
60 opportunities
61 torpedoes
62 wolves
63 classrooms
64 debts
65 responsibilities
66 tornadoes
67 radios
68 mackintoshes

Standard and Non-standard English

1

(A) 1 She **goes** to football practice every Wednesday.
2 We **were** sure the shop stayed open late on a Thursday.
3 Boys **cry** just as much as girls!

(B) 1 The gardener had **grown** the most beautiful roses.
2 She **drank** two glasses of orange juice.
3 The wind **blew** fiercely.

(C)
infinitive	past simple tense	past perfect tense
to give	gave	had given
to choose	chose	had chosen
to do	did	had done
to freeze	froze	had frozen
to hide	hid	had hidden
to write	wrote	had written

2

1 The discussion wasn't getting them anywhere./The discussion was getting them nowhere.
2 You can't have any ice cream!
3 I didn't see anything.

3

1 That phone is **broken**.
2 I think you're **mad/crazy**!
3 **Move** over.

147

4 Goodbye.
5 I need a **nap/to sleep**.
6 What are you **talking** about?
7 That film was **great/amazing**.
8 This is **easy**.

4

1 I need to **borrow** a pencil.
2 Mum took my friend and **me** to the pictures.
3 They could **have** got lost.
4 I didn't know **what** to do.
5 **Those** shoes need polishing.
6 I did **my** project on the computer.
7 You should put **less** salt on your food.
8 We were **taught** some French today.

Let's Write

" **Hello**. How **are** you **doing**?" said Fred.
" **All right**," replied Grace.
"What **have** you been **doing**?" asked Fred.
"**Nothing** much. I **wrote my** story for school. Miss Green **taught** us direct speech again **because** everyone **gets it wrong**."
" We **were doing** that as well. I don't **understand** it," moaned Fred.
"It's **easy**! I **get** it **right** all the time," boasted Grace.
" Can you **teach** me?" asked Fred.
"**That won't be a problem**. You won't **have any** problems when I **teach you**," said Grace.

Suffixes

(A) 1 operation 2 fierceness
    3 responsibility 4 decision
(B) 1 managing 2 acting
    3 brutish 4 dangerous
(C) 1 straighten 2 terrorise
    3 modernise 4 punctuate

Verbs

1

infinitive	present simple	past simple	future
to look	I look	I looked	I shall look
to smile	He smiles	He smiled	He will smile
to follow	It follows	It followed	It will follow

2

(A) 1 The goats **are chewing** the grass.
    2 He **is reading** his book.
    3 I **am cleaning** my teeth.
(B) 1 We **search** for our cat.
    2 My friend **feels** unwell.
    3 The wind **howls** down the chimney.

3

(A) 1 He **was planting** the bulbs.
    2 They **were copying** the questions.
    3 I **was reading** the instructions.
(B) 1 She **managed** very well.
    2 The cat **clawed** at the tree.
    3 The men **painted** the fence.

(C) 1 The blackbird **sang**.
    2 We **drove** to the coast.
    3 They **built** sand castles.

4

(A) 1 The flight commander <u>had grounded</u> the planes because of bad weather.
    2 The swallows <u>have returned</u> to their nest in the barn.
    3 He <u>had broken</u> his arm playing rugby.
    4 They <u>have known</u> each other for a long time.
(B) 1 They **had spoken** on the phone.
    2 I **had seen** a beautiful rainbow.
    3 The birds **had flown** away.

(C)

infinitive	past simple tense	perfect tenses
to awake	awoke	awoken
to beat	beat	beaten
to bite	bit	bitten
to choose	chose	chosen
to fall	fell	fallen

5

(A)

Present tenses	Past tenses	Future tenses
explain is existing are embarrassing recommend	had recognised was developing wrote has interfered had appreciated were exaggerating	will achieve shall suggest

(B) 1 I **shall** go to the shops.
    2 They **will** play in the park.
    3 We **shall** ride our bicycles.
(C) 1 We will get lost.
    2 They shall regret it.

6

(A) 1 We <u>could</u> go for a bike ride if you want.
    2 <u>May</u> I have some more orange juice?
    3 Our team <u>should</u> win.
    4 We <u>might</u> be able to see the shooting stars tonight.
    5 I <u>would</u> like to finish my book.
    6 You <u>must</u> tidy your room!
(B) 1 They **can** catch the early train.
    2 The scouts **may** camp in my field.
    3 I wonder if he **can** beat me in this race?
    4 Mum says I **may** have a friend to tea if I **can** help prepare it.
(C) Individual answers

7

(A) 1 The cliffs were battered by the waves.   P
    2 This book was written by Charles Dickens. P
    3 The squirrel gnawed the nut.   A
(B) 1 The team was chosen by William.
    2 The treasure was found by the pirate.
(C) Individual answers
(D) Individual answers

8

1 She is demanding that there be explanation.
2 He requested that he attend the meeting.
3 It is essential the work be finished.

Grammar and Punctuation Skills Finder

Category	Book 1A	Book 1B	Book 2	Book 3	Book 4	Book 5	Book 6
Adjectives	Unit 3/Unit 4/ Unit 13	Unit 6/ Unit 13	Unit 1/Unit 2/ Unit 28				
comparatives			Unit 16/Unit 20	Unit 3/Unit 9			
superlatives				Unit 3/Unit 9			
number order				Unit 13			
formation				Unit 17			
phrases				Unit 21	Unit 6		
possessive					Unit 13	Unit 2	
synonyms						Unit 11	
(relative) clauses						Unit 17/Unit 25	Unit 26
Adverbs			Unit 9/ Unit 21				
comparatives			Unit 26	Unit 6/Unit 12			
superlatives			Unit 26	Unit 6/Unit 12			
phrases				Unit 23	Unit 6		
pairs					Unit 10		
clauses					Unit 16/ Unit 23 Unit 27	Unit 5/Unit 25 Unit 5	Unit 26
fronted					Unit 27	Unit 19	
descriptive writing						Unit 20	
sequencing						Unit 23	
Alphabet	Unit 1/Unit 6						
Antonyms		Unit 13	Unit 2				
Apostrophes							
contractions			Unit 7/ Unit 14/ Unit 18			Unit 14	
possession			Unit 17		Unit 24/ Unit 26	Unit 6/ Unit 14	
Articles				Unit 1			
Brackets						Unit 27	
Capital letters	Unit 11/ Unit 14		Unit 6/Unit 12	Unit 19			
Colon							Unit 21
Commas							
in lists			Unit 15				
direct speech				Unit 20	Unit 4/ Unit 25	Unit 4	
fronted adverbials					Unit 23/ Unit 27	Unit 5 Unit 19	
to avoid ambiguity						Unit 26	
Confusing words			Unit 24		Unit 18	Unit 22	Unit 9/Unit 14
Conjunctions		Unit 10	Unit 8/Unit 23/ Unit 25	Unit 25			
Dashes						Unit 27	
Determiners				Unit 1	Unit 17		Unit 12
Ellipsis							Unit 11
Exclamation marks		Unit 5	Unit 6/Unit 12				
Full stops	Unit 11/ Unit 14		Unit 6/Unit 12				
Homonyms						Unit 13	Unit 3
Homophones			Unit 24			Unit 9	Unit 3
Hyphens							Unit 15/Unit 25
Improving writing							Unit 11/Unit 13
Nouns							
common	Unit 2/Unit 4	Unit 14	Unit 1/Unit 27				
proper	Unit 9	Unit 4/Unit 7/ Unit 11	Unit 5				
collective			Unit 3				
compound			Unit 11				
abstract				Unit 16	Unit 3		

Category	Book 1A	Book 1B	Book 2	Book 3	Book 4	Book 5	Book 6
singular possessive			Unit 17		Unit 24/ Unit 26	Unit 6	
plural possessive					Unit 24/ Unit 26	Unit 6	Unit 12
phrases					Unit 17		
Paragraphs				Unit 26	Unit 19/ Unit 28	Unit 20	Unit 22
Prefixes		Unit 13	Unit 2	Unit 22		Unit 21	
Prepositions				Unit 18			
Pronouns							
personal			Unit 13				
subject			Unit 13	Unit 11			
object				Unit 11			
reflexive				Unit 11			
possessive					Unit 8	Unit 2	
ambiguity					Unit 21		
relative						Unit 12	Unit 4
repetition and clarity						Unit 16	
Question marks		Unit 2	Unit 6/Unit 12				
Semicolon							Unit 21
Sentences	Unit 11/ Unit 14	Unit 2/Unit 5	Unit 6/Unit 12	Unit 4			
direct speech				Unit 10/ Unit 20	Unit 4/ Unit 25	Unit 4/Unit 7	Unit 16
main clauses				Unit 28	Unit 2	Unit 25	Unit 26
subordinate clauses					Unit 2		Unit 26
subject and object					Unit 11		Unit 1
indirect speech					Unit 14	Unit 7	
double negatives					Unit 20		
subject and predicate						Unit 15	Unit 2
improving writing						Unit 28	Unit 11/Unit 13
relative clauses						Unit 17/ Unit 25	Unit 6/ Unit 26
multi-clause							Unit 8/Unit 10/ Unit 26
conditional clauses							Unit 20
Singular and plural	Unit 8	Unit 9	Unit 3	Unit 2/Unit 5/ Unit 15	Unit 7/ Unit 26	Unit 1	
Standard English							Unit 19/Unit 24/ Unit 28
Suffixes		Unit 14	Unit 27/ Unit 28	Unit 24	Unit 5		
Synonyms					Unit 22	Unit 11	
Verbs							
present simple tense	Unit 5/Unit 7						
present progressive tense	Unit 10/Unit 12	Unit 3	Unit 4				
past simple tense		Unit 8/Unit 12	Unit 10	Unit 8			
past progressive tense			Unit 19/Unit 22				
future tense				Unit 14			
perfect tense				Unit 27	Unit 9		
past perfect tense					Unit 12/Unit 15		
common mistakes					Unit 18		
synonyms					Unit 22		
formed with suffixes						Unit 10	
auxiliary						Unit 18/ Unit 24	Unit 17
modals						Unit 24	Unit 5/Unit 17
prefixes						Unit 21	
active and passive							Unit 18/Unit 23
clause round-up							Unit 26
subjunctive							Unit 27

SATs Practice Paper Answers

Test A
Section I

Question	Answer and mark scheme	Allocation
1	**I am reading** this book while the twins **are having** their tea.	1 mark

Skill: present progressive

Question	Answer and mark scheme	Allocation
2	The horse **had jumped** the first fence before it stumbled.	1 mark

Skill: past perfect

Question	Answer and mark scheme	Allocation
3	They will go to the park after school.	1 mark

Skill: modals

Question	Answer and mark scheme	Allocation
4	The travellers plodded through the <u>silent</u> wood. They were <u>cold</u> and <u>hungry</u>, and longing for <u>comfortable</u>, <u>warm</u> beds.	Up to 5 marks

Skill: Adjectives

Question	Answer and mark scheme	Allocation
5	The dog barked and **it** jumped up at the stranger.	1 mark

Skill: pronouns to avoid repetition

Question	Answer and mark scheme	Allocation
6	After the match had finished, the spectators went home. **1 mark** for the correct positioning of the adverbial phrase and **1 mark** for the comma.	2 marks

Skill: frontal adverbials and comma

Question	Answer and mark scheme	Allocation
7	**My** sister has **a** friend who lives in **the** country.	3 marks

Skill: determiners

Question	Answer and mark scheme	Allocation
8	Isn't that the lady **who** lives next door to you? That's the dog **which** chased out cat!	2 marks

Skill: relative pronouns and relative clauses

Question	Answer and mark scheme	Allocation
9	The doctor bandaged her arm <u>after</u> he had cleaned the cut. [subordination conjunction] He has a burger <u>after</u> the match. [preposition] <u>After</u> I had been looking for ages, I found the key! [subordinating conjunction]	

Skill: subordinating conjunctions and prepositions

Question	Answer and mark scheme	Allocation
10	Later that morning, the <u>postman</u> delivered a (parcel).	2 marks

Skill: subject & object

Question	Answer and mark scheme	Allocation
11	It is important that everyone **be on time** for the concert.	1 mark

Skill: subjunctive verb forms

Question	Answer and mark scheme	Allocation
12	There are three things we must do before your cousins arrive: change the beds; buy the food; fill the car with petrol.	3 marks

Skill: colons & semi colons

Question	Answer and mark scheme	Allocation
13	**Big Cats /The Cat Family** These are members of the cat family / These are big cats: • lions • tigers • cheetahs Award 1 mark for each of: heading; introductory sentences; bullet points.	3 marks

Skill: bullet points

Question	Answer and mark scheme	Allocation
14	Sally, thinks John, is nosey! Sally thinks John is nosey! Accept answers to the effect of: in the first sentence, John's opinion of Sally is that she is nosey/ John is doing the thinking; in the second sentence, Sally's opinion of John is that she thinks he is nosey/ Sally is doing the thinking.	2 marks

Skill: commas to clarify meaning

Question	Answer and mark scheme	Allocation
15	The gardener dug up the daffodils and tulips. Accept 'The gardener dug up the daffodils and the tulips.'	1 mark

Skill: ellipsis

Section 2

Question	Answer and mark scheme	Allocation
1	Accept: They have letters missed out. The apostrophe stands in place of a missing letter.	1 mark

Skill: apostrophes to mark contracted forms

Question	Answer and mark scheme	Allocation
2	swift	1 mark

Skill: synonyms and antonyms

Question	Answer and mark scheme	Allocation
3	replied	1 mark

Skill: G8.1 synonyms and antonyms

Question	Answer and mark scheme	Allocation
4	legs / trees	1 mark

Skill: grammatical difference between plural s and 's

Question	Answer and mark scheme	Allocation
5	Shows possession: the legs belonging to Hare	1 mark

Skill: grammatical difference between plural s and 's

Question	Answer and mark scheme	Allocation
6	fronted adverbial	1 mark

Skill: fronted adverbials

Question	Answer and mark scheme	Allocation
7	I've time for a little rest because Tortoise is so slow.	1 mark

Skill: clauses

Question	Answer and mark scheme	Allocation
8	The exclamation mark ends the sentence which shows the unexpected / a surprise.	1 mark

Skill: exclamation marks

Question	Answer and mark scheme	Allocation
9	The words in the brackets are 'extra information'. The sentence would function equally well without them.	1 mark

Skill: parenthesis

Question	Answer and mark scheme	Allocation
10	crowd = collective noun as = conjunction soon = adverb the = determiner thought = verb	Up to 5 marks

Skill: conjunctions

Total marks available: 42

The table below shows the end-of-year expectations which are tested by the different questions.

Section I

Questions	National Curriculum for England 2014 Programme of Study
	Year 1
1, 4	Year 2
2	Year 3
5, 6, 7,	Year 4
3, 8, 9, 14	Year 5
10, 11, 12, 13, 15	Year 6

Section 2

Questions	National Curriculum for England 2014 Programme of Study
4	Year 1
1, 5, 7	Year 2
	Year 3
6, 10	Year 4
9	Year 5
2, 3,	Year 6

Test B

Section I

Question	Answer and mark scheme	Allocation
1	I **was looking** for my bag when someone **knocked** on the door.	1 mark

Skill: past progressive

Question	Answer and mark scheme	Allocation
2	He <u>has mended</u> the vase that the cat knocked off the table.	1 mark

Skill: present prefect

Question	Answer and mark scheme	Allocation
3	rained = verb the = determiner sun = noun we = pronoun beautiful = adjective	Up to 5 marks

Skill: nouns

Question	Answer and mark scheme	Allocation
4	I agreed to meet my friend **although** I was very tired.	1 mark

Skill: conjunctions

Question	Answer and mark scheme	Allocation
5	possessive pronouns: theirs/mine/hers possessive adjectives: my/her/their	Up to 6 marks

Skill: possessive pronouns

Question	Answer and mark scheme	Allocation
6	She stayed <u>behind</u> to tidy up, as she <u>often</u> did.	2 marks

Skill: adverbs of time and place

Question	Answer and mark scheme	Allocation
7	We stayed in the car for a few minutes <u>because</u> it was raining.	I mark

Skill: subordinate clauses

Question	Answer and mark scheme	Allocation
8	With that ticket you can visit the museum **and** the house **or** gardens, **but** not the stables. OR With that ticket you can visit the museum **or** the house **and** gardens, **but** not the stables.	3 marks

Skill: co-ordinating conjunctions

Question	Answer and mark scheme	Allocation
9	Can you see <u>those strange-looking plants</u>?	1 mark

Skill: noun phrases

Question	Answer and mark scheme	Allocation
10	He was going/went to the shops and he bought an ice cream and was eating / ate it on the way home.	2 marks

Skill: tense agreement

Question	Answer and mark scheme	Allocation
11	Invitations for the party were sent out by Jas. OR Invitations were sent out by Jas for the party.	1 mark

Skill: active & passive

Question	Answer and mark scheme	Allocation
12	the visitors' car the children's dog	2 marks

Skill: apostrophes to mark plural possession

Question	Answer and mark scheme	Allocation
13	"When the wind gets up," said Dad, "we will go out and fly the kite."	Up to 7 marks

Skill: inverted commas

Question	Answer and mark scheme	Allocation
14	I <u>done</u> my homework on Friday because we <u>was</u> going away for the weekend. I **did** my homework on Friday because we **were** going away for the weekend.	2 marks

Skill: subject – verb agreement

Question	Answer and mark scheme	Allocation
15	This letter has been **re-sent**. Are you **recovering** from your cold?	2 marks

Skill: hyphens

Section 2

Question	Answer and mark scheme	Allocation
1	is = are teaches = teach thinked = thought easy = easily were = was an = a passed = past won = beat of = have might = must	10 marks

Skill: verb agreement, verbs, modal verbs

Question	Answer and mark scheme	Allocation
2	My list : find books on the pyramids; make notes ; draw a map. Sasha's project was about tigers. They were really fierce! After she had finished drawing a beautiful picture , she wrote all about tigers. Raju said, "I have finished my project, Miss. Will you read it? It's really good."	Up to 10 marks

Total marks available: 57

The table below shows the end-of-year expectations which are tested by the different questions.

Section I

Questions	National Curriculum for England 2014 Programme of Study
	Year 1
6, 9	Year 2
1, 2, 4, 7, 8, 10	Year 3
5, 12, 13	Year 4
	Year 5
11, 14, 15	Year 6

Section 2

Questions	National Curriculum for England 2014 Programme of Study
	Year 1
	Year 2
	Year 3
2 (parts 2 and 3)	Year 4
	Year 5
1, 2 (part 1)	Year 6

Glossary

Adjectives

Adjectives are also known as *describing words*. They describe nouns and pronouns.
Many simple adjectives describe appearance, e.g.
    a *tall* man

Colours
Colour words are adjectives, e.g.
A few colour words can be nouns, e.g.
    an *orange* (fruit)

Cardinal numbers
Numbers are adjectives, e.g.
    one boat
    eight books

Ordinal numbers
Words that describe numerical order are adjectives, e.g.
    He was *second* in the race.
    It was the *fourth* time she had missed the bus.

Comparative adjectives
Comparative adjectives compare two nouns or pronouns.
Short, regular comparative adjectives are usually formed by adding *er*, e.g.
    dark   darker

Sometimes forming comparative adjectives requires an adjustment to the spelling, e.g.
    heavy   heavier   (*y* to *i* then add *er*)
    brave   braver   (just add *r*)
    big   bigger   (double last consonant)

Longer adjectives form their comparative with *more*, e.g.
    important   more important

Superlative adjectives
Superlative adjectives compare three or more nouns or pronouns.
Short, regular superlative adjectives are usually formed by adding *est*, e.g.
    dark   darker   darkest

Sometimes forming superlative adjectives requires an adjustment to the spelling, e.g.
    heavy heavier *heaviest* (*y* to *i* then add *est*)
    brave braver *bravest* (just add *st*)
    big bigger *biggest* (double last consonant)

Longer adjectives form their superlative with most, e.g.
    important   more important   most important

Irregular comparative and superlative adjectives
A few adjectives change completely in their comparative and superlative forms, e.g.

bad	worse	worst
good	better	best
little	less	least
much	more	most
many	more	most
some	more	most

Forming adjectives
Adjectives can be formed by adding suffixes, e.g.
    pain   *painful*   *painless*

Adjectives can be formed from e.g.
nouns: peril   *perilous*   a *perilous* journey
verbs: to grow *grown* the *grown* man

Some nouns and verbs can be used as adjectives, e.g.
nouns: a *city* dweller   a *library* book
verbs: the *running* track the *managing* director

Adjective phrases
An adjective phrase is a group of words without a finite verb. It is used to describe a noun or a pronoun, e.g.
    The *angry, frightened old* man got off the bus.

Possessive adjectives
Possessive adjectives show who or what possesses (owns) a noun, e.g.
    my hat   *your* book   *his* stick

Adjective (relative) clauses
An adjective clause:
– is a subordinate clause containing a finite verb
– describes a noun or pronoun
– is used in multi-clause (also known as complex) sentences
– begins with a relative pronoun (*who whom whose which that*), e.g.
    I work for the man *who runs the garden centre*.
    They bought the horse *which looked calm and gentle*.
    I want to find the key *that fits this lock*.

Adverbs

Adverbs are words that give us extra information about verbs.

Adverbs tell us how, when or where something happens or is done, e.g.

how   He ran *quickly*.
when   She arrived *late*.
where   The car stopped *here*.

Comparative adverbs

Comparative adverbs are used to compare the actions of two people or things. Some adverbs follow the same rules as adjectives, e.g.

late   later

Adverbs ending in *ly* usually form their comparative with *more*, e.g.

soundly   *more* soundly

Superlative adverbs

Superlative adverbs are used to compare the actions of three or more people or things. Some adverbs follow the same rules as adjectives, e.g.

late   later   latest

Adverbs ending in *ly* usually form their superlative with *most*, e.g.

soundly   *most* soundly

Irregular comparative and superlative adverbs

A few adverbs change completely in their comparative and superlative forms, e.g.

well   better   best
badly   worse   worst

Adverb phrases

An adverb phrase is a group of words without a finite verb, used to describe how, when or where actions take place, e.g.

how   The horse galloped *like the wind*.
when   *Before sunset*, we had pitched camp.
where The cottage stood *at the edge of the wood*.

Adverb pairs

Adverbs can be used in pairs to add further detail to the action, e.g.

how: He ran *very quickly*.
when: She arrived *extremely late*.
where: The car stopped *near here*.

Adverb clauses

An adverb clause contains a subject, verb and conjunction.
Adverb clauses begin with conjunctions, e.g.

  The boy fell *when the branch broke*.
  I will go out *after I have washed my hands*.
  She went to that shop *because it is just around the corner*.

An adverb clause can come at the beginning of the sentence. It is separated from the main clause by a comma, e.g.

  When the branch broke, the boy fell.
  After I have washed my hands, I will go out.
  Because it is just around the corner, she went to that shop.

An adverb clause:
– is a subordinate clause containing a subject, verb and conjunction
– indicates how, when or where the action of the verb takes place
– is used in multi-clause (also known as complex) sentences
– begins with a subordinating conjunction, e.g.
  The boy fell, *when the branch broke*.

An adverb clause can come at the beginning, middle or end of the sentence, e.g.

  When the branch broke, the boy fell.
  The boy fell, *when the branch broke*, and hurt his arm.

Alphabet

The alphabet contains 26 letters from which all English words are formed.

5 vowels   =   a   e   i   o   u
21 consonants

The letter *y* can sometimes act as a vowel, e.g.
  sky   *cry*

The letters can be written in lower case (small), e.g.
  a   b   c   d   e   etc.

The letters can be written in upper case (capitals), e.g.
  A   B   C   D   E   etc.

Alphabetical order

To put letters or words into alphabetical order is to arrange them so that the first letter of each word is in the order in which it appears in the alphabet, e.g.
  ant   baby   cot   desk

Words beginning with the same letter are arranged by the second letter and so on, e.g.
  air   ant   apple   attack

Apostrophes

Apostrophes are used for:
1 contractions, e.g.   *can't didn't let's*
2 possessive nouns, e.g.   *Sam's bicycle*
                                     the girls' bags

Articles

The indefinite article is *a* or *an*, e.g.
   a car   *a* box
   an orange   *an* ice cream

The definite article is the, e.g.
   the car   *the* orange

Articles are a type of determiner.

Capital Letters

Capital letters are used for:
- the pronoun I   **M**y brother and **I** are twins.
- the beginning of   **A**nyone want to play
  a sentence   football?
- people's names   **M**rs **O**live **B**rown
- days of the week   **S**aturday
- months of the year   **N**ovember
- names of places   **Y**orkshire **M**oors
- book titles   **T**he **F**ive **C**hildren and **I**t
- plays   **T**wo **G**entlemen of **V**erona
- films   **B**atman **B**egins

Capital letters are also used for headings and subheadings in non-fiction writing.

Colons and Semicolons

Colons are used for:
   – introducing a list
   – introducing a result or an example
   – balancing one statement against another.

Semicolons are used for:
- separating two or more statements in a sentence which are related to each other;
- separating a list of items in a sentence when the items are a phrase rather than a single word.

Commas

- **lists**

When a sentence contains a *list*, commas are used to separate the items in the list. The final two items are joined by a *conjunction*, e.g.
   We need paint, wallpaper, brushes, paste *and* a ladder.
   I am good at painting, wallpapering, woodwork *but* not plumbing.

- **direct speech**

Commas are used to separate spoken and non-spoken words in direct speech, e.g.
   "The highest mountain is Mount Everest," said Tom.
   Tom said, the highest mountain is Mount Everest.
   "The highest mountain," Tom said, "is Mount Everest."

- **fronted adverbials**

Adverbial phrases and clauses coming before a main clause are demarcated by a comma, e.g.
   Later in the day, we were expecting snow.
   Although the sky was clear now, we were expecting snow.

- **parenthesis**

Commas, along with brackets and dashes, are used to separate extra information in a sentence from the main sentence.

Words between the commas (brackets/dashes) can be left out and the sentence still make sense, e.g.
   The birthday cake, *made for my sister*, turned out really well.
   On the following day (*Monday 23rd*) the snow began to thaw.
   The lighthouse keeper – *an old man of nearly eighty* – still enjoys his job.

- **to avoid ambiguity**

A missing comma, or a comma in the wrong place, can change the meaning of a sentence, e.g.
   May we eat Mum?   (May we eat, Mum?)
   Stop cattle crossing.   (Stop, cattle crossing)
   Ed thought Ben was   Ed, thought Ben,
   on holiday.   was on holiday.

Conjunctions

Conjunctions are also known as *joining words*. The conjunctions and/but/or are co-ordinating conjunctions. All other conjunctions are subordinating conjunctions.

They are used to join sentences, e.g.
   The boy kicked the ball. He scored a goal.
   The boy kicked the ball *and* he scored a goal.
   I have found the key. I can't open the door.
   I have found the key *but* I can't open the door.
   I might go out this evening. I might stay in.
   I might go out this evening *or* I might stay in.
   She needed some eggs. She went to the shops.
   She needed some eggs *so* she went to the shops.

Fred was late getting home. He missed the bus.
Fred was late getting home *because* he missed the bus.
I am going swimming. I don't feel well.
I am going swimming *although* I don't feel well.

Contractions

A contraction is a shortened form of a word with an *apostrophe* to show where a letter or letters have been omitted.

Contractions are often used when writing direct speech to reflect natural speech patterns.

The apostrophe, when used in this way is known as the *apostrophe of omission*, e.g.

I am	I'm
he is	he's
you have	you've
it has	it's
did not	didn't

There are some words that have other changes in their contracted form, e.g.

| will not | won't |

Determiners

A determiner begins a noun phrase.
Determiners can be:
 – the definite article   *the*
 – an indefinite article   *a/an*
 – demonstrative pronouns, e.g.   *this/that/these/those*

Determiners are used to say whether a noun is specific, e.g.
   My banana   That book
Or general, e.g.
   Some grapes   Other children

Ellipsis

Ellipsis is when one or more words have been omitted from a sentence because they are understood or expected, e.g.

The girl went into the kitchen and she reached for an apple.

Ellipsis also refers to a punctuation mark [...] which is used to show that a word or words have been omitted.

Homonyms

Homonyms are words that are spelled and pronounced the same but are different parts of speech and have different meanings, e.g.

The sun *rose* in the morning.	verb
The *rose* smelled beautiful.	noun
This is a *grave* matter.	adjective
We put flowers on the *grave*.	noun

Homophones

Pairs or groups of words can be confusing if they sound the same but are spelled and used differently. These words are *homophones*, e.g.
   meet   meat
These *homophones* are most often confused:

- **to/too/two**

to can be used as part of the verb family name (infinitive), e.g.
   to go   *to* bake
to can also be used to denote *movement towards*, e.g.
   We went *to* the shops.
two is used to denote a *quantity*, e.g.
   I need *two* eggs to make this cake.
too can be used to denote *as well as*, e.g.
   I need some flour, *too*
too can also be used to denote *more or different to what is expected*, e.g.
   The oven was *too* hot.

- **there/their/they're**

There is used to denote *place* (notice the word here is in there), e.g.
   We have to go over *there*.
Their is used to denote *ownership*, e.g.
   Their holiday was a great success.
They're is the contraction of they are, e.g.
   They're (They are) having a wonderful time.

- **where/were/we're**

Where is used to denote *place* (notice the word here is in where), e.g.
   I don't know *where* I put it.
Were is part of the past tense of the verb *to be*, e.g.
   We *were* at the hospital yesterday.
We're is a contraction of *we are*, e.g.
   We're (We are) not going out just yet.

Hyphens

Hyphens are used to form:
- compound words, e.g.
    - *water-ski*   *two-seater*
- adverb phrases not ending in *ly*:
    - *well-known*   *good-looking*
- numbers from 21 to 99:
    - *thirty-one*   *eighty-five*
- fractions:
    - *two-fifths*   *one-quarter*
- words with prefixes:
    - *self-respect*   *pre-elect*

Nouns

Nouns are also known as *naming words*.

Common nouns
Most nouns are common nouns, e.g.
   bat   *ship*   *piano*   *boy*

Proper nouns
Proper nouns begin with a *capital letter* and are the names of *specific things*, e.g.
- people   *Sarah   Chris   Mrs Patel   Dr Leigh*
- days of the week   *Monday   Tuesday*, etc.
- months of the year   *January   February*, etc.
- places   *Australia   Mount Everest   High Street*

Collective nouns
Collective nouns are words used to denote a *group or collection of things*, e.g.
   a *flock* of sheep

Nouns formed from adjectives
The suffix *ness* can be added to adjectives to form nouns, e.g.
   dark   *darkness*

Sometimes the spelling has to be adjusted, e.g.
   happy   *happiness*   (*y* to *i* then add *ness*)

Nouns formed from verbs
The suffixes *er* and *ing* can be added to verbs to form nouns, e.g.
   paint   *painter*   *painting*

Sometimes the spelling has to be adjusted, e.g.
   write   *writer*   (just add *r*)
          writing   (drop the *e*, add *ing*)

Compound nouns
Compound nouns are made up of two nouns joined together, e.g.
   foot + ball = *football*
   rain + coat = *raincoat*

Abstract nouns
Abstract nouns denote qualities, feelings and times, e.g.

qualities: He was known for his *heroism*.
             His *stupidity* was unbelievable.
feelings: Her *happiness* knew no bounds.
             The old woman's *gratitude* was touching.
times: The *morning* was cool and damp.
         The *celebration* was a great success.

Abstract nouns can be formed from other parts of speech by using suffixes, e.g.
   adjective   =   silent
   abstract nouns   =   silence
   verb   =   alter
   abstract noun   =   alteration

Singular possessive nouns
Singular possessive nouns use the apostrophe of possession to show ownership.
The apostrophe comes after the singular owner, e.g.
   the *dog's* lead

Plural possessive nouns
Plural possessive nouns use the apostrophe of possession to show ownership.
The apostrophe comes after the plural owners, e.g.
   the *dogs'* leads

If the noun makes a plural without the final *s*, then *'s* is added, e.g.
   the *children's* coats

Noun phrases
Noun phrases can be made with:
– articles
– possessive adjectives
– possessive nouns
– demonstrative adjectives (also called demonstrative pronouns when not followed by a noun)
– adjectives including 'ing' participles
– infinitives

Paragraphs

Paragraphs are groups of sentences within a longer piece of writing that have a common theme or topic. The beginning of a paragraph (except for the initial one), is indicated by indenting 20 mm from the left-hand margin.

Paragraphs in stories

Paragraphs in stories often signal the passing of time in the narrative sequence, e.g.
> *In the morning...*
> *Later that day...*

Narrative paragraphing can also be determined by a change of location, e.g.
> *Arriving at the airport...*
> *When we boarded the plane...*

Paragraphs in non-fiction writing

Usually, each paragraph in information writing covers a particular aspect of the topic. In discursive writing, each paragraph deals with an argument for or against the topic under discussion.

Prefixes

A prefix is a group of letters added to the front of a word to *modify its meaning*, e.g.

adjectives:	happy	*un*happy
	suitable	*un*suitable
verbs:	wrap	*un*wrap
	lock	*un*lock

Some prefixes form opposites, e.g.

suitable	*un*suitable
valid	*in*valid
prudent	*im*prudent
agree	*dis*agree
logical	*il*logical
climax	*anti*climax

Some prefixes have specific meanings, e.g.

uni	one	*uni*form
bi	two	*bi*ped
tri	three	*tri*angle
super	extra good/large	*super*market
pre	before	*pre*viously
post	after	*post*humous

Prepositions

A preposition is a word that shows the relationship of a noun or a pronoun to other words in a sentence.

Prepositions of place

Some prepositions show where an object or person is positioned in relation to something else, e.g.
> The boxes were *in* the cupboard.
> I could see the garage *behind* the house.
> They built a road *alongside* the stream.

Some prepositions show a relationship in time, e.g.
> *at* one o'clock   *in* June   *on* my birthday

Pronouns

Pronouns stand in place of nouns.

Personal pronouns

Subject pronouns: *I/you/he/she/it/they/we*

A personal pronoun can be used instead of a noun when the noun is the subject of the sentence, e.g.
> Mary ate an apple.   *She* ate an apple.

Object pronouns: *me/you/him/her/it/us/them*

An object pronoun can be used instead of a noun when the noun is the object of the sentence, e.g.

> Sam fed the dog.   Sam fed *it*.
> Mum waved to Ben and me.   Mum waved to *us*.

Reflexive pronouns

Reflexive pronouns are used when we refer back to the subject of the sentence or clause.

singular: *myself/yourself/himself/herself/itself*
plural: *ourselves/yourselves/themselves*

Possessive pronouns

Possessive pronouns show ownership or possession, e.g.
> That scarf is *his*.
> This book is *mine*.
> Those clothes are *theirs*.

The possessive pronouns are:
> *mine   yours   his   hers   its   ours   theirs*

Relative pronouns

Relative pronouns have two functions:
1 to take the place of nouns
2 to act as conjunctions related to the noun that comes before them in a sentence, e.g.
> Here is the ball *which/that* I found in the garden.
> Do you know the lady *who* has moved in next door?

The relative pronouns are:
> *who   whom   whose   which   that*

Sentences

A sentence:
- begins with a capital letter;
- ends with a full stop/question mark/exclamation mark
- makes sense

e.g.
> Harry is riding his bicycle. (statement = full stop)
> Is Harry riding his bicycle?
>   (question = question mark)

163

Look out, Harry!

(exclamation = exclamation mark)

- **direct speech**

Some sentences show the actual words that someone has said. These sentences need special punctuation.

Inverted commas " " (also known as speech marks) go at the beginning and end of the spoken words, e.g.

"I need to see the head teacher."

If the spoken words are followed by details of the speaker, e.g.

said Fred

then a comma is placed before the closing inverted commas, e.g.

"I need to see the head teacher," said Fred.

If the spoken words are a question, then a question mark is placed before the closing inverted commas, e.g.

"May I see the head teacher?" asked Fred.

If the spoken words are an exclamation, then an exclamation mark is placed before the closing inverted commas, e.g.

"I must see the head teacher!" insisted Fred.

If the words indicating who is speaking come first, then a comma separates the non-spoken and spoken words, e.g.

Fred said, "I need to see the head teacher."

If the spoken words signal the end of a sentence, then a full stop, question mark or exclamation mark is used before the closing inverted commas, e.g.

Fred said, "I need to see the head teacher."
Fred asked, "May I see the head teacher?"
Fred insisted, "I must see the head teacher!"

Sometimes direct speech is split by the unspoken words, e.g. *said Jane*

"I need to see the head teacher," said Jane, "and I need to see her now!"
"Please tell me why you need to see her," said Paul. " I will go and see if she is free."

- **indirect speech**

Indirect or reported speech is when we write about what someone has said but do not use the actual words spoken, e.g.

direct speech
"My tyre has a puncture," said Rita.
indirect speech
Rita said that her tyre had a puncture.

- **clauses**

A main clause carries the core meaning of a sentence and contains a finite verb. A main clause can be a sentence in itself, e.g.

The dog growled angrily.

A subordinate clause is of secondary importance and is joined to a main clause by a conjunction, e.g.

The dog growled angrily when the cat came into view.

The main clause does not have to come first in the sentence, e.g.

When the cat walked by, the dog growled angrily.

Adverbial clauses are introduced by a conjunction, e.g.

when   after   because

Relative (adjectival) clauses begin with relative pronouns, e.g.

which   that   who

Conditional clauses begin with a subordinating conjunction, e.g.

if   unless   as long as

All clauses contain finite verbs.

- **subject and object**

Simple sentences have a **subject**, **verb** and an **object**.

Subjects and objects are nouns and pronouns.

The **subject** tells you who or what the sentence is about.

The **object** tells you who or what is having something done to it, e.g.

subject   object
↓   ↓
The **girl** kicked the **ball**.

- **double negatives**

Contractions which end in *n't* and the words *no, not, nothing, never* and *nowhere* are negative words.
In English, double negatives are not grammatically correct, e.g.

I *don't* want *no* pudding. = I do want *some* pudding.
Correctly written this is = I *don't* want *any* pudding.

- **subject and predicate**

The *subject* is the thing or person the sentence is about.

The *predicate* is the rest of the sentence, e.g.

The man cleaned the car.
The man   = subject
cleaned the car = predicate

The predicate always contains the verb.

= cleaned

The subject can be more than one or two words, e.g.

The energetic young man

The predicate can be made interesting, e.g.
> vigorously cleaned the valuable vintage car.

- **Single-clause sentences**

A single-clause sentence is one main clause, e.g.
> The tractor was stuck in the mud.
> The farmer couldn't move it.

A multi-clause sentence can consist of two main clauses joined with a co-ordinating conjunction, e.g.
> The tractor was stuck in the mud and the farmer couldn't move it.

This is sometimes known as a compound sentence. Both parts of the sentence are sentences in their own right.

A multi-clause sentence can also consist of two or more clauses joined with a subordinating conjunction. The main clause can stand as a sentence by itself, but the other clauses (known as subordinate clauses) cannot, e.g.
> The road was covered with broken eggs *which fell from the lorry*.

This is sometimes known as a complex sentence.

Singular And Plural

Both nouns and verbs have *singular and plural forms*.

Verbs

In the present simple tense, the *third person singular* has an *s* or *es*, e.g.
> he *looks*   she *looks*   it *looks*
> he *watches*   she *watches*   it *watches*

Nouns

Nouns form their plurals in a variety of ways.
- The most common way is to add and *s*, e.g.
  bat   *bats*
  leg   *legs*
  panda   *pandas*
- For nouns ending in *s/ch/sh/x*, add *es*, e.g.
  grass   *grasses*   match   *matches*
  bush   *bushes*   box   *boxes*
- For nouns ending consonant + *y*, change the *y* to *i* and add *es*, e.g.
  pony   *ponies*
- For nouns ending vowel + *y*, just add *s*, e.g.
  tray   *trays*
  boy   *boys*
- For nouns ending in *f* or *fe*, change the *f* or *fe* to *ve* and add *es*, e.g.
  knife   *knives*
  loaf   *loaves*

There are some exceptions, e.g.
  cliff – *cliffs*   sheriff – *sheriffs*
  reef – *reefs*   gulf   – *gulfs*   etc.

Some can also have both plural forms, e.g.
  hoof – *hoofs/hooves*
  wharf – *wharfs/wharfs*   etc.

For most nouns ending in *o*, add *es*, e.g.
  tomato   *tomatoes*

If the noun is related to music, such as the name of a musical instrument or type of voice, just add *s*, e.g.
  piano   *pianos*

Some nouns have *irregular plurals* that follow none of the rules above, e.g.
  child   *children*   fungus   *fungi*
  tooth   *teeth*   cactus   *cacti*

Some nouns are the same in the plural as the singular, e.g.
  cod   sheep   deer

Suffixes

Suffixes are groups of letters added to the end of a root word to modify the meaning.

- **Verb tenses**

A suffix can change the tense of a verb, e.g.
  infinitive: to jump
  progressive tenses   jump*ing*
  past tenses   jump*ed*

- **Comparative and superlative**

A suffix added to an adjective or adverb forms the comparative and superlative, e.g.
  bright   bright*er*   bright*est*

- **Changing part of speech**

A suffix can change a word from one part of speech to another, e.g.
  adjective   =   happy
  abstract noun   =   happiness
  verb   =   to build
  noun   =   builder

Synonyms

Synonyms are words that mean the same or nearly the same, e.g.
  verbs
  said   *announced/stated/shouted/boasted*
  walked   *trudged/strolled/sauntered/ambled*
  adjectives
  happy   *pleased/content/satisfied*
  cold   *icy/freezing/wintry*

Verbs

Verbs are also known as *doing or being words*.

- **verb family name**

This is the infinitive and always begins with 'to', e.g.
   to follow   to dig   to travel

- **verb tenses**

The tense of a verb tells you *when* the action was done, e.g.

present simple tense	*I walk*
present progressive (continuous) tense	*I am walking* *You are walking*
past simple tense	*I walked*
past progressive (continuous) tense	*I was walking* *They were walking*
present perfect tense	*I have walked* *She has walked*
past perfect tense	*I had walked*
future tense	*I shall walk* *He will walk*

Some verbs have irregular past tenses, e.g.
   I **buy a newspaper**.
   I **bought** a newspaper
   I **have bought** a newspaper.

Some verbs have a past participle that is different from the past simple tense, e.g.
   I **write** a letter.
   I **wrote** a letter.
   I **have written** a letter.

- **the verb to be**

The verb *to be* is often used as an auxiliary verb to form tenses, e.g.

present progressive tense	*I am* walking
past progressive tense	*I was* walking
future tense	*I shall* walk/ *He will* walk

These are important tenses of the verb to be:

present simple	**past simple**	**future**
I am	I was	I shall be
you are	you were	you will be
he is	he was	he will be
she is	she was	she will be
it is	it was	it will be
we are	we were	we shall be
you are	you were	you will be
they are	they were	they will be

- **subject/verb agreement**

A singular subject must have a singular verb, e.g.
   The *girl sings* in the choir.
   I *am* bored.
A plural subject must have a plural verb, e.g.
   The *girls sing* in the choir.
   We *are* bored.

- **forming verbs**

Verbs can be formed with the use of suffixes, e.g.
   from nouns:
      captive   captivate
   from abstract nouns:
      strength   strengthen

A prefix can be added to a verb to adjust or qualify its meaning but does not alter the spelling of the word it is being added to, e.g.
   to charge: *recharge   undercharge   overcharge*

- **auxiliary verbs**

Auxiliary verbs are known as 'helper verbs' and are used to show tense, e.g.
   to be   We *were going*.
   to have   We *have gone*.

Modal verbs are also auxiliary verbs, e.g.
   I *can* jump as high as you.
   You *may* have a biscuit.
   He *might* get a dog for his birthday.
   She *must* get to the station on time.
   We *would* like to pass our exams.
   We *should* pass our exams if we work hard.
   We *could* pass our exams if we worked harder.

- **active and passive**

In the active mood, the subject does the action, e.g.
   The dog chased the rabbit.
In the passive mood, the subject receives/is affected by the action. The subject of an active sentence becomes the 'agent' in a passive sentence, e.g.
   The rabbit was chased by the dog.

- **subjunctive**

This is rarely used except in very formal writing. The form is the same as the infinitive without 'to', and is always the same no matter what the tense, e.g.
   He commands that we leave immediately.
   He commanded that we leave immediately.